The Political Content of Bri
and Financial

Gary James Merrill

The Political Content of British Economic, Business and Financial Journalism

A Deficit of Perspectives

palgrave
macmillan

Gary James Merrill
University of Roehampton
London, UK

ISBN 978-3-030-04011-6 ISBN 978-3-030-04012-3 (eBook)
https://doi.org/10.1007/978-3-030-04012-3

Library of Congress Control Number: 2019932929

Cover illustration: © Alex Linch/shutterstock.com
Cover design by eStudioCalamar

This Palgrave Macmillan imprint is published by the registered company Springer Nature Switzerland AG
The registered company address is: Gewerbestrasse 11, 6330 Cham, Switzerland

Preface

In the years following the 2008 Financial Crisis, academics began to take closer interest in economic, business and financial (EBF) journalism. Traditionally, these areas of the news media had received little attention. But such was the impact, reach and severity of the Crisis that researchers were prompted to turn the spotlight onto these interrelated spheres.

Many early works debated the role of journalism in the prelude to the Financial Crisis. Although there is some disagreement, particularly in the USA, the consensus among scholars and practitioners alike was that journalists somehow failed to sufficiently warn the public of looming danger. Some academics concentrated on the relationship between journalists and their sources, and British research revealed widespread reliance on corporate public relations (PR) which, by extension, meant sceptics and dissenters were given little opportunity to air their views. Other reasons given—typically by practitioners—for journalism's inadequacies include: the rigidity of reporting beats; deficiencies in training; restrictions on airtime and page space; cuts to newsroom budgets; and the complexities of financial markets.

While the immediate post-Financial Crisis corpus is valuable, it only offers a partial explanation of EBF journalism, primarily because it is focussed on a single, albeit important, episode. Furthermore, most early studies were journal articles and conference papers and, consequently, limited in scale. Some were based on relatively small numbers of interviews with practitioners, and others were predominantly learned commentary and analysis with little empirical grounding. Book-length studies were published later in the decade after the Crisis, and, naturally, these benefited from the passage of time, deeper reflection and more comprehensive analysis. One of the most welcome developments in this subcorpus was the recognition that the history of EBF journalism is crucial to understanding present challenges. The 2008 Financial Crisis was an exceptional event, but it was not totally unprecedented, and it would be misguided to view it in isolation.

Although the understanding of EBF journalism has deepened and widened, there is still a distinct lack of focussed and comprehensive content analyses of the news product, and certainly no substantial, data-rich study that concentrates on its political content. This book attempts to address this deficiency by assessing the extent to which the British news media gives exposure and credence to different political interpretations of economics and business. In doing so, it provides empirical evidence to inform the largely theoretical debates about the presence of neoliberal assumptions in news.

Like other recent works, this book was inspired by the Crisis. But instead of focussing on the characteristics of journalism in the immediate prelude, attention is turned to three issues in the preceding decade. In doing so, this study analyses the characteristics of British EBF news in what might be described as 'normal times'. Also, by looking at the reporting of the same issues over the same periods by a selection of news organisations, this book offers a comparative dimension. More precisely, it evaluates the coverage given to disparate political discourses in three different contexts by four different news organisations over a ten-year period.

Chapter 1 begins by emphasising that EBF journalism has a long track record of over-optimism. The chapter then considers previous British and international research around a sociological framework of analysis. As will be shown, past studies have found a propensity for journalists to give only a partial representation of political economic opinion, with ideas from the left of the spectrum often sidelined, dismissed or criticised in ways that right-wing perspectives are not.

The second chapter covers the research design and discusses the scope of analysis. First, it justifies the choice of case studies: economic globalisation; private finance and public services; and Britain's largest supermarket company, Tesco. It then explains the selection of time periods, and the chosen news media, and outlines each publication's political position. The main part of the chapter consists of three contextualising sections, one for each case study, which outline the competing narratives that were evident in the mediated debates. The chapter concludes by describing the methodology.

With the foundations established, this book then systematically analyses how the three contentious issues were covered at specific points in time by a selection of British news providers. Hence, each case study compares in detail how three organisations reported the same issues over the same periods. In total, some 1600 articles are meticulously analysed, and distinct patterns in reporting are uncovered.

The book concludes with a discussion of the collective findings. The most revealing is that the British news media tends to reinforce neoliberal assumptions in its reporting and gives only limited exposure and credence to interpretations of the economic environment from the left. This deficit of perspectives is most evident in sourcing patterns, but it is also apparent in the choice of stories, how they are framed, and the portrayal of economic actors. These patterns are consistent across the three case studies, and, to varying degrees, across all four of the news providers that were scrutinised.

There are currently vigorous debates about the relationship between politics and journalism, the news media's portrayal of figures from the fringes of politics and its coverage of political ideas. Events over the last decade—such as the British EU Referendum, the election of President Trump, the election and re-election of Jeremy Corbyn as British Labour Party leader—surprised many commentators, and it is likely that academic interest in this sphere will expand. This study is, therefore, well-timed as it provides researchers with a solid and detailed foundation of empirical data that will help inform their own studies.

This book will appeal to scholars of journalism studies, particularly those interested in the sociology of journalism, and political communications. It is also relevant to people in other university departments who are interested in the political content of news, and the role of the news media in a democracy. These might include teachers, students and researchers in media, political science, sociology, business and PR.

London, UK
December 2018

Gary James Merrill

Contents

About the Author

Gary James Merrill is a senior lecturer in journalism at the University of Roehampton, London. After graduating with a degree in Business Administration from the University of Bath in 1986, Gary spent the first half of his professional life working in and then writing about the technology industry, both as a journalist and a PR. For much of the second half, he has taught journalism at British universities, and in 2015, he completed Ph.D. at Goldsmiths, University of London.

List of Figures

List of Tables

CHAPTER 1

The Nature and Nurture of EBF Journalism

Audiences, History, Production, Sources, Political Economy and Content

Introduction

Although journalism's role in the 2008 Financial Crisis certainly sparked renewed interest from academics, the corpus remains underdeveloped and there are many opportunities for scholarly analysis. To gain a fuller understanding of EBF (economic, business and financial) journalism, therefore, the more recent studies need to be synthesised with the somewhat sparse and disjointed research prior to the Crisis. Hence, this chapter describes, evaluates and aggregates existing work in the sphere of EBF news. Because of the relative shortage of British academic studies, this chapter also includes international research, and contributions from news media practitioners to help gain a fuller picture.

As will become apparent, there is a paucity of detailed studies of the sociology of EBF journalism and there has been no ethnography, nor any wide-reaching analysis, that comes close to matching the depth, range and influence of the classic works in other areas of British journalism.[1] Indeed, there is a considerable body of work in the sociology of journalism, but it would be impossible to give a comprehensive summary within the limits of this chapter. Instead, by using a sociological framework of analysis, this chapter concentrates on subsets of the grand corpus with the view of augmenting the EBF-focussed work. Hence, assuming theories that have been developed in the context of general journalism may

[1] For example, Tunstall (1971), Schlesinger (1978) and Hetherington (1985).

G. J. Merrill, *The Political Content of British Economic, Business and Financial Journalism*, https://doi.org/10.1007/978-3-030-04012-3_1

be equally relevant to EBF news, this chapter will help identify the focus of this book.

The first section discusses research related to the audiences of EBF news. The next gives a brief overview of the history of EBF journalism and considers how it has delivered on the needs of the general public at key moments. The third section focusses on factors that influence the production of EBF news. The fourth concentrates on sourcing patterns, and the fifth covers political economy. The final section of this chapter turns the attention to the news product itself and investigates the political content of economics, business and finance journalism.

Audiences

Before embarking on the analysis, it is important to first delineate economics, business and financial journalism. Although they are interrelated and often cover similar territory, these are not synonyms, and there are considerable differences in their respective foci and audiences. Previous scholarly work, however, has tended to blur the lines and some researchers[2] attach the adjective 'financial' to all journalism in the broader field. Hayes (2014: 60) argues that it is difficult to differentiate and consequently, 'business…has become the "catchall" term'. Shaw (2016) draws a distinction between financial journalism (focussed on investors) and business journalism (aimed at the general public). For the purposes of this book, the acronym EBF will be used when discussing general studies, and for more specific work, the following categorisations apply: economic is concerned with macroeconomic issues (inflation, trade, wages, poverty, etc.); business relates to the activities of companies and industries; and financial applies to financial markets, investments and consumer finance reporting.

The lack of agreement in nomenclature is perhaps symptomatic of the historically low levels of interest awarded to EBF journalism (Gavin and Goddard 1998: 451; Wahl-Jorgensen and Hanitzsch 2009: 13). This neglect is somewhat ironic because, although EBF journalism might appear to deal in abstract concepts, the subject matters affect every consumer, employee, investor and citizen, and so accurate and engaging news is fundamental to 'civic empowerment' (Doyle 2006: 435).

[2] For example, Doyle (2006) and Parsons (1989).

The EBF news media establishes 'a community of economic discourse' (Parsons 1989: 7) and plays a vital role in furnishing the public with knowledge of the economic environment which is a prerequisite of 'democratic development' (Corner et al. 1997: 91). Given that EBF news is anthropocentric—in that its normative function is to inform and engage people about their economic environments—the scarcity of audience studies is striking.

Most work is concerned with popular audiences rather than those who are deemed to be specialists, such as the readers of the *Financial Times*, whom have more interest in EBF issues and greater knowledge of related concepts. The most detailed analyses of audience understanding in the UK were carried out by researchers at Liverpool University. The Liverpool Project, as it became known, found that, despite the inherently abstract nature of the economy, viewers do engage with economic news but in a way that is 'complex and ambiguous' (Gavin 1998: 184). A related study revealed cynicism over economic data and, at times, sheer incomprehension (Corner et al. 1997) and Richardson (1998: 235) noted that some viewers were sceptical about news of unemployment: 'the text is convincing but (the viewer) is not convinced'. This inconsistency—between economic news and people's own experiences—was also raised in a comparative international study which discovered that Japanese and American TV viewers thought coverage of the economy was too negative, while Dutch participants thought it excessively optimistic (Arts et al. 2002). The net effect of this fracture was 'disinterest in hard news' which, the researchers believed, was 'closely related to its content' (ibid.: 2, 11).

In the USA, Wu et al. charted the complex relationship between recession news, the state of the economy and public perceptions. This comprehensive study[3] revealed that these factors reinforce and influence each other, and the presence of 'distinctive predictive relationships' between the three (2002: 29). Although far from conclusive, this research suggests: a greater interest in economic news during downturns; public expectation is influenced more by actual conditions than news coverage; and the centrality of people's own circumstances when decoding news. The findings were echoed in Schifferes and Coulter's (2012) study of BBC News online in the post-Credit Crunch

[3]It covered the period 1987–1996 and included data from 3000 participants.

period—September to December 2008—which revealed a huge increase in traffic and usage of the business pages compared with less traumatic times. In addition to accessing more news in this period, audiences actively sought out further information, particularly from blogs of senior journalists. A related audience study found that only half of the British public were satisfied with the coverage of the aftermath of the 2008 Financial Crisis, and a similar proportion expressed 'a deep-seated mistrust' of business journalists' objectivity. There was also:

> scepticism about their motivation and use of sources and a belief that they are out of touch with the needs and wants of the general public. (Schifferes 2015: 156)

With some notable exceptions, much audience research is somewhat dated and tends to be rather pessimistic. Two British studies, however, suggest some grounds for optimism. In his 2007 analysis, Neil Gavin found that economic news does not have a uniform effect on audiences: 'only some people, some of the time, pay attention', and among newspapers, the effect on the reader is rather weak and inconsistent (Gavin 2007: 175). But, in terms of presenting balanced, engaging and informative reports about the economy, the broadcast media are: 'more than just holding the line against the corrosive forces that assail the modern media' (ibid.: 4). Also in 2007, Alan Budd's report on the impartiality of BBC business reporting found that the Corporation was regarded by audiences as a trusted source of accurate, relevant and balanced business news. It also revealed that those most interested in BBC business news were middle-aged men in the 'AB social class' and other groups (e.g. young people and women) had low levels of engagement (Budd 2007). This study—and others—highlighted another challenge for EBF journalisms: namely, matching content with the needs of a heavily segmented audience (Knowles et al. 2017; Peston in Smith 2008).

Some studies show that audiences will engage with EBF news in certain circumstances, but overall the research suggests British economic and financial journalists constantly struggle to explain, contextualise and maintain the interest of diverse, lay audiences, and the challenge is exacerbated by the limits of airtime and page space (Corner et al. 1997: 91; Tambini 2008: 20). News is intrinsically polysemic and it cannot be assumed that audiences make the same meanings (McQuail 1997: 19). Hence, consumers, investors, employees, the unemployed, the retired and other subgroups require different information, have varying levels of interest and understanding, and will decode messages in their own, unique ways. In the USA, the investor audience tends to be given the priority in business news (Starkman 2014; Croteau and Hoynes 2000: 168) and this preference has also been highlighted in the UK (Knowles et al. 2017; Milne 2009; Marron et al. 2010). The universal centrality of economics, business and finance, combined with the inherent complexities of these subjects, places a considerable burden on the news media to capture and hold the audience's attention. Doyle's assessment of the overall record is particularly stark: 'the task of facilitating a sound public grasp over the significance of financial and economic news developments is largely being neglected' (2006: 433).

In the light of previous audience research, there is clearly potential to strengthen the relevance of EBF journalism to mainstream audiences. But one should be careful, however, not to be too optimistic. Corner et al. added a caveat about mass audiences which is equally relevant today:

> It is useful to be wary of the radical idealism issuing from parts of the Academy, which can project wholly unrealistic expectations about sustained popular engagement with public issues. (1997: 90)

A Brief History of EBF Journalism

Research that has taken a historical perspective has invariably found that the deficiencies of EBF journalism are most evident in times of economic trauma. Far from alerting the public to nascent dangers, studies have repeatedly shown that the news media habitually sustains booms which can lead to speculative bubbles and, hence, financial crises which inevitably impinge negatively on the public. The most vivid example is the 2008 Financial Crisis, but this was just the latest in a succession of episodes.

In one form or another, the media has been reporting on business and finance since the Dutch 'Tulip mania' of the 1630s, and in the early eighteenth century, coffee house gossip combined with enthusiastic newspaper reports and 'fed the frenzied trading of speculators' prior to the bursting of the South Sea Bubble in 1720 (Shiller 2001: 71; Dale 2004: 17). Financial journalism followed the development of liberal capitalism, expanded towards the end of the nineteenth century and continued into the early decades of the twentieth when the link between bubbles and the media strengthened, despite huge improvements in communication technology:

> ...from the 1920s to 2000, the flaws of business journalism in writing about stock markets have remained almost the same: their reporting is too enthusiastic (or positive) and uncritical... (Ojala and Uskali 2006: 1)

The EBF news media grew rapidly for the rest of the century. The BBC reported stock market news as early as the 1920s and business featured regularly on British TV schedules from the late 1960s and more programmes followed from the 1970s onwards (Kinsey 2009: 161; Tumber 1993: 455). This was, in part, a response to the government-commissioned *Annan Committee on the Future of Broadcasting* which, in 1977, described the BBC and ITV's coverage of business and industry as 'dingy and unimaginative' (Mills 2016: 171). In contrast, from the 1930s to the 1980s, the financial press had been a vibrant forum for political debate among prominent economists and their journalistic supporters (Parsons 1989). But with the 'Big Bang' liberalisation of the London financial market in 1986 and the subsequent wave of privatisations, share ownership became popularised which generated a demand for financial information from a far wider demographic. Press coverage expanded (Tumber 1993: 248) and even the 'red top' tabloids began devoting pages to business and finance (Parsons 1989: 210), in many cases, at the expense of the coverage of labour and industrial issues (Mills 2016: 169–170).

EBF journalism became more prevalent as neoliberalism displaced Keynesianism in other industrialised countries. Thus, the British experience was mirrored in the news media of other Western democracies, such as the Nordic region (Kjaer and Slaatta 2007: 137), and France and Canada (Augey and Brin 2004). Similarly, in the US coverage boomed from the 1970s, business journalism rapidly expanded in the early 1980s and a decade later, the 'New Economy' accelerated the trend (Henriques 2000: 18; Uskali 2005: 5). Lewis Simons estimated that the number of American business journalists rose from 4800 in 1988 to over 12,000 by 2000 (Roush 2006: 198). Newspaper coverage of business doubled in the same period, the number of business magazines increased from 358 to 694 and 'formerly staid business sections' were revamped as 'Money' (Shiller 2001: 29). As in the UK, business replaced the once-common reporting of labour issues (McChesney 2003: 313), and in 1980, the launch of CNN brought 24-hour, rolling news to TV screens and provided a template for specialist business channels such as CNBC and Bloomberg. In the late 1990s, numerous websites devoted to financial matters sprang up, most notably TheStreet.com in the USA (Cassidy 2002: 178). Across all media, national and global, economics, business and finance became part of the standard news offering.

This brief history[4] is revealing because, despite the rapid growth of EBF news media, there is little evidence of an improvement in the effectiveness of the journalism. In the period immediately before the Wall Street Crash of 1929, for example, even the most cautious of the American financial media seemed to believe the boom would continue indefinitely (Bow 1980: 447). Such optimism was mirrored in the prelude to the Asian Financial Crisis of 1997 (Yun et al. 2002), and in the same decade, the American news media was instrumental in hyping the 'New Economy' boom that spectacularly crashed in 2000. Thomas Frank maintains that journalists were complicit during this episode because they eagerly promoted the 'democratisation' of the stock market with little regard for the risks (2001: 123). Robert Shiller asserts that, in comparison with previous extreme bull markets, much of the reporting was incredulous rather than overtly inflammatory, but the media undoubtedly amplified a climate of confidence (2001: 113). Lionel Barber (2009) concedes that the 'financial media could have done a better job... ahead of the dotcom crash' but other critics are more pointed in their criticism. John Cassidy, for example, writes: 'Despite some honourable exceptions, the overall standard of reporting on the internet stock phenomenon was dismal' (2002: 326).

Prior to 2008, Enron was the definitive example of EBF journalism's weaknesses. Until the company collapsed in autumn 2001, business journalists were seemingly oblivious Enron's dubious accounting practices. Just months before its downfall, Enron 'had been the business media's poster child, praised for its "innovative" practices and consistently listed among the top American corporations' (Nieman Reports 2002: 4). In heaping such adoration on the company, the news media 'actively helped create the Enron scandal' (Madrick 2003: 3), and yet, according to Bob McChesney: 'Despite the vast resources devoted to business journalism in the 1990s, the media missed the developing story *in toto*' (2003: 314). Some argue that Enron was an exception and to

[4]Other studies include comprehensive accounts of the historical development of EBF journalism (e.g. Schifferes and Roberts 2015; Butterick 2015; Mills 2016).

cite it as an example of widespread, endemic problems in business journalism is unfair. However, Danny Schechter (2009) writes: 'there is an unfortunate dialectic between financial failures and media failures'. This view is supported by Dyck and Zingales who in their detailed analysis of previous investment bubbles found that the media's inability to warn of Enron's impending collapse was: 'not an occasional lapse, but a systematic problem that emerges during stock market booms' (2003: 99).

In one of the earliest post-2008 Financial Crisis studies, Damian Tambini posed a series of questions that underpinned much subsequent research:

> Why didn't we know this (the Crisis) was coming? Did the journalists fail to put the financial system under proper scrutiny? Are they equipped to deal with the continuing complex story? Is this representative of a wider problem with the news media? (Tambini 2008: 2)

Although questions about journalists' role in the Crisis are still relevant, they evoke a sense of *déjà vu*. Similar inquiries were made in the wake of Enron's demise in 2001 and yet it is debatable whether journalism's inadequacies were addressed over the seven intervening years. The apparent immutability was emphasised in a longitudinal, tri-nation content study of financial news which analysed some 1200 articles covering the recession of the early 1990s; the dot-com boom in 2000; and the 2008 Crisis. The authors found a general lack of scepticism in news reports; a narrowing range of sources; a dependency on overarching, official narratives; and, perhaps most worrying, evidence of a *decline* in standards of reporting over the three decades covered by the study (Knowles et al. 2017).

News Production

When amalgamated, previous audience studies and historical analyses suggest that EBF journalism has deep-seated characteristics that somehow prevent it from providing the information the public needs, particularly at crucial times. This pushes the analysis towards the production of news. Despite the absence of detailed ethnographic studies of EBF journalism, it is possible to deepen understanding by considering some important production factors highlighted by earlier works, many of which are based on interviews with practitioners.

As noted above, recent EBF journalism research has tended to revolve around issues raised by the 2008 Financial Crisis. While some elements of this sub-corpus argue that journalists engaged well with audiences and explained the reasons for the Crisis *after* the event,[5] others, notably Damian Tambini (2010) in the UK and Dean Starkman (2014) in the USA, have addressed an important question which is fundamental to EBF journalism, namely whether reporters have a more wide-ranging, watchdog role that would benefit the broader society. The EBF news media may indeed be adept at reporting events and *post-mortems* but journalism that anticipates far-reaching economic problems requires a different approach. Starkman argues that investor audiences benefit from journalists' focus on scoops and privileged information, but citizens need journalists to explain complex problems, expose corporate wrongdoing and hold the powerful to account. Mike Berry (2012) agrees that this type of journalism necessitates a wider range of sources, but he also argues that it is not the source type per se that restricts debate but the absence of competing perspectives. Berry's paper brings an added dimension to the post-Financial Crisis research by emphasising the inherently political nature of economics and, by extension, business and finance. This element is absent from other studies that have tended to focus solely on the allegiance of sources, and yet it is crucial to understanding EBF journalism.[6]

EBF studies that have revealed disagreement among reporters about their purpose tally with research about the wider profession which has noted a 'plurality of roles and role perceptions', and not all practitioners consider themselves as 'active players in a democratic system' (Zelizer 2004: 57). In his comprehensive study of the American news media, Starkman (2014) gives a particularly compelling explanation of the plurality of roles in an EBF context. He argues that, in the prelude to the 2008 Financial Crisis, reporters became so embedded within the corporate information machine that they were unable to produce critical work. Starkman suggests that contemporary business and financial journalism is driven by 'access' to key sources rather than 'accountability' to the general public, and this tilts reporting in the favour of those who benefit from rising financial markets. Starkman's differentiation between access

[5] For example, Marron et al. (2010) and Schifferes and Coulter (2012).

[6] The political content of EBF news is discussed in detail below.

and accountability reporting also resonates in the UK. Indeed, by asking the simple question 'what are financial journalists for?' Tambini (2010) uncovered uncertainty among British practitioners. Only a minority believed they had any wider 'public interest' remit and most restricted their 'watchdog role' to individual companies and corporate wrongdoing, rather than the economy as a whole. Also in the UK, Gillian Doyle found that some EBF journalists *do* see themselves performing Fourth Estate functions but most: 'would not immediately recognise their role as embodying any broad public responsibilities' (2006: 450). In the wake of the Financial Crisis, the profession showed signs of reassessing such roles. At a public debate, Larry Elliot, economics editor of *The Guardian*, said journalists: 'should be professional sceptics and doubters' (Elliot 2009) and senior BBC economics correspondent, Hugh Pym, agreed that financial journalists do have a watchdog responsibility, but it was not the BBC's role to be critical outside of the political-economic consensus (Pym 2009; Manning 2014: 186).

Research has also identified three occupational factors that are particularly relevant to EBF journalism, namely: ethics and regulation; routines; and journalist knowledge. Firstly, given that the EBF media has the 'the power to move markets' (Tambini 2008: 9; Hayes 2014), journalists have an ethical responsibility to cover events accurately but without inducing panic (Wu et al. 2002: 21; Kinsey 2009: 167; Marron et al. 2010: 274). Unlike other specialists, financial journalists also need to be wary of breaking criminal laws, such as 'market abuse' (Tambini 2010[7]). Secondly, routines and beats strongly influence EBF news production. 'Diary events'—such as government economic reports and corporate results—are marshalled by news agencies and provide an orderly and scheduled flow of ideas for stories for EBF journalists (Doyle 2006: 448). This might be convenient for editorial staff, but a predictable schedule of pre-packaged news means coverage becomes event-centred and episodic, journalists tend to move as a herd, become reliant on newswires and PR and thus, there is an increased risk of producing 'churnalism' (Davies 2008).

A third occupational factor that is particularly relevant in EBF news production is journalist knowledge. A lack of training is commonly cited by practitioners as a reason for the failure to spot the warning signs of

[7]The main areas of potential market abuse are: insider trading, market manipulation, conflict of interests and non-disclosure (Tambini 2010: 162–163).

the 2008 Financial Crisis (Barber 2009; Brummer 2009: 40) but some academics have noted that it has been an unresolved, neglected issue for years, particularly for business reporters in the non-specialist mainstream media (Tambini 2008: 19; Davis 2007: 163). The lack of skills is so manifest, argues Doyle (2006), that journalists are unable to hold companies to account. This was evident in journalists' response to criticism about the news media's failure to spot the warning signs before Enron's crash in December 2001. As with the 2008 Crisis, there was a mismatch between journalists' knowledge and financial complexity. A year after the Enron scandal broke Marjorie Scardino, CEO of Pearson, which owned the *FT* at the time, offered a *mea culpa* by proxy: 'We could have done a lot more digging... but business journalists often don't know a lot about business' (Cassy 2003). This stark and surprisingly candid admission could also be applied to senior editorial staff elsewhere who may be accused of being ignorant—or at least unaware—of the importance of EBF issues. Consequently, EBF journalists find it difficult to 'sell stories' to editors (Elliot 2009). Some British scholars (e.g. Tulloch 2009), however, are not convinced that training is the central issue, but others wonder if financial journalists should have a formal accounting qualification before being allowed to practise (Tambini 2009).

Sources

Research covering the sourcing patterns of EBF journalism generally concurs with studies in other areas that have found a tendency to gravitate to elite sources. For Michael Schudson (2011: xv), this is a defining factor because the relationship between journalists and their sources determines the substance of news. There is, however, some disagreement between scholars and practitioners. The professional code of objectivity ensures that it is sources rather than journalists who express their views, so the selection of sources largely determines the way stories are framed. Journalists may claim that they dispassionately collect facts, 'much as a geologist collects rocks for research' but '...what is selected (as a fact) depends on what the selector thinks important' (Edwards and Cromwell 2009: 239). This explains why journalists are attracted to sources whom they deem to be experts and authorities (Berry 2012; Machin and Niblock 2006), particularly if the source can quickly supply them with the right type of information, and sources who offer alternative perspectives tend to be 'ignored, devalued, delegitimised and villainised' (Schlosberg 2013: 201). Hence, primary sources are typically characterised by official authority, social status or commercial success. Such sources tend to be well resourced and organised, with spokespeople and regular releases of information which save the journalist effort. News organisations are eternally constrained by cost, time and space, and so journalists tend to justify their dependence on certain sources in purely pragmatic terms.

Some scholars have characterised the association between journalists and their sources as a form of combat—'a tug of war' (Gans 1979: 117)—but others perceive a symbiotic relationship with information traded for publicity (McNair 1998: 147; Tunstall 1971: 7). Irrespective of which party gains most, the consequence of the routine gravitation to elite sources is: 'political news comes to the public from the top-down' (Gans 2003: 46), the citizen's perspective is rarely given, and news from the periphery is seldom awarded coverage. In the latter case, the reason is not because such news lacks interest or impact, rather it doesn't have 'official sponsorship' (Schudson 2011: 34). Intended or not, 'journalists help legitimate and even glorify the sources and strata from which they report. In effect, journalists "follow the power"' (Gans 2003: 47). Furthermore, in using the same language as their sources, reporters inevitably reproduce the attitudes of the elite (Fowler 1991: 23).

Although there is a diversity of research in the sourcing patterns of EBF journalism, both from the UK and elsewhere, the findings generally agree that business people and politicians have far more presence in reports than representatives of other stakeholder groups, such as consumers, employees, local communities, taxpayers and citizens. Consequently, economics, business and finance tend to be portrayed by the news media as the domains of the elite and, with little input from those who might offer different perspectives, issues are rarely contested. Some believe that this tendency is so pronounced that, in the words of Aeron Davis (2011), 'financial journalism (in the UK) … has been "captured" or neutralised by those it is meant to hold to account'. American researchers have observed similar patterns: according to Jonathan Weil,[8] for example, journalists have: 'outsourced their critical thinking skills to Wall Street analysts' (in Sherman 2002: 28).

[8]Jonathan Weil worked for the *Wall Street Journal* and was one of the few reporters who raised questions about Enron's stock market valuation before its collapse.

This is an important issue because primary sources—such as stockbrokers, investment bankers or economists employed by financial organisations—often have a vested interest (Gans 2003: 66; Madrick 2003) and self-serving commentaries from sources whose 'agendas and biases are naturally instilled into the reporter' (Schiffrin 2006: 189) can influence the trajectory of investments (Doyle 2006). Crucially, such information can be disseminated with little regard for the impact on the financial system (or indeed the economy) as a whole (Manning 2010: 14). Indeed, if journalists favour certain source types over others, the balance and objectivity of EBF reporting, and, therefore, its value to informed decision-making by citizens, is disputable.

These brief summaries are derived from a considerable body of empirical, content-based research over the last four decades that has illustrated the extent to which politicians and the business elite dominate EBF news reports. In the USA, for example, Lasorsa and Reese (1990) analysed the reporting of the causes and effects of the 1987 stock market crash and calculated that 'Wall Street' accounted for nearly half of all quoted sources, and in contrast, academics made up just 7%. Powell and Self (2003) discovered that government officials provide most of the commentary during business crises, and an evaluation of sources in four business publications[9] revealed heavy dependence on senior executives (McShane 1995). Indeed, in the American news media, business people and government officials are nearly always consulted on economic issues, and consumer advocacy groups and trade unions rarely (Croteau 1998; Gans 2003: 63). This was reflected in a major British study[10] by Lewis et al. (2008: 3) which found that business is three times more successful than NGOs, charities and civic groups in turning PR activity into news. More recently, a content analysis of BBC *News at Six* revealed that business spokespeople outnumbered the representatives of trade unions by a factor of five to one in 2007, and 19 to one in 2012 (Berry 2013). This imbalance was surprising, argued Berry, in the context of immigration and the EU which are of particular interest to trade unions, and yet: 'out of 806 source appearances, not one was… a representative of organised labour' (ibid.).

[9] *Fortune, Business Week, Canadian Business* and *Report on Business.*

[10] The researchers analysed 2207 newspaper articles and 402 broadcast segments. The former did not include the business pages.

The exclusion of trade union—and workers'—voices from economic news has been a recurring phenomenon since the Glasgow University Media Group's [GUMG] pioneering work (1976, 1980, 1982) which found that, in the reporting of industrial disputes, employees and their representatives were often marginalised while disproportionate credence, airtime and context were given to management and the government. The GUMG's research was criticised[11] partly because it challenged deeply held beliefs, particularly within the BBC, that TV news is impartial, and other British research has disputed the key findings. For example, Dennis McQuail's comprehensive study of newspaper content, published a year after the GUMG's first volume, revealed that trade union representatives accounted for 41% of all sources, compared to 24% for government and a 'relative invisibility' of management (McQuail 1977: 137, 145). Also, Neil Gavin's study of the reporting of unemployment suggested that economic news does *not* favour elite sources. Instead, he found a: 'wide and expansive commentary… sharply at odds with the dismal picture painted [by the GUMG]' (Gavin 2007: 72). Even so, this research must be seen in the context of numerous other studies that have noted the omission of dissenting voices (particularly those of trade union leaders, striking workers, etc.). Notable examples can be seen in Britain (O'Neill 2007), South Africa (Kariithi and Kareithi 2007), Ireland (Fahy et al. 2010), and the USA, Chomsky (1998: 187) and Bekken (2005).

The tendency to rely on elite political and business sources at the expense of others, notably workers, was also highlighted by Alan Budd in his report about impartiality in BBC business reporting (Budd 2007: 20). The BBC was also the focus of Mike Berry's study of BBC Radio 4's morning news programme, *Today*, in the six weeks following the collapse of Lehman Brothers in September 2008 (Berry 2012). This was a crucial period for the British economy and the government had proposed a 'bail out' of debt-stricken banks which was the subject of much media attention. Berry revealed that over one-third of sources appearing on the programme were representatives of financial or other City of London

[11] For a summary of the criticism, see Deacon in Cottle (2003: 102). Alastair Hetherington was particularly critical. The GUMG, according to Hetherington, represented 'the most obvious case' of the 'Marxist tendency' in journalism research. Their first book (GUMG 1976) 'scored… a bull's-eye' but the next two (GUMG 1980, 1982) 'offered prejudiced evidence and suspect statistics' (Hetherington 1985: 20).

institutions, and a further 32% were politicians, most of whom were in favour of 'free markets and light touch regulation'. In contrast, organisations that might offer counter-arguments barely featured: for example, there was only a single appearance by a trade union leader; and perhaps surprisingly, investors accounted for less than 2% of the total (ibid.: 257–258). As noted above, Berry also argued that it is not the source type per se that limits debate but the exclusion of certain viewpoints.[12]

Researchers who have endeavoured to find explanations for such dominance have often highlighted the prevalence of public relations (PR). Some authors[13] suggest that PR tends to be an insidious force, primarily because of its use by the wealthy and powerful to influence the media's reporting in their favour and thus, to bend public opinion. The history of PR gives some credence to this viewpoint. Public relations and lobbying grew rapidly in the USA from the 1930s onwards, as corporate, free-market advocates attempted to roll back the social and economic reforms of Roosevelt's New Deal (Ewen 1996), and it enjoyed a second boom from the late 1970s when American business mounted a 'ideological offensive' on public opinion to redress the perceived anti-business bias of the media (Dreier 1982). The parallel between the rise of the neoliberalism and the expansion in corporate PR is also visible in the UK where consultancy income grew by around 25% per annum in the 1980s (Davis 2000: 283) with even greater growth in the 1990s (Tambini 2008: 21). In these terms, PR seems to confirm its reputation as the servant of neoliberalism. However, although corporations have the greatest fiscal means and, therefore, the most powerful PR operations, the discipline is not inherently pro-business. By developing their own in-house departments and using external consultants, non-commercial organisations such as trade unions, pressure groups and NGOs have had some success in persuading the media to cover their stories (Davis 2002; Wolfsfeld 2003; Bennett et al. 2004; Gavin 2007: 173) and they too can master the 'grammar of news' and learn how to exploit the needs of journalists (McNair 1998: 154). This is not to say, however, that non-commercial sources are equally successful in their hunt for publicity. The largest UK companies generally have an enviable record in turning their PR activities into news items in the financial media

[12] This crucial distinction is addressed in detail below.

[13] For example, Davies (2008) and Rampton and Stauber (1995).

(Davis 2006: 11) and up to 80% of financial news is directly influenced by PR (Hobsbawm 2006: 2).[14]

Over the last decade, researchers have argued that PR is becoming an evermore powerful force in EBF journalism. Paul Manning noted that journalists used to be able to approach senior contacts—such as chief executives—directly, but these days the PR professional has: 'effective control over information flows' (2010: 11). Some scholars have charged EBF journalists with being far too close to their nominal adversaries, and even deifying elite sources (McChesney 2003: 313; Starkman 2014). Indeed, Aeron Davis noted that reporters: '... tend to move in small exclusive circles consisting almost exclusively of City sources' (2000: 285). This is perhaps unsurprising when one considers that journalism textbooks emphasise the importance of building relationships in the pursuit of exclusive stories: 'contacts are a (business) reporter's life blood...make them almost friends', advised Hayes (2014: 31). To compound matters, financial news reporters are more dependent on PR than other specialists and they are the least critical of their sources (Davis 2006: 11). Such reluctance to ask probing questions might be because sources are the sole repositories of information (Tambini 2008; Doyle 2006), or because the journalist fears a loss of access (Robinson 2008), or to compensate for the generally poor level of journalist knowledge. The net result is that EBF journalists have become embedded with the corporate and government officials they are supposed to hold to account (Schechter 2009: 19; Marron et al. 2010: 273; Starkman 2014). A quarter of a century ago, Wayne Parsons warned of the consequences of such integration:

> The danger is that, as in the past, the financial press may become more participants and puffers than observers and more extensions of PR companies than independent commentators and reporters. (1989: 213)

According to Starkman (2014), Parsons' prophecy was evident in the prelude to the 2008 Financial Crisis. The reason that American journalists missed the 'brewing crisis', he suggests, was they did not consult dissenters. This was a consequence of an endemic, insular approach to reporting:

[14]The proportion of general news in UK newspapers composed wholly or mainly from PR and/or newswire copy is estimated at 60% (Davies 2008: 52). In the USA, the equivalent figure is between 40 and 70% (Machin and Niblock 2006: 28).

'an insistence on looking at (the) subject through frames set by the institutions' (ibid.: 144) which, by their nature, have little interest in systemic, wide-ranging problems. Hence, by fostering harmonious relationships with sources in the financial industry, journalists habitually give the investor's perspective. In their defence, journalists note that they have little time to write stories, particularly if they work for TV news organisations, like CNBC and Bloomberg, in which rapid analysis of an endless stream of news releases and data is the main currency (Schifferes and Coulter 2012; Starkman 2014: 156). This is certainly a factor but the inevitable result, as noted by one of Aeron Davis's interviewees, is: 'the national (UK) financial press are written for the City by the City' (Davis 2011).

Political Economy

As demonstrated in the preceding sections, research in both EBF and general news production has revealed recurring patterns. These are the inevitable consequences of shared working practices that, in turn, are determined by the bureaucratic needs of the news production process. However, this process does not take place in an economic or political vacuum: on the contrary, routines are determined by 'the goals and policies of a larger social structure and how power is exerted within it' (Reese 2001: 181). In most instances, such structures are news organisations that are privately owned, either by wealthy individuals or companies quoted on the stock market. For some critical political economy theorists, this means that senior managers of media companies are compelled to hold pro-business sympathies, support government policy that promotes neoliberalism and be active participants in public debate. Although journalistic staff *appear* to have considerable latitude in determining the content of the publication, the news product will inevitably be influenced by the economic and political goals of the owners. Consequently, journalists are discouraged from producing work that is critical of neoliberalism, large corporations and the political status quo, and conversely, argues Fowler, the press is: 'bound to be preoccupied with the ogres of socialism and trade unionism and to condemn them because (they are) antagonistic to the business of making money' (1991: 20).

This scholarly interpretation is compelling, but it clashes with journalists' own perceptions because few are ever told explicitly to suppress or change a story. This is probably true but the political-economic forces that influence news are subtle: hierarchical power is exercised 'periodically, implicitly and covertly', and journalists effectively self-censor by anticipating organisational boundaries (Reese 2001: 182). Compliance is achieved by appointing editors who can be relied upon to steer the reporting in a direction advantageous to the proprietor's interests. Hence, editors intuitively 'second guess' the news values and framing preferences of the owners and so the journalism will be largely consistent with the organisation's needs (Petley 2011: 85). The structured nature of the organisation noted Jackie Harrison in her study of British TV news: '… ensures that the real power is located at the top of the hierarchical pyramid' (2000: 133). Such explanations tally with the Gramscian conception of hegemony—'the voluntary yielding to authority' (Zelizer 2004: 73)—in that the news media habitually defines normality and sets the news agenda in the interests of the powerful. In effect, journalists are 'ideological agents who secure agreement by consensus rather than forced compliance' (ibid.).

Central to critical political economy is the question of whether journalists can be effective watchdogs of democracy if they are employed by organisations owned by the rich and the powerful. This was addressed in Herman and Chomsky's seminal 1988 study which argued the American news media is subject to filters that remove the vast majority of critical perspectives. The research was conducted during a time of polarised Cold War politics and the authors' 'Propaganda Model' became very influential. Although it has arguably less relevance in a modern British context, the work still provides a useful framework for analysing the broad characteristics of news. Taken at face value, Herman and Chomsky present a rigid view of a news media: '…working hand in glove with other large corporations to stifle dissent' (Schudson 2005: 177) but this interpretation is problematic. As shown above protestors, striking workers, social reformers and other radical voices are not totally excluded from news reports, and examples journalism that have exposed the abuse of power, corporate misdeeds and political corruption are often cited as evidence that the news media is an efficient watchdog for society. In a British context, however, Schlosberg (2013: 196) argues that even some of the most celebrated examples of journalism that seemingly brought the powerful to account:

> … painted a picture of transparency or restorative justice that was ultimately in tune with elite sources, to the exclusion or marginalisation of alternative frames.

In these terms, dissent is not totally silenced but the news media generally: 'reinforce the established society, uphold law and order and accept social reform only gradually' (Hetherington 1985: 12). By gravitating to elite sources, who are unlikely to be radical reformers, the media make existing power structures seem normal, and hence opposition becomes: 'unreasonable, quixotic or utopian' (Schudson 2005: 177).

With much of the UK—and virtually all the US—news media privately owned, it would be surprising 'if the press was a hot bed of radical thought' (Schudson 1989: 268–269). Indeed, some scholars argue that the news media has been a crucial part of the establishment—and hence, antagonistic to dissenting perspectives—since at least the late nineteenth century (Petley 2009a: 188). Other authors suggest that the tendency to under-report dissent is becoming more pronounced (Davies 2008). The rise of online news and social media has intensified the pressure on print and broadcast organisations to focus on economic imperatives at the expense of probing journalism. In the UK, the five national broadsheets lost an average of 22% of paying readers in less than nine years (*Guardian* 2001, 2010). To reduce costs, British news organisations have cut thousands of journalism jobs: a Newspaper Society survey in 2007, for instance, revealed a decline in employment of 30% in five years (Nel 2010) and another study found almost 10,000 journalism job losses were reported between January 2007 and June 2009 alone (AJE 2010).

It has been a similar story in broadcasting where the digital revolution has intensified competition and fragmented audiences. As a publicly funded, public service organisation, the BBC has a different set of priorities to profit-driven broadcasters, but it still needs to attract audiences to justify its licence fee and operates as an increasingly commercialised entity (Gavin 2007: 8; Harrison 2000: 203). Under such conditions, news organisations focus on delivering safe and entertaining news, largely generated by corporate PR machines and newswires to a selected audience, thus attracting premium advertising (Davies 2008). The net result of declining audiences, plunging advertising revenues and reduced editorial staff is a diminishing ability to perform Fourth Estate duties. Despite the noble intentions of journalists, uncovering deception and exposing injustice is inherently more difficult if newsrooms are under-resourced, and owners are increasingly reluctant to alienate their advertising clients and members of their elite social circles.

Research has also touched on the effect that political-economic factors have specifically on the production of EBF news. According to Starkman (2009), the commercial challenges of the American business media began with the bursting of the dot-com bubble in 2000 when advertising revenues plunged and never recovered. Stock market values of newspaper groups shrank and: 'the drip of newsroom cuts became a deluge - newspapers lost 13,000 jobs [in 2008] - and business news hasn't been spared'. The UK business media has endured similar experiences and there is little optimism for a return to a perceived golden age. As noted by Aeron Davis, 'Like most news sections, financial media has suffered from an increase in output demands at the same time as news resources have declined' (2011). One solution is to reduce staff and replace original journalism with 'inexpensive syndicated material and fluff' (McChesney et al. 1998: 18). Under these circumstances, reporters hoping to honour their civic responsibilities will be frustrated because investigations require time and resources. As Gillian Doyle's interviews with British financial journalists revealed:

> ...the circumstances and constraints (reporters) work within ... make it unlikely that financial irregularities obscured within company accounts will be detected on a routine or consistent basis. (2006: 433)

Furthermore, business news is more susceptible to political-economic pressures than other specialisms—for example, sports journalism—because it is supported by advertising from the same entities upon which it reports. Hence, media organisations have little incentive to raise doubts over a booming economy, a buoyant industry or the activities of individual corporations (Shaw 2016). Some authors, notably Davies (2008), dismiss charges of explicit links between commercial needs and journalistic decisions as a 'conspiracy' but editors are 'all too aware that advertisers like their advertisements to appear within a sympathetic editorial ambiance' (Petley 2011: 82). Consequently, the commercial EBF news media is simply not designed to put investigative journalism—accountable to the public rather than investors—ahead of financial demands (Starkman 2014).

This point resurrects questions about the purpose of EBF journalism. As noted above, there is little agreement among scholars and practitioners. The image is blurred further when one considers Keith Butterick's contention that business and financial journalism has two functions: it is the 'sphere through which the corporate world prefers to interact with society'; *and* 'the vehicle through which economic ideas... are discussed and promulgated' (2015: xi). This coexistence has been present since the seventeenth century, maintains Butterick, when joint-stock companies, the forerunners to modern public companies, were formed to exploit international trade. From the British railway mania of the nineteenth century, through the Great Depression and the subsequent rise and fall of Keynesian economics, onto the ascent of neoliberalism and the 2008 Financial Crisis, the business and financial media has done much more than report on the activities of companies; it has also been at the heart of political debate.

Ibrahim Seaga Shaw, however, identifies tension between two antagonistic principles. Business journalists, he wrote, walk a 'tightrope' and have repeatedly failed to 'strike a balance' between competing forces: on the one side is the social liberalism that allows—and expects—them to openly and freely criticise power on behalf of the public, and on the other is neoliberalism upon which journalists depend for financial sustenance (2016: xii). This is perhaps not surprising when one considers that 'journalism based on the neoliberal capitalist model breathes and lives capitalism' and so any crisis in capitalism will clearly have a damaging effect on news organisations (ibid.: 14). In short, it is not the interests of EBF journalism to be overtly critical of the dominant economic paradigm.

The Political Content of EBF Journalism

While the financial media is generally recognised by academics as having a key role in 'influencing events and policy response' (Schifferes and Roberts 2015: xvi), the political content of the news product is invariably underplayed by scholars, and sometimes it is neglected altogether. This is a grave omission because the three closely interrelated disciplines of economics, business and finance are inherently susceptible to different interpretations, policies and remedies. Consequently, politics, or more precisely, political ideas, narratives and assumptions are present in all EBF reporting. In modern times, of course, the prevailing economic paradigm has been neoliberalism. But, as Butterick underlines, neoliberalism is 'more than an economic philosophy; it is also a social philosophy which aims to radically transform society' (2015: 168). Understanding *how* neoliberalism is reported, therefore, is a vitally important element in the quest for better EBF journalism. Citizens of democratic societies, blessed with pluralistic news media, might reasonably expect that all political ideas are critically analysed by journalists as a matter of course. Research, however, suggests they are not.

Before assessing previous studies in this area, it is important to emphasise some key characteristics of neoliberalism. At its core is the belief that 'human wellbeing can be best advanced by liberating entrepreneurial freedoms and skills' (Harvey 2005: 2). Hence, markets are the 'primary means of organising society' (Mansell 2011: 20) and together with low taxation; low inflation; and minimal government intervention, proponents hope to create a fertile environment in which private enterprise can create wealth (Heywood 1992: 81–86). True to its roots in classical liberalism, neoliberalism places faith in the individual rather than the collective, and business, particularly the joint-stock company, is seen as the engine of economic success. It is vital to stress, however, that economics is an inherently subjective discipline and neoliberalism is just one of many models. For centuries theorists and politicians have striven to find a framework that can deliver enhanced, sustained and universal well-being. Such debates are perpetual and there is no definitive answer to the basic economic problem of reconciling finite resources and infinite wants. The same is true of business: the modern corporation, owned by public shareholders and focussed on maximising investor returns, is just one form of commercial entity. Others include worker cooperatives, state-owned enterprises, family-run businesses and freelances.

Alternatives to neoliberalism clearly exist and yet, over the last two decades, there has been scant evidence of mainstream political debate. Acknowledging Francis Fukuyama's (1992) proclamation that the demise of the Communist bloc represented the 'end of history' and proved the superiority of capitalism, Žižek suggests that by adopting the tenets of neoliberalism, traditionally left-wing parties had negated its negation (2008: 189). Although few political parties during the period covered by the case studies offered a: 'convincing alternative grand narrative capable of challenging neoliberalism' (Cammaerts 2011: 48), the doctrine still has plenty of credible opposition. For example, Nobel Prize winner Joseph Stiglitz questioned the neoliberal assumption that markets are self-correcting and serve the public interest well (Mansell 2011: 20) and others have focussed on the social consequences of this particularly brutal form of capitalism that prioritises unfettered profit maximisation over everything else (Klein 2000; Monbiot 2001; Pilger 2002; Bakan 2004; McChesney in Chomsky 1999). Consequently, in the absence of coordinated criticism from left-of-centre parties, counter-arguments to neoliberalism typically come from trade unions; anti-poverty, environmental and development NGOs; think tanks; and a scattering of intellectuals (Cammaerts 2011: 48).

For this reason, journalism researchers typically deduce the presence of different interpretations of the economic environment from the source type, but this can be misleading. For example, a business person could conceivably argue for policies that are normally the domain of NGOs or trade unions. Also, the narrative of a news item could take a different political stance than the sources might suggest, or in the case of an opinion piece, a journalist could argue for a particular policy without quoting a single source. Hence, one could argue that it is not the source profile of news per se that is important but whether a diversity of perspectives are provided. This is somewhat more difficult to gauge than simply categorising source types, and few scholars even acknowledge that EBF news has an inherently political element. Even so, there is sufficient research to suggest that much news reporting has normalised neoliberalism, and arguments that might question its assumptions are rarely aired.

This was particularly evident in Mike Berry's study of BBC Radio 4's *Today* programme[15] (2012). As well as analysing sources, Berry also assessed the extent to which competing arguments about the UK government's bank rescue plan were given exposure. Injecting public money (the 'bank bailout') was just one of several options and was supported by virtually all key sources—mostly from the City of London—and yet an alternative policy, nationalisation, was barely mentioned or quickly dismissed (ibid.: 260–261). These findings mirrored similar content studies by the GUMG (1976, 1980, 1982) and by Aeron Davis (2000) in his analysis of the takeover of Forte by Granada, in which the investor perspective dominated and, in contrast, just 7% of articles mentioned the impact on workers, and 4% on customers.

Despite such empirical evidence, some maintain that business is unfairly represented in news reports. This charge is frequently levelled at the BBC which, because of its statutory obligation to impartiality, is institutionally sensitive to charges of imbalance (Gavin 2007: 10). Such accusations are surprising, however, when one considers the development of business journalism at the BBC. Coverage increased significantly

[15]A subsequent paper by this author focussed on BBC News at Ten's coverage of the UK's public deficit debate in 2009. Again, political and financial elite sources dominated and the news 'reproduced a very limited range of opinion' (Berry 2016).

during Margaret Thatcher's period in office, and by the early 1990s, 'a certain social democratic paradigm that had been institutionalised... in reporting had been displaced' by an acceptance of neoliberalism (Mills 2016: 189). Over the next decade, successive director generals gave greater priority to business reporting. Both John Birt and then Greg Dyke appointed pro-market journalists to senior editorial positions,[16] in which the incumbents set 'the tone of the journalism rather than providing management oversight' (ibid.: 180–205). The BBC's first business editor, Jeff Randall, who joined in 2001, arrived with a perception that the Corporation was: 'culturally and structurally biased against business' (in Boyle 2008: 416). This widely shared view was the catalyst for a major study of the impartiality of BBC business reporting chaired by Alan Budd.[17] Although the author found no 'evidence of systemic (anti-business) bias', he did discover a 'polarisation of views between business and consumer' and a neglect of news from the perspective of investors, as well as workers (Budd 2007).

Academics, however, tend to be far more critical. As noted by Tom Mills, by 2007, economics and business reporting at the BBC had become 'hopelessly conflated as the "economic life of the nation" (and) was covered ever more from the viewpoint of the corporate elite' (Mills 2016: 106). This was also evident during the industrial disputes of the 1970s and 1980s, when the BBC's coverage 'barely featured' perspectives of workers, and during the 1984/5 miners' strike in particular, news reports were 'overwhelming favourable' to the perspectives of government and managers (ibid.: 174). The exclusion of arguments from trade unions—and employees in general—is a recurring theme in EBF research. This could be a simple reflection of societal changes: unions are less powerful, have fewer members and have been in decline for four decades, so one might expect less coverage (McNair 1998). But although trade unions are able to set the parameters of debate, and many unions believe that media coverage improved in the 1990s (Davis 2002), organised labour seems to be treated by the British media with, at best, indifference: 'Unions believe ... that the world of work does not really feature on the BBC – and even when it does it is without the workers' (Budd 2007: 20).

[16] In his account of the development of BBC business journalism, Mills briefly describes the previous careers of three editors—Peter Jay, Evan Davis and Jeff Randall—who were 'thoroughly committed to orthodox economic theory' (Mills 2016: 185).

[17] Mills describes Budd as 'the neoliberal economist' (2016: 198).

The findings of these British studies are largely consistent with research from other countries that shows EBF reporters habitually accept and reinforce neoliberalism. In the USA, for example, Herbert Gans (2003: 46) observed the irony that, although there are far more workers than bankers in the US economy, journalists reporting on worker issues tend to gravitate towards officials in the Treasury and Federal Reserve. Similarly, there has been very little mediated debate about whether 'markets work' (Sherman 2002: 28), and the view that reduced corporate regulation and 'free markets' have delivered widespread prosperity has been largely accepted as 'conventional wisdom' (Goozner 2000: 24). Taking a global perspective, Kantola (2006) analysed the *Financial Times*' coverage of 32 elections between 2000 and 2005 and discovered that candidates in favour of pro-market reforms were repeatedly favoured. This is, perhaps, to be expected from the *FT* but similar phenomena were also observed in the popular news media of South Africa (Kariithi and Kareithi 2007) and Finland (Ainamo et al. 2006: 630). In both of these examples, the news media also played an active role in delegitimising conflicting (left-wing) perspectives: 'In doing so', argued Kariithi and Kareithi, 'the mass media rendered as common sense and natural the logic of the contemporary neoliberal global economy'. Indeed, other studies confirm that EBF reporters seem to accept neoliberalism as a fact of life. For example, Gillian Doyle's interviews with British journalists revealed: 'passivity in relation to pro-market ideologies' (2006: 446), a mindset that tallies with Tumber's (1993: 358) observation that most business news is: 'supportive, complimentary and consonant with the media's role in reproduction of the dominant ideology'.

Neoliberalism has become a pervasive, hegemonic discourse which makes it: 'part of the common-sense view of the world' (Thussu 2007: 134). It is also a subtle discourse: many economic and business concepts are abstract, so metaphors are commonly used by reporters (Augey and Brin 2004). By characterising 'the economy' or 'the market' in anthropomorphic, meteorological, biological or mechanical terms,[18] it becomes a reified, mysterious force outside of the control of people or even government (Emmison 1983, 1986; Jensen 1987). The language and images: 'which serve to constitute (the economy) are produced without reflection. It has become the 'natural' way to see ... a world

[18]For example, 'a machine requiring fixing' or 'as a beast or animal... in varying degrees of health' (Emmison 1986: 91).

of normality' (Emmison 1983: 154). What's more, by aggregating the needs of groups with opposing interests—for example, workers who want higher wages and shareholders who want increased dividends—'the economy' itself becomes a constructed, ideological category applied to the public as a whole (Emmison 1986; Mills 2016: 169).

This 'one-size-fits-all' approach is vividly apparent when news reports equate the health of the economy to stock market movements and, hence, the contentment of the investor community (Croteau and Hoynes 2000: 169). Such assumptions were also evident in the pre-2008 boom, suggests Keith Butterick, when 'too many' business and financial journalists had 'become the willing or unwilling apostles of neoliberal, low tax, less government interference, loose labour laws policies and the transfer of wealth from the poor to the rich' (2015: xii). According to British journalists Hugh Pym and Nick Kochan, the acceptance of this modern form of capitalism is a simple reflection of the convergence of mainstream political opinion (2008: 3). There is evidence, however, that the world's publics are not so convinced. In 2009, one year after the Financial Crisis, a major international survey[19] found widespread disillusionment. In only two countries did more than 20% of people think capitalism was working well, and a higher proportion thought it 'fatally flawed'. Globally, there was also significant support for more government regulation of business and a fairer distribution of wealth (BBC World Service 2009).

Although this survey was conducted at a particularly traumatic time, it confirmed that the mainstream political consensus is not universally accepted. Hence, one might expect a pluralistic news media to give voice to critics of neoliberalism, but the research suggests the more vociferous are demonised. In the 1970s and 1980s, for example, Ken Livingstone, Tony Benn and other left-wing politicians were pilloried by the British press (Curran et al. 2018) and this tendency is still apparent in political and popular dissent against neoliberalism.[20] For example, Thomas Friedman's[21] description of World Trade Organisation protestors

[19]The researchers questioned 29,000 people in 27 countries.

[20]In recent years, Jeremy Corbyn has received similarly negative coverage in the British news media (Couldry and Cammaerts 2016; Schlosberg 2016).

[21]Friedman wrote *The Lexus and the Olive Tree* (1999), a seminal text for the advocates of (neoliberal) globalisation.

in 1999 was indicative of a common representation of misguided misfits fighting against an inevitable tide: 'a Noah's ark of flat-earth advocates, protectionist trade unions, and yuppies looking for their 1960s fix' (in Goozner 2000: 24).

NGOs, trade unions and popular movements may have better access to the media than ever before, but it is debatable whether they have made much progress in the 'contest over meaning' (Wolfsfeld 2003: 94). Even if the news media does pay attention, a preoccupation with violent protest often ignores or undermines the merit of the political arguments (Solomon 2000; Smith et al. 2001; Cottle 2003: 158). This 'protest paradigm' has been evident since the anti-Vietnam War demonstrations of the 1960s and was also apparent in the representation of the 'anti-globalisation' movement in the late 1990s (Gitlin 1980; Jha 2007; Gavin 2007). *Ad hominem* attacks by journalists on protestors, strikers or socialist politicians may be deemed acceptable because, in Daniel Hallin's (1986) terms, they are in the 'zone of deviance', outside of what mainstream culture accepts as normal, and hence beyond the professional journalistic codes of objectivity and fairness. In Stuart Hood's words, journalists define 'impartiality as the acceptance of that segment of opinion which constitutes parliamentary consensus' (Curran and Seaton 1991: 200). Hence, if political parties do not offer a plurality of interpretations, then journalists feel no obligation to find and present views from outside of the mainstream spectrum (Petley 2009a: 606).

With neoliberalism normalised, reified and constantly reinforced, it is perhaps inevitable that EBF journalism has a patchy record in warning of economic hazard. By the same token, the news media are also criticised for neglecting endemic problems associated with neoliberalism. Poverty, unemployment, shortages of affordable housing and social deprivation are long-term, interrelated issues that necessitate widespread and frequent mediated debate if they are to be resolved, and yet EBF news tends to be episodic, dealing with: '...single issues that emerge, occupy journalists' and the public's attention and then recede' (Wu et al. 2002: 33). Bob McChesney gave a blunt assessment of this propensity in American journalism:

> ... the virtual absence of news concerning the working class and poor is taken for granted by professional journalists. It is not seen as "self-censorship" to shape the news in such a manner. That is the genius of professionalism as a form of regulation. (2003: 313)

There are signs, however, that popular movements and campaigns orchestrated by NGOs and can make an impact,[22] and there are times when 'radical' voices are allowed to contribute to debates about underlying systems and structures (Schudson 1989: 267; Tumber 1993: 358). However, such deliberations in the mainstream media are rare (Milne 2009; Payne 2008) and the balance of reporting is still strongly tilted in favour of elite institutions, like the World Economic Forum, governments, business and, hence, the neoliberal status quo (Bennett et al. 2004: 437; Smith et al. 2001: 1414; Jha 2007).

The inability to address economic issues critically and as part of a bigger picture characterised the non-reporting of warning signals in the prelude to the 2008 Financial Crisis. Paul Manning argues that evidence of impending disaster *was* available to journalists but 'few began to develop a comprehensive or holistic approach that might point to the broadest dangers' (2010: 6). Professor Alistair Milne echoed Manning's assertion and said journalists rarely analyse the capitalist system itself, and its impact on society as a whole (Milne 2009). 'Systemic criticism' was also absent in the Irish news media in the days of the 'Celtic Tiger' economic boom, and it was not until the scale of the Crisis became apparent that previously marginalised voices were heard in news reports (Fahy et al. 2010). It would appear that meaningful and informed public debate about the foundations of neoliberalism only occurs in difficult economic times.

In the light of these findings, it is useful to resurrect questions about the purpose of EBF journalism. As Tambini (2010), Starkman (2014) and other scholars have noted, there is a public need for journalists to be critical about the structures of economic systems, not just individual actors, companies and events. Despite journalists showing signs of contrition over their profession's performance in the prelude to the 2008 Financial Crisis, research has revealed few examples of practitioners acknowledging that they need to make any substantial changes to their approach. Some of Paul Manning's interviewees, for instance, were surprised how much they had embraced: 'received economic wisdom… a set of assumptions about the nature of the political and economic world that were profoundly ideological' (2014: 186) and yet they showed little

[22] For example, Make Poverty History in 2005.

sign of challenging beliefs or practices. Crucially, these assumptions[23] were shared with the business community and politicians, and as members of the same broad social group, EBF journalists do not believe it is their role to question the elite consensus (Pym in Manning 2014: 186). Hence, suggests Mike Berry, if the British news media, especially public service broadcasters, simply report on 'shades of opinion at Westminster', then citizens are inevitably offered a restricted range of debate and are: 'denied the information necessary to make informed political decisions' (2012: 267–268).

Conclusion

History demonstrates that EBF journalism has developed in tandem with economic doctrines and is the inevitable product of its past. Furthermore, the political economy of the EBF news media is largely consistent with that of the profit-focussed organisations upon which their journalists report, and executives depend upon for advertising income. It follows that the news media will habitually convey ideas, arguments and policies that present neoliberalism in positive terms. EBF journalists have also become too close to their sources to be effective critics and the symbiotic relationship between the financial media and public companies is deeply rooted. Hence, a political monoculture exists in which media executives, editors, reporters and their sources all hold neoliberal assumptions. Consequently, from an audience perspective, argues Butterick: 'neoliberalism is now embedded into our common sense and our language'. Indeed, the pervasiveness of neoliberalism is evident at the end of every BBC news report with the single figure assessment of the health of the economy: the FTSE 100. The normality of this data is 'so entrenched that many cannot conceive of any alternative' (Butterick 2015: 127, 171).

Although the media are not simply 'passive transmission belts of capitalist propaganda' (Dreier 1982: 123) and theories of elite domination are far from infallible, previous research suggests that the UK—and other Western democracies—does not have an inclusive EBF news media that might facilitate informed public debate about the economic environment. Furthermore, reporting from the point of view of citizens, rather

[23]Manning gives the example: 'dominant neoliberal discourses promoting deregulated financial services as an unquestioned success' (2014: 186).

than consumers or shareholders, would necessitate a fundamental change in working practices and sourcing strategies. Even with the benefit of post-Financial Crisis hindsight, however, Gillian Doyle's assessment still holds true: 'commercially-led financial news production… is not really designed for and is unlikely to succeed in any public educational role' (Doyle 2006: 451).

References

Ainamo, A., Tienari, J., & Vaara, E. (2006). Between West and East: A Social History of Business Journalism in Cold War Finland. *Human Relations, 59*, 611–636.

AJE. (2010). *UK Journalism Cuts a Third of Jobs in Decade*. Association for Journalism Education. Retrieved from http://www.ajeuk.org/2010/09/09/uk-journalism-cuts-a-third-of-jobs-in-decade. Accessed November 22, 2014.

Arts, F., Takeshita, T., & Becker L. (2002, July 21–26). *Economic News and Perceptions of the Economy: Results from the Netherlands, Japan and United States*. Presented at the Annual Conference of the IAMCR, Barcelona, Spain.

Augey, D., & Brin, C. (2004, May 12–15). *Media and Manias: News and Economic Decision-Making*. Presented at Sixth World Media Economics Conference, Montréal, Canada.

Bakan, J. (2004). *The Corporation: The Pathological Pursuit of Profit and Power*. Toronto: Viking Canada.

Barber, L. (2009, April 21). *On Why Journalists Missed the Impending Financial Crisis*. Poynter Fellowship Lecture at Yale University. Retrieved from http://cjrarchive.org/img/posts/LionelBarber-lecture.pdf. Accessed January 27, 2010.

BBC World Service. (2009). *Wide Dissatisfaction with Capitalism—Twenty Years After Fall of Berlin Wall*. Opinion Poll Produced in Conjunction with PIPA and Globescan. Retrieved from www.globescan.com/news_archives/bbc2009_berlin_wall. Accessed January 1, 2010.

Bekken, J. (2005). The Invisible Enemy: Representing Labour in a Corporate Media Order. *The Public, 12*(1), 71–84.

Bennett, W., Packard, V., Iozzi, D., Schroeder, C., Lagos, T., & Caswell, C. (2004). Managing the Public Sphere: Journalistic Construction of the Great Globalization Debate. *Journal of Communication, 54*(3), 437–455.

Berry, M. (2012). The Today Programme and the Banking Crisis. *Journalism, 14*(2), 253–270.

Berry, M. (2013, August 23). Hard Evidence: How Biased Is the BBC? *New Statesman*.

Berry, M. (2016). No Alternative to Austerity: How BBC Broadcast News Reported the Deficit Debate. *Media, Culture and Society, 38*(6), 844–863.

Bow, J. (1980). The Times' Financial Markets Column in the Period Around the 1929 Crash. *Journalism Quarterly, 57*(447–450), 497.

Boyle, R. (2008). From Troubleshooter to The Apprentice: The Changing Face of Business on British Television. *Media Culture Society, 30*, 415.

Brummer, A. (2009). Far from Scaring People, the Press Were Providing Readers with Reliable Information. In J. Mair & R. Keeble (Eds.), *Playing Footsie with the FTSE? The Great Crash of 2008* (pp. 38–41). Bury St Edmunds: Abramis Academic.

Budd, A. (2007). *Report of the Independent Panel for the BBC Trust on Impartiality of BBC Business Coverage*. Retrieved from http://www.bbc.co.uk/bbctrust/our_work/other/business_news.shtml. Accessed January 1, 2010.

Butterick, K. (2015). *Complacency and Collusion: A Critical Introduction to Business and Financial Journalism*. London: Pluto Press.

Cammaerts, B. (2011). Disruptive Sharing in a Digital Age: Rejecting Neoliberalism? *Continuum, 25*(1), 47–62.

Cassidy, J. (2002). *Dot Con: The Real Story of Why the Internet Bubble Burst*. London: Penguin.

Cassy, J. (2003, January 6). Let's Not Do Lunch.... *Guardian*. Retrieved from http://www.guardian.co.uk/media/2003/jan/06/financialtimes.mondaymediasection. Accessed January 24, 2010.

Chomsky, N. (1998). Propaganda and Control of the Public Mind. In R. McChesney, E. Meiskins Wood, & J. Foster (Eds.), *Capitalism and the Information Age: The Political Economy of the Global Communication Revolution* (pp. 179–190). New York: Monthly Review Press.

Chomsky, N. (1999). *Profit Over People: Neoliberalism and Global Order*. London and Toronto: Seven Stories Press.

Corner, J., Gavin, N., Goddard, P., & Richardson, K. (1997). Television News and Public Knowledge: Understanding the Economy. *Hermes, 21*, 81–93.

Cottle, S. (Ed.). (2003). *News, Public Relations and Power*. London: Sage.

Couldry, N., & Cammaerts, B. (2016). *Journalistic Representations of Jeremy Corbyn in the British Press: From Watchdog to Attack Dog*. London School of Economics. Retrieved from http://www.lse.ac.uk/media@lse/research/pdf/JeremyCorbyn/Cobyn-Report-FINAL.pdf. Accessed February 13, 2017.

Croteau, D. (1998, July/August). *Challenging the "Liberal Media" Claim: On Economics, Journalists' Private Views Are to Right of Public*. Extra! FAIR.

Croteau, D., & Hoynes, W. (2000). *Media Society: Industries, Images and Audiences*. Thousand Oaks, CA: Pine Forge.

Curran, J., & Seaton, J. (1991). *Power Without Responsibility: The Press and Broadcasting in Britain*. London: Routledge.

Curran, J., Gaber, I., & Petley, J. (2018). *Culture Wars: The Media and the British Left* (2nd ed.). Abingdon: Routledge.

Dale, R. (2004). *The First Crash: Lessons from the South Sea Bubble*. Princeton, NJ: Princeton University Press.

Davies, N. (2008). *Flat Earth News: Falsehood, Distortion and Propaganda in the Global Media*. London: Vintage.

Davis, A. (2000). Public Relations, Business News and the Reproduction of Corporate Elite Power. *Journalism, 1*(3), 282–304.

Davis, A. (2002). *Public Relations Democracy: Public Relations, Politics and the Mass Media in Britain*. Manchester and New York: Manchester University Press.

Davis, A. (2006). The Role of the Mass Media in Investor Relations. *Journal of Communication Management, 10*(1), 7–17.

Davis, A. (2007). Economic Inefficiency of Market Liberalisation: The Case of the London Stock Exchange. *Global Media and Communication, 3*(2), 157–178.

Davis, A. (2011). News of the Financial Sector: Reporting on the City or to It? *Open Democracy*. Retrieved from https://www.opendemocracy.net/ourkingdom/aeron-davis/news-of-financial-sector-reporting-on-city-or-to-it. Accessed August 15, 2014.

Deacon, D. (2003). Non-governmental Organisations and the Media. In S. Cottle (Ed.), *News, Public Relations and Power* (pp. 99–115). London: Sage.

Doyle, G. (2006). Financial News Journalism: A Post-Enron Analysis of Approaches Towards Economic and Financial News Production in the UK. *Journalism, 7*(4), 433–452.

Drier, P. (1982). Capitalism vs. the Media: An Analysis of an Ideological Mobilisation Among Business Leaders. *Media, Culture and Society, 4*(2), 111–132.

Dyck, A., & Zingales, L. (2003). The Bubble and the Media. In P. Cornelius & B. Kogut (Eds.), *Corporate Governance and Capital Flows in a Global Economy* (pp. 83–103). New York and Oxford: Oxford University Press.

Edwards, D., & Cromwell, D. (2009). *Newspeak in the 21st Century*. London: Pluto Press.

Elliott, L. (2009, December 2). *Saints or Sinners: The Role of the Financial Media in the Financial Crisis*. Conference, City University, London. Retrieved from http://www.city.ac.uk/whatson/2009/12_dec/021209-media-financial-crisis. Accessed December 23, 2009.

Emmison, M. (1983). The Economy and Its Emergence in Media Discourse. In H. Davis & P. Walton (Eds.), *Language, Image, Media* (pp. 139–155). Oxford: Blackwell.

Emmison, M. (1986). Visualizing the Economy: Fetishism and the Legitimation of Economic Life. *Theory Culture Society, 3*, 81–95.

Ewen, S. (1996). *PR! A Social History of Spin*. New York: Basic Books.

Fahy, D., O'Brien, M., & Poti, V. (2010). From Boom to Bust: A Post-Celtic Tiger Analysis of the Norms, Values and Roles of Irish Financial Journalists. *Irish Communications Review, 12*(2), 5–20.
Fowler, R. (1991). *Language in the News: Discourse and Ideology in the Press.* London: Routledge.
Frank, T. (2001). *One Market Under God: Extreme Capitalism, Market Populism and the End of Economic Democracy.* London: Secker & Warburg.
Friedman, T. (1999). *The Lexus and the Olive Tree.* London: HarperCollins.
Fukuyama, F. (1992). *The End of History and the Last Man.* New York: Free Press.
Gans, H. (1979). *Deciding What's News: A Study of CBS Evening News, NBC Nightly News, Newsweek, and Time.* Evenston, IL: North-western University Press.
Gans, H. (2003). *Democracy and the News.* New York: Oxford University Press.
Gavin, N. (1998). *The Economy, Media and Public Knowledge.* London: Leicester University Press.
Gavin, N. (2007). *Press and Television in British Politics: Media, Money and Mediated Democracy.* Basingstoke: Palgrave Macmillan.
Gavin, N., & Goddard, P. (1998). Television News and the Economy: Inflation in Britain. *Media, Culture and Society, 20,* 451–470.
Gitlin, T. (1980). *The Whole World Is Watching; Mass Media in the Making and Unmaking of the New Left.* Berkeley, CA: University of California Press.
Glasgow University Media Group. (1976). *Bad News.* London: Routledge.
Glasgow University Media Group. (1980). *More Bad News.* London: Routledge.
Glasgow University Media Group. (1982). *Really Bad News.* London: Routledge.
Goozner, M. (2000). Blinded By the Boom: What's Missing in the Coverage of the New Economy? *Columbia Journalism Review, 39*(November/December), 23–35.
Guardian. (2001). *National Newspaper Circulation—Dailies.* Retrieved from http://media.guardian.co.uk/presspublishing/tables/0,,592183,00.html. Accessed April 6, 2010.
Guardian. (2010, February). *ABCs: National Daily Newspaper Circulation.* Retrieved from http://www.guardian.co.uk/media/table/2010/mar/12/abcs-dailies-february-2010. Accessed April 6, 2010.
Hallin, D. (1986). *The Uncensored War: The Media and Vietnam.* New York: Oxford University Press.
Harrison, J. (2000). *Terrestrial TV News in Britain.* Manchester: Manchester University Press.
Harvey, D. (2005). *A Brief History of Neoliberalism.* New York: Oxford University Press.
Hayes, K. (2014). *Business Journalism: How to Report on Business and Economics.* London: Apress.

Henriques, D. (2000). Business Reporting: Behind the Curve. *Columbia Journalism Review, 39*(November/December), 18–21.

Herman, E., & Chomsky, N. (1988). *Manufacturing Consent: The Political Economy of the Mass Media*. New York: Pantheon Books.

Hetherington, A. (1985). *News, Newspapers and Television*. Basingstoke: MacMillan Press.

Heywood, A. (1992). *Political Ideologies: An Introduction*. Basingstoke: MacMillan Press.

Hobsbawm, J. (2006). *Where the Truth Lies: Trust and Morality in PR and Journalism*. London: Atlantic Books.

Jensen, K. (1987). News as Ideology: Economic Statistics and Political Ritual in Television Network News. *Journal of Communication, 37*(1), 8–27.

Jha, S. (2007). Exploring Internet Influence on the Coverage of Social Protest: Content Analysis Comparing Protest Coverage in 1967 and 1999. *Journalism & Mass Communication Quarterly, 84*(1), 40–57.

Kantola, A. (2006). On the Dark Side of Democracy: The Global Imaginary of Financial Journalism. In B. Cammaerts & N. Carpentier (Eds.), *Reclaiming the Media: Communication, Rights and Democratic Media Roles*. Bristol: Intellect.

Kariithi, N., & Kareithi, P. (2007). It's off to Work You Go! A Critical Discourse Analysis of Media Coverage of the Anti-privatisation Strike in South Africa in October 2002. *Journalism Studies, 8*(3), 465–480.

Kinsey, M. (2009). Reporting Business, Finance and the City. In J. Chapman & M. Kinsey (Eds.), *Broadcast Journalism: A Critical Introduction* (pp. 159–170). London: Routledge.

Kjaer, P., & Slaatta, T. (2007). *Mediating Business: The Expansion of Business Journalism*. Copenhagen: Copenhagen Business School Press.

Klein, N. (2000). *No Logo*. London: Flamingo.

Knowles, S., Phillips, G., & Lidberg, J. (2017). Reporting the Global Financial Crisis. *Journalism Studies, 18*(3), 322–340.

Lasorsa, D., & Reese, S. (1990). News Source Use in the Crash of 1987: A Study of Four National Media. *Journalism Quarterly, 67*, 61–71.

Lewis, J., Williams, A., Franklin, B., Thomas, J., & Mosdell, N. (2008). *The Quality and Independence of British Journalism: Tracking the Changes Over 20 Years*. MediaWise Journalism and Public Trust Project.

Machin, D., & Niblock, S. (2006). *News Production: Theory and Practice*. Abingdon: Routledge.

Madrick, J. (2003). Financial Reporting: Lessons of the Enron Collapse. *Harvard International Journal of Press/Politics, 8*(1), 3–7.

Manning, P. (2010, January 7). *News Sources, News Agencies and the Banking Crisis*. Conference paper MeCCSA, London School of Economics.

Manning, P. (2014). Financial Journalism, News Sources and the Banking Crisis. *Journalism, 14*(2), 173–189.

Mansell, R. (2011). New Visions, Old Practices: Policy and Regulation in the Internet Era. *Continuum: Journal of Media and Cultural Studies, 25*(1), 19–32.
Marron, M., Sarabia-Panol, Z., Sison, M., Rao, S., & Niekamp, R. (2010). The Scorecard on Reporting of the Global Financial Crisis. *Journalism Studies, 11*(2), 270–283.
McChesney, R. (1999). Introduction. In N. Chomsky (Ed.), *Profit Over People: Neoliberalism and Global Order* (pp. 7–16). Toronto: Seven Stories Press.
McChesney, R. (2003). The Problem of Journalism: A Political Economic Contribution to An Explanation of the Crisis in Contemporary US Journalism. *Journalism Studies, 4*(3), 299–329.
McChesney, R., Meiskins Wood, E., & Foster, J. (Eds.). (1998). *Capitalism and the Information Age: The Political Economy of the Global Communication Revolution*. New York: Monthly Review Press.
McNair, B. (1998). *The Sociology of Journalism*. London: Arnold.
McQuail, D. (1977). *Analysis of Newspaper Content. Royal Commission on the Press*. London: Her Majesty's Stationery Office.
McQuail, D. (1997). *Audience Analysis*. Thousand Oaks, CA: Sage.
McShane, S. (1995). Occupational, Gender, and Geographic Representations of Information Sources in U.S. and Canadian Business Magazines. *Journalism and Mass Communication Quarterly, 72*, 190–204.
Mills, T. (2016). *The BBC: The Myth of a Public Service*. London: Verso.
Milne, A. (2009, December 2). *Saints or Sinners: The Role of the Financial Media in the Financial Crisis*. Conference, City University, London. Retrieved from http://www.city.ac.uk/whatson/2009/12_dec/021209-media-financial-crisis. Accessed December 23, 2009.
Monbiot, G. (2001). *Captive State: The Corporate Takeover of Britain*. London: Pan Books.
Nel, F. (2010). How Many Journalists Are There in the UK? *Media Blog*. Retrieved from http://forthemedia.blogspot.co.uk/2010/08/how-journalists-are-there-in-uk-this-is.html. Accessed November 22, 2014.
Nieman Reports. (2002). *Reporting on Business: Enron and Beyond, 56* (2), 4–5.
Ojala, J., & Uskali, T. (2006, August 24). Any Weak Signals? *The New York Times and the Stock Market Crashes of 1929, 1987 and 2000*. Paper presented at XIV International Economic History Congress, Helsinki, Finland. Retrieved from http://www.helsinki.fi/iehc2006/papers1/Ojala.pdf. Accessed December 26, 2009.
O'Neill, D. (2007). From Hunky Heroes to Dangerous Dinosaurs. *Journalism Studies, 8*(5), 813–830.
Parsons, W. (1989). *The Power of the Financial Press: Journalism and Economic Opinion in Britain and America*. Aldershot: Edward Elgar.

Payne, G. (2008). Structural and Social Forces Restricting Media News Content in Democracies: A Critical Perspective. *Journal of Humanities and Social Science, 2*(1), 1–10.

Petley, J. (2009a). Impartiality in Television News: Profitability Versus Public Service. In S. Allan (Ed.), *The Routledge Companion to News and Journalism Studies* (pp. 602–613). Abingdon: Routledge.

Petley, J. (2009b). What Fourth Estate? In M. Bailey (Ed.), *Narrating Media History* (pp. 184–195). Abingdon: Routledge.

Petley, J. (2011). Rules, Recycling, Filters and Conspiracies: Nick Davies and the Propaganda Model. In B. Franklin & M. Carlson (Eds.), *Journalists, Sources and Credibility: New Perspectives* (pp. 75–89). London: Routledge.

Pilger, J. (2002). *The New Rulers of the World*. London: Verso.

Powell, L., & Self, W. (2003). Government Sources Dominate Business Crisis Reporting. *Newspaper Research Journal, 24*(2), 97–106.

Pym, H. (2009, December 2). *Saints or Sinners: The Role of the Financial Media in the Financial Crisis*. Conference, City University, London. Retrieved from http://www.city.ac.uk/whatson/2009/12_dec/021209-media-financial-crisis. Accessed December 23, 2009.

Pym, H., & Kochan, N. (2008). *What Happened? And Other Questions Everyone Is Asking About the Credit Crunch*. London: Old Street Publishing.

Rampton, S., & Stauber, J. (1995). *Toxic Sludge Is Good for You*. London: Robinson Publishing.

Reese, S. (2001). Understanding the Global Journalist: A Hierarchy of Influences Approach. *Journalism Studies, 2*, 173–187.

Richardson, K. (1998). Signs and Wonders: Interpreting the Economy Through Television. In A. Bell & P. Garrett (Eds.), *Approaches to Media Discourse* (pp. 220–250). Oxford: Blackwell.

Robinson, J. (2008, October 12). Why Didn't the City Journalists See the Financial Crisis Coming? *The Observer*. Retrieved from http://www.guardian.co.uk/media/2008/oct/12/pressandpublishing-creditcrunch. Accessed January 24, 2010.

Roush, C. (2006). The Need for More Business Education in Mass Communication Schools. *Journalism and Mass Communication Educator, 61*(2), 196–204.

Schechter, D. (2009). Credit Crisis: How Did We Miss It? *British Journalism Review, 20*(1), 19–26.

Schifferes, S. (2015). Why the Public Doesn't Trust the Business Press. In S. Schifferes & R. Roberts (Eds.), *The Media and Financial Crises: Comparative and Historical Perspectives* (pp. 153–168). London and New York: Routledge.

Schifferes, S., & Coulter, S. (2012). Downloading Disaster: BBC News Online Coverage of the Global Financial Crisis. *Journalism, 14*(2), 1–25.

Schifferes, S., & Roberts, R. (2015). *The Media and Financial Crises: Comparative and Historical Perspectives*. Abingdon: Routledge.

Schiffrin, A. (2006). PR in Developing Countries. In J. Hobsbawm (Ed.), *Where the Truth Lies: Trust and Morality in PR and Journalism* (pp. 184–193). London: Atlantic Books.

Schlesinger, P. (1978). *Putting Reality Together (BBC News)*. London: Constable.

Schlosberg, J. (2013). *Power Beyond Scrutiny: Media, Justice and Accountability*. London: Pluto Press.

Schlosberg, J. (2016). *Should He Stay, or Should He Go? Television and Online News Coverage of the Labour Party in Crisis*. Media Reform Coalition. Retrieved from http://www.mediareform.org.uk/wp-content/uploads/2016/07/Corbynresearch.pdf. Accessed February 13, 2017.

Schudson, M. (1989). The Sociology of News Production. *Media, Culture and Society, 11*(1), 263–282.

Schudson, M. (2005). Four Approaches to the Sociology of News. In J. Curran & M. Gurevitch (Eds.), *Mass Media and Society* (pp. 172–197). Hodder Headline: London/New York.

Schudson, M. (2011). *The Sociology of News*. New York, NY: W. W. Norton.

Shaw, I. (2016). *Business Journalism: A Critical Political Economy Approach*. Abingdon: Routledge.

Sherman, S. (2002, March/April). Enron: Uncovering the Uncovered Story. *Columbia Journalism Review, 40*(6), 22–29.

Shiller, R. (2001). *Irrational Exuberance*. Princeton, NJ: Princeton University Press.

Smith, P. (2008, March 19). How Money Matters Made Front-Page News. *Press Gazette*.

Smith, J., McCarthy, J., McPhail, C., & Augustyn, B. (2001). From Protest to Agenda Building: Description Bias in Media Coverage of Protest Events in Washington, DC. *Social Forces, 79*(4), 1397–1423.

Solomon, W. (2000). More Form Than Substance: Press Coverage of the WTO Protests in Seattle. *Monthly Review, 52*(1), 12–20.

Starkman, D. (2009, January/February). How Could 9,000 Business Reporters Blow It. *Mother Jones*. Retrieved from http://motherjones.com/politics/2009/01/how-could-9000-business-reporters-blow-it. Accessed January 14, 2010.

Starkman, D. (2014). *The Watchdog that Didn't Bark: The Financial Crisis and the Disappearance of Investigative Reporting*. New York: Columbia University Press.

Tambini, D. (2008). *What Is Financial Journalism for? Ethics and Responsibility in a Time of Crisis and Change: A Polis Report*. London, UK: Polis, LSE.

Tambini, D. (2009, December 2). *Saints or Sinners: The Role of the Financial Media in the Financial Crisis*. Conference, City University, London. Retrieved from http://www.city.ac.uk/whatson/2009/12_dec/021209-media-financial-crisis. Accessed December 23, 2009.

Tambini, D. (2010). What Are Financial Journalists For? *Journalism Studies, 11*(2), 158–174.

Thussu, D. (2007). *News as Entertainment: The Rise of Global Infotainment.* London: Sage.

Tulloch, J. (2009). From Amnesia to Apocalypse: Reflections on Journalism and the Credit Crunch. In J. Mair & R. Keeble (Eds.), *Playing Footsie with the FTSE? The Great Crash of 2008* (pp. 99–109). Abramis: Bury St Edmunds.

Tumber, H. (1993). Selling Scandal: Business and the Media. *Media, Culture and Society, 15*(1), 345–361.

Tunstall, J. (1971). *Journalists at Work.* London: Constable.

Uskali, T. (2005). Paying Attention to Weak Signals—The Key Concept for Innovation Journalism. *Innovation Journalism, 2*(4), 19.

Wahl-Jorgensen, K., & Hanitzsch, T. (2009). *The Handbook of Journalism Studies.* Abingdon, UK: Routledge.

Wolfsfeld, G. (2003). The Political Contest Model. In S. Cottle (Ed.), *News, Public Relations and Power* (pp. 81–95). London: Sage.

Wu, H., Stevenson, R., Hsiao-Chi, Chen, & Guner, N. (2002). The Conditioned Impact of Recession News: A Time-Series Analysis of Economic Communication in the United States, 1987–1996. *International Journal of Public Opinion Research, 14*(2), 19–35.

Yun, C. H., Wei, K. S., Peng, T. H., & Xiaoming, Hao. (2002). Stock-Market Forecasts by Singapore Newspapers Before and After the 1997 Asian Financial Crisis. *Asian Journal of Communication, 12*(1), 100–125.

Zelizer, B. (2004). *Taking Journalism Seriously: News and the Academy.* London: Sage.

Žižek, S. (2008). *In Defense of Lost Causes.* London: Verso.

CHAPTER 2

Research Design

Case Studies, News Media, Political Positions and Methods

Introduction

EBF journalism is a vital element of public debate as it furnishes all stakeholders—investors, workers, consumers, citizens, etc.—with information about economic events, problems and possible solutions. Economics, business and finance are inherently political disciplines and are open to a range of interpretations and solutions. The somewhat disjointed academic research, however, suggests a persistent deficit of perspectives with certain viewpoints frequently excluded from mediated debates. Scholars have also found that dissenters—left-wing politicians, trade unionists, environmentalists, protestors, etc.—are often belittled, side-lined and demonised. Such a modus operandi inevitably produces news that gives only a partial view of the economic environment, a phenomenon that was apparent prior to the 2008 Financial Crisis.

Like much EBF journalism research of the last decade, this book was inspired by the Financial Crisis. But instead of focussing on the characteristics of news in the prelude to this episode, attention is turned to three issues in the preceding decade that were not directly related to the Credit Boom nor the subsequent Crisis. In doing so, this study analyses the manifest characteristics of British news in what might be described as 'normal times'. Although the understanding of EBF journalism has deepened and widened in recent years, there is still a lack of focussed and comprehensive content analyses of the news product, and certainly no substantial, data-rich study that concentrates on its political content.

G. J. Merrill, *The Political Content of British Economic, Business and Financial Journalism*, https://doi.org/10.1007/978-3-030-04012-3_2

This book attempts to address this deficiency by assessing the extent to which the news media gives exposure and credence to different political interpretations of economics and business. In doing so, it provides data-rich evidence to inform the largely theoretical debates about the presence of neoliberalism in news. Also, by analysing the reporting of the same issues over the same periods by a selection of news organisations, this study offers a comparative dimension. More precisely, it assesses the coverage given to disparate political ideas, narratives and assumptions in three different contexts by four different news organisations over a ten-year period.

This chapter covers the research design. First, it explains the choice of case studies and the news media. After sketching a left–right spectrum of economic thought, the main part of the chapter consists of three contextualising sections, one for each of the case studies, which outline the competing arguments and narratives that were evident in the mediated debates. The final part briefly describes the methodology with particular emphasis on how the political content of news items was assessed through a combination of quantitative content analysis and critical discourse analysis.

Case Studies

The three issues covered by the case studies were chosen primarily because each was particularly contentious, and subjected to competing political interpretations, in the decade before the 2008 Financial Crisis. Hence, one might expect a high degree of interest from the news media. In addition, for each case study it was possible to centre the sample periods on important events.

For economic globalisation, this was the World Trade Organisation (WTO) Ministerial Conference in Seattle in late November 1999. The Conference represented a crucial moment in the development of modern economic globalisation, and negotiations among senior politicians were accompanied by street demonstrations. Indeed, the future of world trade was heavily contested at the time with developed-world governments favouring a model that removed tariffs, subsidies and other hindrances to 'free trade', while trade unions, environmental and developmental NGOs, and numerous authors arguing for a more sustainable, humanised form of economic globalisation.

The first key moment for the second case study occurred in September 2002 when delegates at the British Labour Party Conference defeated a motion to back the Private Finance Initiative (PFI) as government policy.

PFI was highly contentious with trade unions, academics, accountants and others disputing the government's belief that it was the only effective way to finance public services. Despite the Conference defeat, Tony Blair's government remained committed to PFI and yet some of the doubters' concerns were confirmed in May 2007 with the publication of a damning parliamentary report on the performance of PFI contracts. Hence, this case study has two sample points, five years apart.

Similarly, the third case study, which focusses on the British supermarket company, Tesco, has three sampling points. The first is in 2006, when the Competition Commission launched an investigation into the UK grocery sector; the second is in 2007, when the Commission released its interim findings; and the third came a year later with the publication of the final report. As with the other two case studies, competing interpretations were evident over the periods of analysis: although supermarket chains provide choice and convenience to consumers, and had generated many new jobs and substantial profits, they also faced criticism of anti-competitive behaviour, having dubious environmental credentials, and homogenising the British High Street.

A further advantage of choosing these case studies is that they represent three tiers of neoliberalism. 'Free trade' as envisaged by the WTO is, by definition, an overarching, international economic model; private finance in public services is a policy of national government; and Tesco epitomises the large corporations that dominate Western economies. Hence, by looking at the economic world from three hierarchical perspectives over ten years, this study offers a broad sphere of analysis, and because the content analysis coding schemes for each case study are functionally identical, one can compare the same characteristics of the news product for three distinct issues.

News Media

A second comparative dimension was obtained by including multiple news organisations. The BBC News website was chosen because, despite increased competition, the Corporation is still the UK's primary news provider (Ofcom 2017). Also, the content is universally, and freely accessible online and the BBC's journalistic output, including financial news, is highly trusted by audiences (BBC Trust 2012). One reason for the BBC's high standing as a reliable source of news is its statutory commitment to impartiality (BBC 2018).

This book was partly inspired by the 2007 Budd Report on the impartiality of BBC Business Journalism (Budd 2007). Although this was a comprehensive study—incorporating written and oral evidence, audience research and content analysis—it took a general perspective with no focus on contentious issues. Nor did it have a comparative angle. Furthermore, Budd's assessment was made against a rather ambiguous definition of impartiality from a previous BBC publication, the Neil Report (2004). Impartiality, it stated, requires the BBC to be:

> ...fair and open minded in reflecting all significant strands of opinion, and exploring the range and conflict of views. (in Budd 2007: 6)

What constitutes: 'significant strands of opinion' is clearly open to debate. The leading British political parties' viewpoints naturally fall into this category, but because none offered an alternative economic discourse to neoliberalism during the periods covered by this study, one could argue that views from beyond the parliamentary horizon are insignificant. However, given neoliberalism's evident fragility, one might expect the BBC, as a public service organisation, to give exposure and credence to a broad range of political interpretations.

Hence, to ensure that a wide variety of opinions were considered in this analysis, three newspaper groups were included. Two newspaper pairings traditionally associated with the right, the *Times-Sunday Times* and the *Daily/Sunday Telegraph*, and the left-of-centre *Guardian-Observer* were selected. British newspapers are free to take positions in public debates and so, by comparing their reporting with the BBC's politically impartial news, a more complete picture of the nature of British EBF journalism will be gained. This approach also facilitates a better appreciation of the BBC's understanding of 'significant strands of opinion' relative to other news providers.

Political Positions

With the case study subjects, the news media, and the sample periods selected, pilot studies were undertaken to check that the LexisNexis database and the BBC News website search facility would yield the appropriate quantity and quality of articles. It soon became apparent that the search must cover the whole article text because some important news items did not include the keywords in the headline or the opening

Table 2.1 Characteristics of left- and right-wing economic thought

Left		*Right*
Common	Ownership of resources	Private
Mutuals, cooperatives	Preferred organisation	Entrepreneurs, corporations
Larger	Public sector	Smaller
Higher	Income and wealth taxes	Lower
Stronger	Workers' rights	Weaker
Stronger	Environmental protection	Weaker
More	Corporate regulation	Less

paragraph. The pilot study also helped fine-tune the search terms and, most importantly, establish the political positions related to each of the three case studies. This was achieved by analysing the competing narratives that were evident across a sample of news items.

The following section gives context for each of the case studies and then defines the political positions. As will be demonstrated, the debates surrounding economic globalisation and private finance in public services could be divided into four general perspectives. For the Tesco case study, however, delineations were somewhat more complex. There were essentially two competing groups: advocates, who supported the business model operated by large supermarkets, and reformers, who argued for a variety of changes to the corporate modus operandi. The advocates had two narratives and the reformers' arguments fell into five categories. These are explained in detail below.

Throughout the analysis, the labels 'left' and 'right' are used to describe political positions. The key differences in left- and right-wing economic thought are encapsulated in Table 2.1. Whereas the left traditionally promotes the collective, common ownership, restrictions on commercial and economic power, and hence, the active redistribution of wealth for public benefit, the right favours *laissez-faire*, private ownership and individualism and, by extension, the pre-eminence of the investor, a smaller public sector, lower taxes, weaker trade union rights and minimal corporate regulation.

It is important to note that political positions are not binary. There are different degrees of belief, and every nation state (and every individual) incorporates some left- *and* right-wing ideas in their economic thinking. For example, on the far right of the spectrum, even the most committed neoliberals typically believe the state should collect *some* taxes (to fund, for instance, a legal system and military). Similarly, few people on the left believe private enterprise should be *entirely* replaced by worker cooperatives and nationalised industries.

Case Study 1: Economic Globalisation

The first case study covers a 61-day period straddling the start of the WTO Ministerial Conference in Seattle on November 30, 1999. Using five key phrases—'globalisation'; 'anti-globalisation'; 'World Trade Organisation'; 'WTO'; and 'anti-WTO'—the LexisNexis database was searched for articles in *The Guardian* and *The Observer*, and *The Times* and *The Sunday Times*. The BBC News website archive was also searched in the same way. In total, the searches generated 488 articles.

The four-day Conference was a pivotal event in the development of economic globalisation and was preceded by the signing of a historic trade deal between the USA and China, which, after 13 years of negotiations, brought the latter a significant step nearer to becoming a full member of the WTO. The Conference itself marked the beginning of the 'Millennium Round' of talks at which representatives from 135-member nations would negotiate the next stage of trade liberalisation with tariff cuts at the top of the agenda. If the Conference achieved its stated goals, the WTO would move closer towards the ultimate objective: 'freeing international movements of commodities and services from government restraint' (Peet 2003: 146). Conference delegates were united in their commitment to the WTO as 'the global policeman of free trade' (Curwen 1999) but there were considerable and complex differences between the developed and developing worlds, individual countries and centre-left political parties. Outside the Conference, a plethora of dissenters broadly agreed that economic globalisation as advocated by the corporate-political elite would create a less just world. Consequently, Seattle attracted '50,000 critics of global capitalism' (BBC 1999a) including some 1200 NGOs (*Times* 1999) which promoted the development of an alternative agenda captured by the phrase 'fair trade, not free trade' (Yuen 2002).

With such a diversity of opinion, it would be misguided to simply divide the political positions at Seattle into 'pro' and 'anti'. Hence, the following four classifications are more accurate representations of the debate. These are guided by related American content studies of the WTO Conference (Wall 2003; Bennett et al. 2004; Jha 2007) and British news items analysed during the pilot study.

Liberalisation

This position resides on the right of the political spectrum and represents the ultimate objective of the WTO (Hutton 1999). It was typified by actors who argued for faster, broader and deeper liberalisation. For example, the Cairns Group of 15 agricultural exporting nations lobbied for the ending of subsidies in the EU and Japan (Jawara and Kwa 2003: 24), and many developing countries argued for unfettered access to the markets of rich countries (Denny 1999). This viewpoint was shared by some development charities, such as Christian Aid and Oxfam, which saw free trade in agriculture as the fastest route out of poverty (Mortishead 1999). Accelerated liberalisation was also promoted by some from the developed world who, for example, pressed for lower taxation and lighter regulation (BBC 1999b).

Protectionism

Few argued for protectionism in the long term, but some countries supported a gradual liberalisation with a more selective transition towards free trade. Typically, this meant the retention of certain restrictions such as tariffs or quotas to protect fragile industries or to garner support from interest groups. This was the position of some industrialised countries who were eager to maintain, for example, subsidies for farmers (such as the European Union's Common Agricultural Policy) or, in the case of the USA, extended quotas on Chinese steel and textile exports (Binyon 1999; BBC 1999c). Also, some developing countries called for slower liberalisation of their own markets (Elliott 1999). Right-of-centre protectionists were differentiated from the left-of-centre progressive reformers because the former argued for the maintenance or gradual phasing out of existing protectionist measures rather than a new agenda.

Progressive Reform

Progressive reformers generally believed the WTO was sound in principle but needed new terms of reference which would put the environment, workers' rights, public health and education, cultural diversity and other social concerns high on the agenda (Burke 1999). At Seattle, the progressives and fundamentalists were excluded from the Conference and they covered a similar spectrum of issues from a left-wing perspective, but their organisation and tactics differed (Wall 2003: 37). The progressives were embodied in a coalition of over 1000 lobbying groups such as development NGOs, trade unions, faith organisations, environmental and other campaigning bodies (Juniper 1999) which promoted their causes through the mainstream media using rational argument and empirical evidence (Wall 2003: 40).

Fundamental Reform

Fundamental reformers, typically associated with the far left of the spectrum, believed that corporate power and capitalism had corrupted the WTO to such an extent that it had become a fatally flawed institution. If it could not be modified to incorporate environmental, labour and diversity concerns, the WTO should be abolished and replaced with a more democratic system (Peet 2003: 195; Monbiot 2003). This position was epitomised in Seattle by the 'protestors' (Jha 2007) and 'street groups' (Wall 2003: 38) such as Reclaim the Streets; EarthFirst! and the Independent Media Centre. The fundamentalists' preferred tactics were protest, direct action and emotive language. They were typically voluntary or poorly funded groups, had fluid hierarchies and used new technology (mobile phones and online message boards) to organise and to promote their causes (ibid.: 40).

Case Study 2: Private Finance and Public Services

In the second case study, the *Guardian-Observer*, the *Daily/Sunday Telegraph* and the BBC News website were searched for two nine-week periods. The first revolves around 30 September 2002 when a motion at the British Labour Party Conference to back PFI as government policy was defeated. The second date is 15 May 2007 when the House of Commons Committee of Public Accounts published an important report about private finance (HCCPA 2007). The four key phrases were: 'Private Finance Initiative'; 'PFI'; 'Public Private Partnership'; and 'PPP', and the searches produced a grand sample of 344 articles.

PFI had been at the heart of Labour Party strategy since Tony Blair formed his first government in 1997. By the time of the 2002 Conference, the Treasury had approved contracts for 40 hospitals and 550 schools, with a further 60 hospitals in the planning stage (*Guardian* 2002). In total, the government had committed to more than £100 billion worth of future payments (BBC 2002a). Although PFI was contentious, the Labour hierarchy had disengaged from intellectual discussions about its merits and limitations (Pollock 2005: 57) but at the Conference, party members had compelled the leadership to justify its position, and 63% of the public supported the unions' call for a review of PFI (Travis and Maguire 2002). Even though the HCCPA report of May 2007 was published in less combative times, many of the problems predicted by critics five years earlier were becoming apparent. The report confirmed some 750 PFI schemes costing over £54 billion had been approved (HCCPA 2007), and it also found that the government was being 'outwitted' when negotiating with consortia (Hencke 2007). In May 2007, during the Labour Party leadership contest, the then chancellor of the exchequer, Gordon Brown, was challenged about PFI by his opponents, and the Scottish Nationalist Party (SNP) renewed its pledge to create a not-for-profit alternative to public–private partnerships (PPP)[1] (SNP 2007: 19). For the first time, the Labour government was faced with focussed parliamentary opposition to private finance. In the same month, concerns about PFI's poor value for money were confirmed by the *Daily Telegraph* which estimated that the government had bought £43 billion worth of services that had a 'long-term cost to taxpayers of £150 billion' (Roberts et al. 2007).

As confirmed by the heated exchanges at the Labour Party Conference, opinion was divided about the merits of private finance in public services during the first decade of the century. The pilot study revealed that the debate was dominated by two political positions: PFI advocacy and PFI scepticism. Two further positions were also present, but they received far less coverage.

Privatisation

Over the sample periods, detailed arguments for outright privatisation never appeared in debates about the funding of public services, but some commentators associated with economically right-wing perspectives did call for an expansion of the private sector involvement beyond PFI. The *Economist*, for example, argued that Blair should be bolder with his reforms of the health service (*Economist* 2006) and senior Conservative politicians promoted 'radical and meaningful – not sham - reforms' (Fox

[1] Public–private partnership (PPP) can be defined as: 'any collaboration between public bodies, such as local authorities or central government, and private companies', and hence, PFI is one type of PPP (BBC 2003b).

in BBC 2002b). The Confederation of British Industry (CBI) also supported an expansion of PPPs with the government turning 'from being a provider of public services to a commissioner…and to introduce more competition and markets into public service provision' (Conway 2007).

PFI Advocacy

The most committed advocates of PFI were Labour government ministers who argued that it would bring greater efficiency, better value for money and faster delivery of new facilities (BBC 2002c). Gordon Brown sometimes acknowledged the existence of alternatives but dismissed the ideas of the left—particularly the trade unions—as 'reckless borrowing', and the right—typically the Conservative Party—as 'privatisation' (Elliott and Wintour 2002). Private finance was often presented as inevitable: Tony Blair conflated it with the broader public sector 'reforms' which, he claimed, would free: 'us from outdated doctrine and practice' (Blair 2002).

PFI Scepticism

Opposition to PFI was multifaceted and the most visible critics were the trade unions which feared the creation of a 'two-tier workforce' (BBC 2002c), but also shared broader concerns with prominent journalists and intellectuals; accountants (BBC 2002d); the Liberal Democrats (Kennedy in Wintour 2002); and dissident Labour MPs.[2] This position and the fourth (see below) were considered left-of-centre and had many arguments in common, but PFI sceptics tended *not* to offer a specific alternative. Indeed, prior to the Labour Party Conference in 2002, the unions softened their opposition by tabling a motion for an independent review of PFI rather than the original moratorium (BBC 2002f).

Social Alternatives

The SNP vowed to: 'halt Labour's privatisation juggernaut dead in its tracks' (Swinney 2002) and was the only political party to explicitly offer a social alternative to PFI, albeit a variation on the traditional model by which the government provides the capital from tax revenues, subcontractors build the project and the asset remains in

[2]For example, Kelvin Hopkins MP called the PFI 'irrational nonsense' and 'less popular than the poll tax' (BBC 2002e).

public ownership (BBC 2002c). There was also opposition to private involvement in public services among the British population and, by extension, a desire to maintain the status quo. In one poll, 60% of respondents said private firms should not run public services (BBC 2003a) and in another, 89% agreed that 'public services should be run by the government or local authorities, rather than by private companies' (Unison 2005).

Case Study 3: Tesco

There was just one keyword for the third case study—'Tesco'—and the *Guardian-Observer*, the *Daily/Sunday Telegraph*, and the BBC News website were searched for any mention of the company during three sample periods of 35 days straddling each of the key dates. The first is 9 May 2006, when the Competition Commission's investigation into the UK grocery sector was announced; the second is 23 January 2007, when interim findings were released; and the third is 30 April 2008, the publication date of the final report. With a total of 789 articles, the universal sample dwarfed the other two.

The issue of supermarket power was more nuanced than economic globalisation and private finance. The pilot study revealed that the debate was contested by two groups: advocates of the status quo and reformists who argued for a variety of constraints. The advocates had two distinct lines of argument, and each of the five reformist subgroups had its own agenda based on the concerns of specific stakeholders.[3] The following section defines these seven narratives in some detail.

Advocacy: Investors

The primary advocate narrative focussed on investors. This is clearly visible on Tesco's website where the foundations of corporate success—customer loyalty, store numbers, geographical expansion, etc.—are prominent alongside key financial data (Tesco 2011a). The narrative is also evident in news of annual results and the continuously updated share prices on financial websites and satellite TV. Indeed, a rising share price

[3]The choice of categories for the reformist arguments was informed by the pilot study and previous critical studies of supermarket power (Simms 2007; Blythman 2007; Monbiot 2001; FoE 2003; NEF 2003).

is paramount to all joint-stock corporations and the leading British supermarket chains are focussed on achieving this goal by placing profit maximisation ahead of all other concerns (Blythman 2007: xvii). The investor narrative is often rather bland, but audiences are intermittently exposed to the single-mindedness of the profit-making process. In 2004, for example, Tesco's then chief executive officer (CEO), Terry Leahy, in a speech to investors, defined the barriers between the company and its goals:

> What saps our strength are high taxes: excessive regulations; inflexible working practices; and the gold plating of EU directives. All of this undermines British businesses… (in Corporate Watch 2004)

In these terms, Tesco is engaged in a struggle against state legislation and organised labour. This economically right-wing position is also evident as a belligerent narrative in books celebrating the success of supermarkets. Indeed, business writers tend to be more candid than CEOs and often reiterate the amoral, natural Darwinian principles that underpin big business: 'creative destruction', for instance, is a force of nature (Seth and Randall 2005: 167) and markets always favour the strong over the weak (Bevan 2005: 169).

Advocacy: Corporate Social Responsibility

The five reformist arguments (see below) were often countered by the advocates' second narrative: Corporate Social Responsibility (CSR). This contrasts sharply with investor arguments: instead of stressing the importance of maximising profit, supermarkets position themselves as responsible corporate citizens whose role is to satisfy the consumer while also remaining sensitive to the needs of other stakeholders (Tesco 2011b). Although it is debatable if supermarkets have succeeded in their quest to become 'green' and ethical (Sunderland et al. 2007), retailers are particularly adept at emphasising the positive consequences of their actions. Tesco, for instance, regularly highlighted its credentials as a 'good neighbour' (Finch 2006) and a 'responsible company' (Cronin 2005). However, while some agree that the investor and CSR narratives can happily coexist, others believe the two are mutually exclusive.[4]

[4]This was evident in the subtitle of Robert Greenwald's 2005 film *Wal-Mart: The High Cost of Low Prices* (Bradshaw 2006).

Some reformists on the left view CSR as a cynical public relations exercise that over-emphasises the company's 'good' works but does little, if anything, to change the corporate modus operandi (Monbiot 2007). In addition, some notable scholars on the *right* believe CSR to be a worrying distraction from the true purpose of business[5] (Bakan 2004: 35).

Reform: Competition and Consumers

Some reformist arguments were founded on the issue of competition and its impact on consumers. With four supermarket groups sharing almost 70% of the grocery market, the UK had one of the most concentrated in Europe (Competition Commission 2008: 29). For the previous two decades, the market had been monitored by government regulators and in 2000, the Office of Fair Trading noted the high profitability of the major chains and referred the case to the Competition Commission (BBC 2000a). Initial findings revealed that claims of relatively high prices in the UK were generally unfounded, and the Commission concluded the market was 'broadly competitive' with the large chains neither making excessive profits nor 'ripping off' customers (Competition Commission 2000). There was, however, a 'complex monopoly situation' and the supermarkets' collective buying power made it difficult for other retailers to compete (Bevan 2005: 6). The next Competition Commission inquiry, announced in 2006, was welcomed by reformists because it was seen as a means to extend the previously restricted view of consumer choice and to assess the impact of supermarkets on the broader society (Monbiot 2007; *New Statesman* 2003). Reformists were also concerned about the self-reinforcing nature of market dominance. By 2006, Tesco had accumulated a 'land bank' that, if developed, would double its size (Simms 2007: 118). Massive profits also financed cross-subsidies that pushed down the cost of staple products, thus putting even more pressure on small retailers (Mesure 2005).

Reform: Suppliers

The second category of reformist arguments relates to supermarkets' relationships with farmers and other elements of the supply chain.

[5] Milton Friedman said corporate executives have just one: 'social responsibility… to make as much money as possible for their shareholders'. According to Harvard Business School Professor Debora Spar, corporations are: '…not set up to be moral entities… they really only have one mission, and that's to increase shareholder value' (Bakan 2004: 34–35).

The Big Four companies were often accused of abusing their commercial power by imposing contracts on food producers that were so punitive that the relationship was akin to 'lord and vassal' (Blythman 2007: xviii). The 2000 Competition Commission inquiry found a 'climate of apprehension' across the supply chain and noted that buying practices: 'adversely affected the competitiveness of some suppliers and distorted competition' (BBC 2000b). Significantly, the Commission instructed supermarkets to develop a new code of conduct. Initially, the code was welcomed by some reformists, but in 2003, a survey of food producers found that the code 'had done little to protect them from the supermarket chains' (Stewart and Treanor 2003). Indeed, the worsening plight of British farmers was highlighted over the first half of the decade and juxtaposed with record profits for the supermarkets. Many farmers were selling below cost price in the 2000s, and this period was characterised by increasing numbers of farm closures, a reduction in supplier diversity and historically low incomes (Bevan 2005: 169–170; Purvis 2003). For Friends of the Earth, the root cause was the 'unchecked growth' of the market-leader, Tesco (in Mesure 2005).

Reform: Communities and Environment

A third group of reformists were focussed on the impact of supermarkets on local communities and the environment. Although advocates reject a causal relationship, there is compelling evidence of a correlation between the expansion of supermarkets and the demise of independent retailers (Monbiot 2001: 166–172). The net effect, argue the critics, is the homogenisation of British High Street and an accompanying diminution of product diversity (Simms 2007). The closure of independent shops also has a negative multiplier effect as other local businesses lose trade which further erodes community cohesion (Blythman 2007: 215). With relatively few supermarket product lines sourced locally, threats to localism extend the debate to the broader environment (FoE 2005). Sourcing products from remote suppliers significantly increases 'food miles': an externalised, largely hidden but considerable cost. To the environmentalists, supermarkets' procurement and distribution policies defied logic: nationally grown fruit and vegetables remain unpicked while comparable produce is shipped halfway around the world (Paxton 1994; Sustain 1999). With free parking in out-of-town locations, critics also argued that supermarkets contribute to congestion, pollution and road accidents (Sunderland et al. 2007).

Reform: Employment

The fourth category of reformist arguments relates to employment. In 2003, the top four supermarket chains employed 650,000 staff, including Tesco's 250,000 (O'Hara 2003), and in these naked terms, claims of significant job creation appear irrefutable. However, research commissioned by the retail industry itself, in the guise of the National Retail Planning Forum, found 'strong evidence' of a 'net negative impact on retail employment' in the catchment area of superstores[6] (Porter and Raistrick 1998). Furthermore, the New Economics Foundation calculated that a supermarket had to take five times as much in sales to create a single job than a small local shop (in Monbiot 2001: 172). Supermarkets were also accused of being miserly employers that engendered 'a social and economic culture of poverty' (Simms 2007: 11) which extended from shop-floor staff to agricultural workers (FoE 2005: 7). In addition, some NGOs were critical of the pay and conditions of developing world suppliers and the lack of Fairtrade products.[7] War on Want, for example, found garment workers in Bangladesh 'slaving in dangerous factories for 80 hours a week for just 5p an hour', and Tesco was one of the companies 'named and shamed' (Sunderland et al. 2007).

Reform: Political Influence

Another group of reformists were concerned about the political influence of supermarkets. Over the period covered by this thesis, the governing Labour Party received advice and funding from several supermarket executives (Oliver 2007). Companies were also represented by the British Retail Consortium which successfully lobbied to sway government policy (Monbiot 2001: 205). As the industry leader, Tesco was first among equals in terms of access and influence. Prior to the 1997 general election, Tesco was invited to join Labour's Industry Forum through which companies were consulted on policy (Osler 2002: 53). The company also made considerable financial donations to the Labour Party and sponsored the Millennium Dome (ibid.: 165, 232) and in 2001, Tesco representatives sat on the boards of six government task forces (Monbiot 2001: 203). Chief executive, Terry Leahy, who was knighted in 2002,

[6] The net impact on employment of 93 new store openings was 25,685 job losses, or 276 per store (Porter and Raistrick 1998).

[7] Less than one per cent of Tesco's product lines were Fairtrade accredited (FoE 2005: 6).

was among a select group of business leaders to have a private meeting with Tony Blair and Gordon Brown in the prelude to the 2001 general election (Osler 2002: 209). Reformists argued that such connections gave supermarket companies—and Tesco in particular—privileged access and, hence, influence over policy that was denied citizens, communities, trade unions and NGOs (Monbiot 2001: 165). Furthermore, supermarkets' lobbying and informal meetings with policy makers occurred largely in private and consequently, they lacked transparency and undermined democracy (Osler 2002).

Methods

Quantitative content analysis is a systematic and replicable method of measuring the manifest characteristics of news. This technique can cope with large quantities of texts and, because variables are measured consistently, it is useful for comparative studies and longitudinal analysis. It is also highly procedural and hence, open to scrutiny and, for these reasons, it has been very popular with media researchers for many years (Hansen et al. 1998: 92; Fiske 2002: 136). Quantitative content analysis provides the foundation for this study, and its design is guided by previous research that has investigated related spheres of journalism, including the coverage of business; protests and social movements; and the representation of trade unions (e.g. Budd 2007; Jha 2007; O'Neill 2007).[8]

Except for the issue-specific variables (article themes, source categories and political positions), the coding schemes for the three case studies are identical. Naturally, the scheme for the first case study took time to develop, but once it had been piloted, modified and proved its robustness, it acted as a template for the other two. Table 2.2 shows the twelve variables in the order the data were recorded. First, the date of publication of each news item was typed into a Microsoft Excel spreadsheet, followed by the appropriate codes for news organisation; topic (home news, international, business, etc.); and the placement of the search term in the article (headline, introduction, etc.). The number of words was also recorded.

Category A variables are unequivocal, but those listed as Category B have various degrees of subjectivity. In most cases, the type of news item

[8] These—and other—studies feature in Chapter 1.

Table 2.2 Quantitative content analysis variables

	Category A		*Category B*
1	Date	6	Item type
2	News organisation	7	Salience
3	Topic	8	Thematic/episodic
4	Placement of search terms	9	Primary theme
5	Article length	10	Secondary theme
		11	Sources
		12	Political positions

(leader, feature article, review, etc.) was evident, but there could conceivably be some variance between researchers. Similarly, assessments of how salient an article is to the search term; whether the article is episodic or thematic; and the themes could differ. There could even be disagreement about the categorisation of sources. The most challenging variable, however, was political position, and much thought was invested into defining the positions for each case study (see above) and devising a sliding scale that could be consistently applied by an imaginary second coder.

Source analysis is a staple component of quantitative content analyses but, as noted in Chapter 1, the source type per se does not necessarily determine if a particular point of view is present in a text. Similarly, individual actors do not always take the line that their responsibilities suggest, and sometimes sources can hold seemingly conflicting opinions simultaneously. Consequently, for the twelfth variable the researcher quantified the extent to which the different political positions were evident in each article. This measurement is important because, clearly, audiences can only judge arguments if they are exposed to them. Hence, if certain viewpoints and interpretations are under-represented in news reports then citizens are ill-equipped to make informed decisions. This part of the analysis was informed by the work of the Glasgow University Media Group whose members have applied this technique to a variety of issues, including industrial relations (GUMG 1980) and the Israel-Palestine conflict (Philo and Berry 2004).

Once the key characteristics and narratives of each position had been written into the code book, the researcher began gauging their visibility in individual articles. This was achieved by taking a holistic assessment of each news item based on: the quantity of words devoted to each position; the general tone and language used to describe ideas and actors; and the prominence of different viewpoints. From the outset,

Table 2.3 Coding political positions and narratives

Code	*Political position/Narrative*
1	Detailed coverage
2	Brief coverage
3	Criticised or dismissed
4	Acknowledged
5	Not acknowledged

it was apparent that this had the potential to be a highly subjective metric, and so the text highlighting function on Microsoft Word was used to colour-code sections of the articles according to their political content. Next, to assess the degree of coverage, a sliding scale was applied to each political position or narrative (see Table 2.3). The researcher soon became proficient at evaluating each positions' exposure and assessing the tenor of the coverage. In most cases, it was apparent if the position was present, merely acknowledged, or criticised/dismissed. The only significant deliberations revolved around the definitions of 'detailed' and 'brief'. The former was selected if the position was described in depth and/or promoted explicitly; and the latter if the article did this more subtly and, hence, the position was deemed valid.

As a notable study of EBF journalism argued: 'news cannot be judged solely on the quantity of coverage or its general tenor' (Gavin 2007: 53). Indeed, discourse sets the: 'parameters of relevant meaning that one uses to talk about things' (Altheide 1996: 31), so *how* something is explained and discussed is just as important, if not more so, than *what* is said. Although discourse analysis has been the subject of much debate among theorists, it is accepted that its main function is to understand how meaning is shared and negotiated in society (Fürsich 2009: 243). Discourse analysis deconstructs texts and looks for patterns of linguistic similarities and differences. It scrutinises the internal structure of texts, their thematic infrastructure, as well as their rhetorical and political leanings. Critical discourse analysis takes these principles further by investigating how power is expressed and reinforced through language, and how mediated discourse reproduces or resists power structures. While it may seem reasonable to assume that language is neutral, it is in fact a 'refracting, structuring medium' which, when used by journalists, presents an inherently subjective view of the world (Fowler 1991: 10). Furthermore, the grammar of news is made meaningful through subtleties such as 'unspoken assumptions, practices and perspectives' (Eldridge 1995: 211) and, ultimately, the language of news is socially constructed and distinctly ideological (Zelizer 2009: 37).

Researchers have consistently found that news reports tend to be written in the same authoritative style which the most frequently accessed sources, politicians and experts, habitually use (Fowler 1991: 23). Consequently, the media tend to reproduce the attitudes of the powerful and, in the process, attempt to convince the public that power structures are 'right and proper' (Matheson 2005: 6). Over time, news becomes self-reinforcing: language is repeated; images are entrenched and: 'key ideological propositions [become] permanent, immutable and to be preferred as the code for reporting and reading the story' (GUMG 1980: 123). In the process, alternative explanations and remedies are ignored, dismissed or belittled (Philo 2007: 177).

As with the quantitative content analysis, the design of the complementary critical discourse analysis was informed by previous studies of EBF journalism. These include research that investigated how the causes and possible remedies for specific economic problems are reported, and whether greater credence is given to the explanations of the elite and the economically powerful.[9] For each case study, the first step was to select samples of news items. Instead of setting temporal boundaries, the researcher initially focussed on editorials and opinion pieces because this is where partisan views would be most evident. Pilot studies discovered plenty of material from the newspapers but none from the BBC News website which, thanks to the Corporation's commitment to impartiality, rarely publishes journalism that carries such overt political opinion. Consequently, the BBC samples consisted mainly of standard news items which covered particularly important announcements and events that could be compared with newspaper reporting at the same time. The next step was to gain a deeper understanding of the various discourses. This involved the detailed reading of political speeches, official statements and first-person perspectives on each of the three issues. This process revealed the arguments and the key linguistic features of the contesting groups' respective narratives. With these established, the researcher then analysed: how the debates were constructed by journalists; how the actors were portrayed; and how journalists described different arguments.

[9] For example, O'Neill (2007), Kariithi and Kareithi (2007), Ainamo et al. (2006).

References

Ainamo, A., Tienari, J., & Vaara, E. (2006). Between West and East: A Social History of Business Journalism in Cold War Finland. *Human Relations, 59*, 611–636.

Altheide, D. (1996). *Qualitative Media Analysis*. Thousand Oaks, CA: Sage.

Bakan, J. (2004). *The Corporation: The Pathological Pursuit of Profit and Power*. Toronto: Viking Canada.

BBC. (1999a, November 30). *Protests Overshadow WTO Talks*. BBC News Website. Retrieved from http://news.bbc.co.uk/1/hi/world/americas/542622.stm. Accessed January 23, 2011.

BBC. (1999b, November 1). *Hague: Cut Taxes to Prosper*. BBC News Website. Retrieved from http://news.bbc.co.uk/1/hi/business/the_economy/501546.stm. Accessed January 23, 2011.

BBC. (1999c, November 13). *Chinese PM Intervenes in Trade Talks*. BBC News Website. Retrieved from http://news.bbc.co.uk/1/hi/business/the_economy/518828.stm. Accessed January 24, 2011.

BBC. (2000a, January 31). *Supermarket Inquiry Steps Up a Gear*. BBC News Website. Retrieved from http://news.bbc.co.uk/1/hi/business/626401.stm. Accessed November 16, 2011.

BBC. (2000b, October 10). *Competition Commission: Findings on Supermarkets*. BBC News Website. Retrieved from http://news.bbc.co.uk/1/hi/business/965773.stm. Accessed November 16, 2011.

BBC. (2002a, September 26). *Brown and Prescott Maul the Unions*. BBC News Website. Retrieved from http://news.bbc.co.uk/1/hi/business/2282328.stm. Accessed April 20, 2011.

BBC. (2002b, October 1). *Blair Backs Foundation Hospitals*. BBC News Website. Retrieved from http://news.bbc.co.uk/1/hi/health/2290300.stm. Accessed April 20, 2011.

BBC. (2002c, October 2). *Call for Workers' Job Security*. BBC News Website. Retrieved from http://news.bbc.co.uk/1/hi/scotland/2290906.stm. Accessed April 20, 2011.

BBC. (2002d, October 11). *Private Funding Comes Under New Fire*. BBC News Website. Retrieved from http://news.bbc.co.uk/1/hi/uk_politics/2318739.stm. Accessed April 20, 2011.

BBC. (2002e, October 21). *Kelvin Hopkins: Profile*. BBC News Website. Retrieved from http://news.bbc.co.uk/1/hi/uk_politics/2119893.stm. Accessed April 20, 2011.

BBC. (2002f, September 6). *Union Leaders' Demands*. BBC News Website. Retrieved from http://news.bbc.co.uk/1/hi/uk_politics/2240692.stm. Accessed May 25, 2011.

BBC. (2003a, February 12). *In Depth—Private Profit, Public Gain?* BBC News Website. Retrieved from http://news.bbc.co.uk/1/hi/in_depth/business/2001/ppp/default.stm. Accessed June 15, 2011.

BBC. (2003b, February 12). *What Are Public Private Partnerships?* BBC News Website. Retrieved from http://news.bbc.co.uk/1/hi/uk/1518523.stm. Accessed June 15, 2011.

BBC. (2018). *Editorial Guidelines: Impartiality*. Retrieved from https://www.bbc.co.uk/editorialguidelines/guidelines/impartiality. Accessed April 30, 2018.

BBC Trust. (2012, November 6). *Seminar on Impartiality and Economic Reporting*. Retrieved from http://downloads.bbc.co.uk/bbctrust/assets/files/pdf/our_work/economics_seminar. Accessed July 15, 2013.

Bennett, W., Packard, V., Iozzi, D., Schroeder, C., Lagos, T., & Caswell, C. (2004). Managing the Public Sphere: Journalistic Construction of the Great Globalization Debate. *Journal of Communication, 54*(3), 437–455.

Bevan, J. (2005). *Trolley Wars: The Battle of the Supermarkets*. London: Profile Books.

Binyon, M. (1999, November 24). Trade Talks Falter Over EU Farm Subsidies. *The Times*.

Blair, T. (2002, October 1). *Speech to Labour Party Conference*. BBC News Website. Retrieved from http://news.bbc.co.uk/1/hi/uk_politics/2290454.stm. Accessed April 20, 2011.

Blythman, J. (2007). *Shopped: The Shocking Power of British Supermarkets*. London: Fourth Estate.

Bradshaw, P. (2006). Film Review: Wal-Mart: The High Cost of Low Price. *The Guardian*.

Budd, A. (2007). *Report of the Independent Panel for the BBC Trust on Impartiality of BBC Business Coverage*. Retrieved from http://www.bbc.co.uk/bbctrust/our_work/other/business_news.shtml. Accessed January 1, 2010.

Burke, T. (1999, November 23). Trade Talks Sleepwalk to Seattle. *The Times*.

Competition Commission. (2000, October 10). *Supermarkets: A Report on the Supply of Groceries from Multiple Stores in the United Kingdom*. Retrieved from http://www.competition-commission.gov.uk/rep_pub/reports/2000/446super.htm#full. Accessed November 16, 2011.

Competition Commission. (2008, April 30). *Groceries Market Investigation: Final Report*. Retrieved from www.competition-commission.org.uk/rep_pub/reports/2008/538grocery.htm. Accessed May 10, 2010.

Conway, E. (2007, May 8). CBI Urges Brown to Cut Spending Plans. *Daily Telegraph*.

Corporate Watch. (2004, October). *Tesco Plc—A Corporate Profile*. Retrieved from http://www.corporatewatch.org/?lid=254. Accessed November 18, 2011.

Cronin, J. (2005, April 12). *Is Tesco Too Big?* BBC News Website. Retrieved from http://news.bbc.co.uk/1/hi/business/4422065.stm. Accessed January 6, 2012.

Curwen, L. (1999, November 12). *The World Trade Organisation: Money Programme*. BBC News Website. Retrieved from http://news.bbc.co.uk/1/hi/events/the_money_programme/517700.stm. Accessed January 26, 2011.
Denny, C. (1999, November 3). Short Attacks Aid Agencies. *The Guardian*.
Economist. (2006, March 11). Why Hospitals Must Be Allowed to Fail.
Eldridge, J. (Ed.). (1995). *News Content, Language and Visuals (Glasgow Media Group Reader, Volume 1)*. London: Routledge.
Elliott, L. (1999, December 2). Who Wants What from the Talks? *The Guardian*.
Elliott, L., & Wintour, P. (2002, September 30). Trust Me on Funding, Says Brown: No Retreat on PFI, Unions Are Warned. *The Guardian*.
Finch, J. (2006, May 11). Tesco Plans to Be Green and a Good Neighbour. *The Guardian*.
Fiske, J. (2002). *Introduction to Communication Studies*. London: Methuen.
Fowler, R. (1991). *Language in the News: Discourse and Ideology in the Press*. London: Routledge.
Friends of the Earth (FoE). (2003, February). *Briefing: Super Markets or Corporate Bullies?* Retrieved from http://www.foe.co.uk/resource/briefings/super_markets_corporate_bullies.pdf. Accessed November 18, 2011.
Friends of the Earth (FoE). (2005, June). *Briefing: The Tesco Takeover*. Retrieved from http://www.foe.co.uk/resource/briefings/the_tesco_takeover.pdf. Accessed March 17, 2012.
Fürsich, E. (2009). In Defence of Textual Analysis. *Journalism Studies, 10*(2), 238–252.
Gavin, N. (2007). *Press and Television in British Politics: Media, Money and Mediated Democracy*. Basingstoke: Palgrave Macmillan.
GUMG (Glasgow University Media Group). (1980). *More Bad News*. London: Routledge.
Guardian. (2002, October 1). Leader: The PFI Needs a Review: Tony Blair Must Address Party Concerns. *The Guardian*.
Hansen, A., Cottle, S., Negrine, R., & Newbold, C. (1998). *Mass Communication Research Methods*. Basingstoke: Palgrave.
Hencke, D. (2007, May 15). Sharp Business People Outwitting Whitehall Over PFI Refinancing Deals, Say MPs. *The Guardian*.
House of Commons Committee of Public Accounts (HCCPA). (2007, May 15). *Update on PFI Debt Refinancing and the PFI Equity Market*. Retrieved from www.publications.parliament.uk/pa/cm200607/cmselect/cmpubacc/158/158.pdf. Accessed May 10, 2010.
Hutton, W. (1999, November 28). On the Eve of Destruction; A New World Trade Organisation Policy Threatens the Very Heart of the National Health Service. *The Observer*.
Jawara, F., & Kwa, A. (2003). *Behind the Scenes at the WTO*. London: Zed Books.

Jha, S. (2007). Exploring Internet Influence on the Coverage of Social Protest: Content Analysis Comparing Protest Coverage in 1967 and 1999. *Journalism & Mass Communication Quarterly, 84*(1), 40–57.

Juniper, T. (1999, November 17). Planet Profit; Is the WTO in the Pocket of Corporate Power? *The Guardian.*

Kariithi, N., & Kareithi, P. (2007). It's Off to Work You Go! A Critical Discourse Analysis of Media Coverage of the Anti-privatisation Strike in South Africa in October 2002. *Journalism Studies, 8*(3), 465–480.

Matheson, D. (2005). *Media Discourses: Analysing Media Texts.* Maidenhead: Open University Press.

Mesure, S. (2005, April 13). Tesco Powers on to Record Profits—But the Backlash Gets Under Way. *The Independent.*

Monbiot, G. (2001). *Captive State: The Corporate Takeover of Britain.* London: Pan Books.

Monbiot, G. (2003). *The Age of Consent.* London: Perennial.

Monbiot, G. (2007, January 23). If Tesco and Wal-Mart Are Friends of the Earth, Are There Any Enemies Left. *The Guardian.*

Mortishead, C. (1999, November 24). Seattle Talking Shop Will Set the Agenda for Us All. *The Times.*

Neil Report. (2004). *The BBC's Journalism After Hutton: The Report of the Neil Report Team.* Retrieved from downloads.bbc.co.uk/aboutthebbc/insidethebbc/howwework/reports/pdf/neil_report.pdf. Accessed July 21, 2013.

New Economics Foundation (NEF). (2003, December 15). *Ghost Town Britain II: Death on the High Street.* Retrieved from http://www.neweconomics.org/sites/neweconomics.org/files/Ghost_Town_Britain_II.pdf. Accessed November 18, 2011.

New Statesman. (2003, January 20). How Supermarkets Damage Society. *Leader.*

Ofcom. (2017, June 29). *News Consumption in the UK 2016.* Retrieved from https://www.ofcom.org.uk/__data/assets/pdf_file/0016/103570/news-consumption-uk-2016.pdf. Accessed June 18, 2018.

O'Hara, M. (2003, January 25). Store Wars: Who Will Be the Casualties? *The Guardian.*

Oliver, J. (2007, June 3). How the Planning Laws Were TESCO-ed. *Mail on Sunday.*

O'Neill, D. (2007). From Hunky Heroes to Dangerous Dinosaurs. *Journalism Studies, 8*(5), 813–830.

Osler, D. (2002). *Labour Party PLC: New Labour as a Party of Business.* Edinburgh: Mainstream.

Paxton, A. (1994). *The Food Miles Report: The Dangers of Long-Distance Food Transport.* London: The Safe Alliance.

Peet, R. (2003). *Unholy Trinity: The IMF, World Bank and WTO*. London: Zed Books.

Philo, G. (2007). Can Discourse Analysis Successfully Explain the Content of Media and Journalistic Practice? *Journalism Studies, 8*(1), 175–196.

Philo, G., & Berry, M. (2004). *Bad News from Israel*. London: Pluto Press.

Pollock, A. (2005). *NHS Plc: The Privatisation of Our Health Care*. London: Verso Books.

Porter, S., & Raistrick, P. (1998, January). *The Impact of Out-of-Town Food Superstores on Local Retail Employment*. Nottingham: National Retail Planning Forum.

Purvis, A. (2003, April). Fifty Years Ago, This Pork Chop Would Have Cost You Twice as Much as It Does Now. *Observer Food Monthly*.

Roberts, D., Halligan, L., Hennessy, P., Watts, R., Pfeifer, S., & Garside, J. (2007, May 6). Does Brown Have a Trick Up His Sleeve? *Sunday Telegraph*.

Scottish Nationalist Party (SNP). (2007). SNP: It's Time. Manifesto for Holyrood Elections 2007, p. 19.

Seth, A., & Randall, G. (2005). *Supermarket Wars: Global Strategies for Food Retailers*. London: Palgrave Macmillan.

Simms, A. (2007). *Tescopoly: How One Shop Came Out on Top and Why It Matters*. London: Constable.

Stewart, H., & Treanor, J. (2003, February 18). Supermarkets Under Fire. *The Guardian*.

Sunderland, R., Stewart, H., & Wood, Z. (2007, August 26). The Good, the Bad and the FTSE. *Observer*.

Sustain. (1999, October). *Food Miles: Still on the Road to Ruin*? Retrieved from http://www.sustainweb.org/foodandclimatechange/archive_food_miles/. Accessed November 19, 2011.

Swinney, J. (2002, September 27). *SNP Conference Speech*. BBC News Website. Retrieved from http://news.bbc.co.uk/1/hi/scotland/2285588.stm. Accessed April 20, 2011.

Tesco. (2011a). *Annual Report and Financial Statements*. Retrieved from www.tescoplc.com/media/417/tesco_annual_report_2011_final.pdf. Accessed November 16, 2011.

Tesco. (2011b). *Corporate Responsibility*. Retrieved from www.tescoplc.com/corporate-responsibility/. Accessed March 13, 2011.

Times. (1999, November 29). Chance in a Millennium. *The Times*.

Travis, A., & Maguire, K. (2002, September 26). Majority Backs Fire Strikes and Wants PFI Halted. *The Guardian*.

Unison. (2005, June). *Positively Public: Briefing*. Retrieved from www.unison.org.uk/acrobat/b1923.pdf. Accessed May 6, 2011.

Wall, M. (2003). Press Conferences or Puppets: NGOs' and Street Groups' Communication in the Battle for Seattle. *Javnost: The Public, 10*(1), 33–48.

Wintour, P. (2002, September 10). Beef Up Employment Rights, Says Kennedy: Lib Dems 'Keener Than Labour' on Consultation. *The Guardian*.

Yuen, E. (2002). Introduction. In E. Yuen, G. Katsiaficas, & D. Rose (Eds.), *The Battle of Seattle: The New Challenge to Capitalist Globalisation* (pp. 215–244). New York: Soft Skull Press.

Zelizer, B. (2009). Journalism and the Academy. In K. Wahl-Jorgensen & T. Hanitzsch (Eds.), *The Handbook of Journalism Studies* (pp. 29–41). New York: Routledge.

CHAPTER 3

The Battle for Free Trade

The Reporting of Economic Globalisation in 1999

Introduction

Globalisation was a defining issue of the 1990s[1] and it was often framed in public discourse as a new phenomenon. Even the British monarch observed: '(It) is not only transforming our economies, it is changing every aspect of our lives' (Windsor in Hamilton 1999). In reality, however, globalisation has existed for as long as humans have traded beyond political and national boundaries. Robbie Robertson (2003) suggests that it began with the pioneering navigators of the fifteenth century, accelerated during the Industrial Revolution and then adopted its modern complexion after World War II with the creation of the General Agreement on Tariffs and Trade (GATT). The liberalisation of global trade was boosted in the late 1970s with the free market reforms in China and a decade later the demise of communism in eastern Europe (Conway 2009: 162). For some, notably Francis Fukuyama (1992), these events represented the natural convergence of humanity's political and economic systems into a universally applicable duet of liberal democracy and free market capitalism. This so-called Washington Consensus appeared, in the

[1] Chanda (2007: 246–247) analysed a database of 8000 newspapers, magazines and reports and found that 'globalization' appeared in just two items in 1981. Appearances increased significantly in the late 1990s and hit 57,235 in 2001.

BBC (1999n).

G. J. Merrill, *The Political Content of British Economic, Business and Financial Journalism*, https://doi.org/10.1007/978-3-030-04012-3_3

1990s, to be unassailable and there was agreement among British political parties that the trend was, as British Prime Minister Tony Blair said: 'irreversible and irresistible' (in Buckman 2004: 5).

GATT was the forerunner of the World Trade Organisation (WTO) which was established in 1995 with the remit of further reducing tariffs to promote free trade. Contemporary opinion polls, however, hinted at widespread ignorance about the central role of the WTO in determining the rules of the globalised economy (Vidal 1999a) but equally, there was public concern that globalisation threatened democracy (Bremner 1999b). Following the completion of the Uruguay Round of WTO trade talks in 1994, the impact of a liberalised trading regime on workers and the environment, and other social consequences, became apparent, and critics became more vocal and better organised (Buckman 2004).

Although there was consensus among political parties in the developed world that the deregulated model of economic globalisation promoted and legitimated by the WTO was desirable and inevitable (Owen 1999; Moore in Juniper 1999; Blair in *Guardian* 1999b), a considerable body of opinion argued it was designed by a neoliberal elite, with no public consultation and little regard for worker and human rights, the poor and the environment (Jawara and Kwa 2003; Monbiot 2003; Peet 2003; Stiglitz 2002; Pilger 2002). The four-day WTO Ministerial Conference in Seattle began on 30 November 1999 and brought together the competing perspectives. Inside the Conference, politicians from around the world debated the trajectory of global trade towards liberalisation. Outside the Conference, however, an informal coalition of 50,000 demonstrators and 1200 NGOs believed globalisation should have a more human dimension (BBC 1999a; *Times* 1999).

The WTO and Globalisation on the News Agenda

The BBC News website was searched for articles published over the 61-day period straddling the Conference that featured any of the five key phrases anywhere in the text.[2] The LexisNexis database was searched for items in the *Times*, the *Sunday Times*, the *Guardian* and the *Observer* in the same way. The raw data immediately revealed a significant difference

[2]The search phrases were: 'World Trade Organisation'; 'WTO'; 'globalisation'; 'anti–WTO'; and 'anti–globalisation'.

in the quantity of reporting with the *Guardian*[3] publishing 205 articles, the BBC 149 and the *Times* 134. On this basis, economic globalisation was clearly deemed more newsworthy at the *Guardian* than at the BBC or the *Times.*

Equally striking was the lack of collocations. Only 13% of articles—62 out of 488 in the universal sample—featured both 'WTO' and 'globalisation' anywhere in the text. Indeed, all three publications were equally likely to *not* include both terms in the same news item. This suggests that journalists did not feel the need to routinely connect the organisation with the phenomenon. Although they are not synonymous, the WTO played a central role in the development of modern globalisation. Naturally, one would not expect every article to contextualise the former with the latter, but with the vast majority of articles not even *mentioning* both words, the prospect for increased audience understanding of globalisation is greatly reduced. This tendency is exacerbated by the dominance of 'WTO' which featured in all bar six of the BBC articles, three-quarters of the *Guardian* sample and two-thirds of the *Times*'. In contrast, 'globalisation' appeared in around 40% of *Times* and *Guardian* articles but in a mere 11% of BBC News items. The initial analysis also revealed that the other search terms—'anti-globalisation' and 'anti-WTO'—were present in just 18 articles. These phrases were used so infrequently by all three media that their value to this part of the analysis is minimal. This does not mean, of course, that dissenting voices were not acknowledged but opponents of WTO policies—or indeed globalisation—were not bracketed in these blunt terms.[4]

The stark difference in the frequency of appearance of 'globalisation' and 'WTO' was mirrored in their respective prominence. The former appeared in just one headline, compared with 100 for the latter, and was generally mentioned just once, away from the top of the article. Across all three publications, 'globalisation' featured prominently in just ten news items, 2% of the universal sample. Clearly, the WTO Conference was considered worthy of detailed coverage but globalisation per se was not. The reporting over this period was distinctly event-centred, rather than issue-centred: the Conference had a specific time and place and attracted

[3]For the sake of brevity, references to the *Guardian–Observer* sample will henceforth be shortened to the '*Guardian*'. Similarly, the *Times–Sunday Times* will become the '*Times*'.

[4]The labels 'anti–capitalists' and 'anarchists' were also attached to dissenters. See below—critical discourse analysis.

the global political elite which consequently drew editorial interest that waned considerably in the aftermath of the Conference. This tendency was evident in the distribution of articles over the nine-week sample period. For all three publications, appearances of the search terms grew from a low base, peaked in week five and then declined to roughly the original level.

Overall, news items containing 'WTO' or 'globalisation' tended to be categorised as 'international' or 'business', with 114 (23%) of articles in the former category and 101 in the latter. The most populous classification for the BBC (56 articles or 38%) was *The Battle for Free Trade*, a special report that ran for much of the sample period. A further 45 BBC articles resided in international sections of the website and 22 fell into 'business'. Very few articles were placed in 'economy', just two in the *Guardian* and four on the BBC website. This was perhaps surprising because the influence of globalisation and the WTO stretch far beyond business.[5] There was also a general trend in the newspapers for stories to move from the business pages to the international and home sections in weeks four and five (reflecting the geographical location of the Conference, the focus on public order and commentary by UK actors). This arguably made the issues more visible. However, with 83% of BBC articles filed as 'international', 'business' or 'trade', audiences with little interest in these topics would rarely be exposed to the debates.

Salience, Themes and Framing

In many news items—typically those with a single occurrence of a search term—the mention of 'globalisation', 'WTO' and their antonyms was purely incidental to the story. Conversely, a search term was sometimes the primary focus of the article, and other stories connected the term to wider debates to varying degrees. Removing the 156 items, a third of the total, with incidental salience to the search terms left 327 articles—127 from BBC News, 122 from the *Guardian* and 78 from the *Times*—to be analysed in greater depth. After this salience filter was applied, the number of articles mentioning globalisation anywhere in the text fell by 51%. This adds further credence to the earlier observation that globalisation per se was not deemed worthy of significant analysis over this key period.

[5]The BBC News website lists 'economy' as a subset of 'business'. This is, arguably, the inverse of what one may expect.

Table 3.1 Primary themes

	BBC News		*Guardian*		*Times*	
	Articles	%	*Articles*	%	*Articles*	%
China and world trade	29	23	4	<4	9	12
World trade	22	17	15	12	15	19
Public order	19	15	7	6	15	19
Political structures, processes etc	16	13	39	32	21	27
Agriculture	9	7	7	6	7	9
Business	7	6	7	6	3	<4
Inequality and poverty	6	5	4	3	0	0
Developing world	6	5	13	11	0	0
Environment	3	<3	7	6	0	0
Labour	3	<3	8	7	1	<2
Other	7	6	11	9	7	9
Total	127	100	122	100	78	100

Fifty-four of the remaining BBC articles were published in the *Battle for Free Trade* special report (BBC 1999n). This was extension of a previous BBC series called *World Trade Wars* which accounted for a further five articles. In both cases, there was a bold graphic below the first paragraph that branded each article with a combative phrase. Hence, almost half of the BBC articles were placed in a bellicose supra-frame and yet, as shown by subsequent analysis of the secondary themes (see below), the text of the articles rarely echoed the degree of conflict promised at the outset ('Battle' and 'Wars') and the combatants were often poorly defined. Hence, it could be argued there was a degree of sensationalism in this strategy. There was no comparable supra-frame in the *Guardian* nor the *Times*, but, as shown in Table 3.1, there were both strong similarities and some important differences between primary themes.

The four most common primary themes for the BBC, *Guardian* and *Times* accounted for 68, 62 and 77% of the totals, respectively. The BBC's top four were shared by the *Times*, albeit in a different order, and two of these ('world trade' and 'political structures') also featured at the top of the *Guardian* rankings with this newspaper's other two preferred themes being 'developing world' and 'labour'. It is perhaps no surprise that 'world trade' was prominent across the board, but articles in this category conceived the key phrases in rather abstract terms. Instead of relating the WTO and globalisation to specific areas of the economy or society (e.g. business, environment, agriculture, etc.), 'world trade' was an over-arching theme which framed the issue in a distant and rather amorphous realm. Indeed, as confirmed by many of the articles that viewed the WTO and globalisation through a political lens, the procedures and rules of economic globalisation are negotiated by the elite, and political structures and exchanges were far more newsworthy than the effects on people. It was only when street protests began that the media, and the *Guardian* in particular, began to ask if those who argued for a more humanised version of globalisation ought to be included in the broader debate. This is apparent in the respective emphases on 'public order', with the BBC and the *Times* between two to three times more likely than the *Guardian* to conceptualise economic globalisation as protest or crime. In contrast, almost a third of *Guardian* articles—and 27% of *Times* articles—saw the WTO and globalisation as primarily political issues, whereas only 13% of BBC items fell into this category.

Overall, in terms of primary themes, the BBC bore a closer resemblance to the *Times* than to the *Guardian*. As well as sharing the same top four themes, and having a stronger propensity to focus on protest, the *Times* and BBC were far less likely to highlight progressive and fundamentalist reformer issues: a quarter of the *Guardian's* articles viewed the search terms in the context of the developing world, environment, inequality and labour, compared to 16% for the BBC and less than 2% for the *Times*. The most striking feature of the BBC's reporting pattern, however, was the prominence given to China. The Sino-American trade negotiations, which culminated in an agreement on November 14 (BBC 1999k), were given far more coverage than by the newspapers. Again, like the 'world trade' theme, China was presented as an elite issue, with the emphasis on exchanges between politicians rather than the wide-ranging economic and social impact of the country's accession to the global market.

The most common primary themes for BBC articles had very different secondary characteristics. These are most clearly expressed in the defining nouns and verbs of the news item. Naturally, 'public order' articles were framed in belligerent terms[6] whereas the lack of agreement at the Conference and the subsequent breakdown of talks were mirrored in

[6]For example, 'fight', 'disorder', 'violence', 'dispute', 'protest', etc.

more moderate secondary themes.[7] Contrary to the BBC's *Battle for Free Trade* supra-frame, however, the period was hardly characterised by combative debate among the elite, and the *Times* was more than twice as likely to place the issues in disputatious terms. The *Guardian's* most common secondary theme reflected the newspaper's support for the progressive reformers with 14 of the 37 articles categorised as 'announcements'[8] published as opinion pieces, five as editorials and four letters to the editor. Although the BBC News website had no direct equivalent of these latter two categories, it still gave exposure to partisan opinion with uncritical news reports of speeches (e.g. Hague in BBC 1999b), sympathetic analysis of the fair-trade argument (BBC 1999l) and opinion pieces written by environmentalists (BBC 1999m). Conversely, the BBC also published articles that were pointedly critical of the reformist causes (Cooke 1999a, b).

Sixty-eight per cent of BBC articles were standard news items compared with 59% for the *Times* and 37% for the *Guardian*. The BBC also published very few longer-format features in comparison with the newspapers, and this is reflected in the average article length with the *Times* at 645 words and the *Guardian* at 757 words, some 40% more than the BBC. These data are largely consistent with the episodic-thematic profiles of the samples. Some 40% of BBC articles were episodic, and 44% were thematic. This ratio reflected a slightly lower propensity to focus on recent and imminent events than the *Times* (58:34) but it was in stark contrast to the *Guardian* ratio which was strongly tilted to detailed, contextualising and explanatory thematic articles (28:63). Taken in isolation, these data are not particularly illuminating but when synthesised with the findings of the primary and secondary theme analysis, patterns emerge.

Across all three publications, the search terms were typically framed as political or economic issues that were debated—at varying levels of intensity—among the elite. The majority of items that reported these discussions and events were relatively short articles which, one might assume, lacked the detail to discuss the complexities of world trade. Although the patterns are rather hazy at this level of analysis, it is apparent that the *Guardian* had a slightly higher propensity to contextualise

[7] For example, 'negotiate', 'discuss', 'debate', 'impasse', 'stalemate', etc.

[8] News items based predominantly on an extended statement, a speech, manifesto or a prediction.

the issues in themes consistent with the dissenters' causes—developing world, environment, labour, etc.—and devoted more space to articles that covered broader debates and macro-trends. In contrast, the BBC and *Times* were appreciably more likely to frame the dissent as a public order problem.[9]

Source Analysis

Initial analysis of the sourcing data revealed that over four-fifths of all articles contained at least one named source. Conversely, none of the news providers had a particular propensity to publish articles with no named sources and each was close to the universal average of 15%. Using the crude measurement of named sources per article, the BBC and *Guardian* were very similar with 1.9 and 2.1, respectively, and the *Times* was noticeably lower with an average of 1.6 sources per article. However, these data are rather misleading because they obscure a surprising inclination to defy journalistic convention by citing just a single source: only 44% of the *Times* articles contained two or more named sources compared to 54% for the BBC and 61% for the *Guardian*. Also noteworthy is the presence of unnamed sources in 60% of BBC articles compared to 38% for the *Guardian* and 26% for the *Times*.

These findings are intriguing, but they say nothing about the diversity of opinion in the samples. Hence, the next step was to organise the sources into six categories: developed world elite; developing world elite; business; progressive reform organisations; grass roots, protestors and street groups; and other, non-aligned. These classifications do not necessarily reflect the political positions described in Chapter 2, but they are useful for gauging the exposure given to different groups' actors and, hence they go some way to understanding journalists' sourcing strategies. Before analysing the data, however, it is important to note the following: first, the elite of the developed and developing worlds had delegations at the WTO Conference, whereas the business community, the progressive reform and grass-roots groups did not. Second, although there were organisational and political differences between the latter two groups, they were bracketed as 'WTO critics' because they shared a general reformist perspective. And third, WTO representatives were

[9] These tendencies are discussed in greater depth in the discourse analysis section.

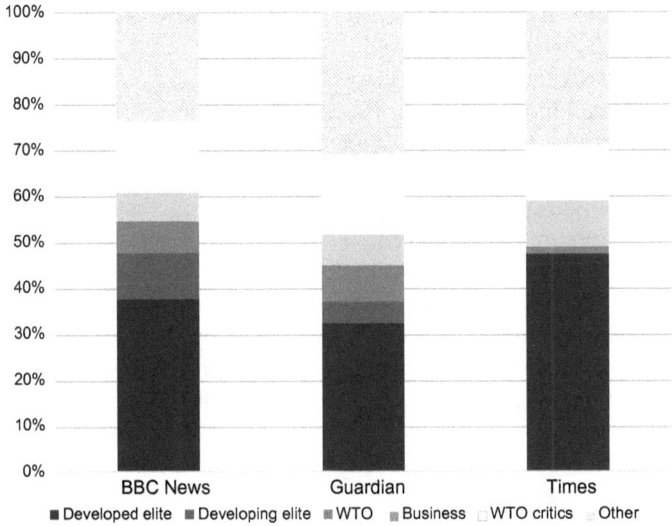

Fig. 3.1 Constitution of named sources

categorised as 'other, non-aligned' but they were included in this part of the analysis as a separate group because the organisation played a central role in the Conference.

As Fig. 3.1 illustrates, actors from groups *within* the Conference—the two political elites and the WTO—accounted for more than half of all named sources in BBC articles, around 50% of *Times'* sources and 45% in the *Guardian*. The *Times* was most dependent on developed elite sources which accounted for almost half of the total. Even though the BBC and *Guardian's* proportions were lower—38 and 32%, respectively—these data suggest that the debate was often expressed in terms preferred by politicians from rich countries. Furthermore, if the two political elites, the WTO and business sources are grouped together—on the basis that all generally supported free trade[10]—and compared with sources critical of the WTO, then the former greatly outnumbered the

[10]The WTO is officially non–partisan but the then WTO director general Mike Moore 'believes that free trade is a force for good and spent his life savings… campaigning for the job of pushing forward the process of liberalisation' (Elliott 1999a).

latter by a ratio of approximately 4:1 across the BBC sample, 6:1 in the *Times*, and 5:2 in the *Guardian*.

The data also illustrate the relatively low frequency of political voices from the developing world with just 38 of the 633 named sources—6%—in the universal sample. This apparent under-representation is ironic because many journalists noted how developing countries felt their views were marginalised at the Conference. Even though they were in Seattle in force, representatives complained about being excluded from discussions that were monopolised by the rich countries (Jawara and Kwa 2003: 18; Vidal 1999c; Vidal and Wintour 1999). Despite noting the exclusion, few journalists attempted to redress the balance by including the developing world elite in their own reports. Just one political representative from these countries was quoted by the *Times*. This was in stark contrast to the BBC's 25 citations, but this was only 10% of the Corporation's total—and a quarter of the developed elite tally—which is insignificant when one considers that three-quarters of the WTO membership were from the developing world (Elliott 1999b). More surprisingly, although the *Guardian* framed the WTO and globalisation as a developing world issue far more than the other two media, members of these countries' political elite made up just 5% of the newspaper's total named sources.

The dependence on sources from rich countries is confirmed in Table 3.2. In around a third of BBC articles a member of the developed elite was the first named source and, hence, was most likely to establish the parameters of debate. If WTO officials are placed in the same political space, then liberalisers accounted for the top four BBC first named sources. In contrast, the WTO critics—progressives and grass roots—were the first source in only 13 articles and developing world sources accounted for a further 12. In the *Times*, it is apparent that WTO critics and developing countries were largely excluded and the rich world dominated. Only in the *Guardian* did the progressive organisations—but not grass-roots voices—gain high visibility. But still, the 13 *Guardian* articles in which an NGO or trade union representative appeared first contrasts sharply with the 37 occasions that a member of the developed political elite opened the debate.

Given that the BBC has often been accused of having anti-business/left-wing sympathies,[11] closer inspection of its source data, and comparison with the traditionally left-of-centre *Guardian*, offers further insight.

[11] See Chapter 1.

Table 3.2 First named source: rankings

Source type	*BBC News N=105*		*Guardian N=107*		*Times N=66*	
	Rank	*Articles*	*Rank*	*Articles*	*Rank*	*Articles*
Leader—developed	1	16	8	6	2	9
WTO official	2	11	4	10	*	*
Minister—developed	3	9	1	15	3	7
Trade rep—developed	4	8	9	5	*	*
Journalist	5	7	2	14	1	13
Progressive groups	5	7	3	13	5	5
Grass-roots groups	7	6	*	*	*	*
Leader—developing	7	6	*	*	*	*
Legal and police	7	6	*	*	*	*
Academic/scientist	*	*	5	8	6	4
Member of public	*	*	6	7	*	*
Civil servant—developed	*	*	6	7	3	7
CEO/senior manager	*	*	*	*	6	4

*Negligible occurrences

If a news organisation tended to favour progressive or radical perspectives, audiences might expect to be frequently exposed to the views of socialist politicians, union members, protestors and social campaigners. These groups' views were indeed represented in the *Guardian* and the BBC, but when compared to other source types, there is little evidence to suggest that either publication was particularly inclined to the left. For instance, grass-roots campaigners were cited as named sources 13 times by the BBC and nine by the *Guardian*. But in both cases, voices of the business community were more prominent at 16 and 18, respectively. The BBC named far more protestors than the *Guardian*, but these were no more prevalent than industry associations, and in the *Guardian* business lobbying organisations were thirteen times more likely to be cited than a demonstrator. Trade unions fared little better with just two appearances in BBC articles and seven in the *Guardian*. Also, in this composite sample of 212 articles, not one UK minority party representative was named and quoted.[12] In terms of non-aligned sources, the

[12]This includes the Green Party, Plaid Cymru, the Scottish Nationalist Party and the Liberal Democrats.

Guardian gave considerable exposure to members of the public with 22 *vox populi* in comparison with the BBC's three. In addition, there was very little supporting data (e.g. poverty or inequality figures) from supra-national bodies such as the United Nations, World Bank or IMF. In the BBC sample, just one economist was quoted—as a fourth source—and a mere seven academics appeared. The figures for the *Guardian* were four and 21, respectively.

Despite the relative lack of input from left-wing sources—and independent sources who *may* hold similar views—the *Guardian* still managed to display distinctly progressive sympathies through its relatively strong coverage of the reformist agenda. By the same measurement, the *Times* was strongly pro-liberalisation[13] and in both newspapers, this could be partially explained by the frequent appearance of a journalist as the pre-eminent source (see Table 3.2). Many of these instances were opinion pieces and editorials but it is perhaps surprising that journalists were the fourth most commonly named source in BBC articles and the second most prevalent unnamed source. Seventeen of the 31 journalistic sources were BBC correspondents[14] and in nine articles, a BBC journalist summed up or gave context to the story. Online news was still in its relatively infancy at the time so this relatively high frequency could possibly be explained by broadcast conventions being naturally extended to written news. Even so, these correspondents guided the reader's understanding to an extent, and in the table of contents page for the *Battle of Free Trade* series, three BBC journalists were named and positioned as guides for those perplexed by global economics (Gallagher 1999; Giles 1999; Walker 1999). As will be described in the discourse analysis, even unnamed BBC journalists' choice of words were sometimes tinged with subjectivity.

The final stage of source analysis considers the sequence in which sources appeared. The person to be quoted first in an article tends to set the parameters of debate and, naturally, will frame the issue in a way that suits his or her position. As illustrated above, members of the developed world elite were the most prominent group. However, so long as sources with contrasting views are included, news items can give credence to a multiplicity of positions, and such articles are more likely to stimulate debate and understanding than those with sources representing just one

[13] Political positions and discourse patterns are discussed in detail below.

[14] The remainder were typically foreign newspaper journalists or anonymous 'correspondents'.

perspective. Hence, to gain a sense of the diversity of perspectives in the sample, developed elite and business sources were amalgamated into one group that shared a liberalising position; the developing world remained a distinct entity; and the progressives and grass roots were reunited as 'WTO critics'. The remaining sources were bracketed as 'others' and assumed to have no political persuasion.

In total, 829 named and unnamed sources were coded for this study, and in half of the 327 articles, one group had a monopoly of sources. The proportion was strikingly similar with around half of each news organisations' articles including spokespeople from just one group, and in each case, the developed elite-business combination was clearly the most likely to dominate. Indeed, WTO critics or representatives from the developing world were totally absent in one-third of BBC and *Guardian* articles and 42% of *Times* articles. Conversely, WTO critics enjoyed a monopoly in just 12% of the BBC articles, 18% in the *Guardian* and 8% in the *Times*. Developing countries fared worse with just 6% of BBC articles devoid of other groups' spokespeople, and none in either newspaper.

In contrast, there was a diversity of source groups in a third of BBC articles, 28% of the *Guardian's* and just 13% of the *Times'*, and again the developed elite-business alliance was the most successful in setting the terms of debate. In the BBC and *Guardian* samples, this group was twice as likely to be quoted before a developing world source or WTO critic than after. Although the BBC did award access to WTO critics, their voices were present in just a quarter of articles compared to a third for the *Guardian*. In contrast, the developed-business elite had a monopoly in 34% of BBC articles and led the debate in a further 21%. Overall, the BBC favoured this group over the WTO critics by a factor of two, marginally lower than the *Guardian*, which favoured the developed-business elite in 48% of articles and WTO critics in 22%, a ratio of 2.2:1.

Coverage of Political Positions

The source analysis demonstrates that representatives from the developed world elite dominated the debate about economic globalisation during the sample period. This was particularly true in the *Times*, but although the *Guardian* and the BBC gave greater access and prominence to dissenting voices, these were distinctly muted when compared to those of rich countries' politicians and their spokespeople. However, within this elite group there were considerable differences in opinion which

Table 3.3 Incidence of criticism and exclusion of political positions

Position	*BBC News % of articles*		*Guardian % of articles*		*Times % of articles*	
	Criticised	*Excluded*	*Criticised*	*Excluded*	*Criticised*	*Excluded*
Liberalisation	6	19	14	22	3	29
Protectionism	6	46	20	48	23	46
Progressive	5	40	4	31	13	41
Fundamentalist	9	73	5	75	28	59

were epitomised in the arguments over the phasing out of tariffs and subsidies. The European Union (EU), Japan and the USA each had protectionist tendencies which co-existed with an over-riding commitment to work towards universal free trade. Hence, it would be reasonable to assume that some articles featuring only developed world sources contained a difference of opinions, namely between liberalisers and protectionists, or indeed between elite advocates of progressive reform.[15] Similarly, even though WTO critics were absent in the majority of articles, this does not necessarily mean that the reformist or radical agendas were not covered. Journalists could, for instance, give credence to this position without citing an NGO spokesperson, a trade union official or a protestor. Hence, to assess the extent to which articles covered the four political positions, multifaceted criteria were applied to each news item.[16]

Almost 10% of the grand sample did not acknowledge any of the four positions and, consequently, these 31 articles gave the reader no indication of the existence of a debate. Exclusion, however, was by no means equal. The fundamental reform perspective was absent from 59% of *Times'* articles and around three-quarters of BBC and *Guardian* news items. Overall, however, *The Times was* the most dismissive and criticised the fundamentalist position in a further 29% of articles, compared with 9 and 5% for the BBC and *Guardian,* respectively. The combined effect was the same with over four-fifths of all articles either ignoring, condemning or ridiculing the fundamentalist cause (see bottom row of Table 3.3). The second most widely disregarded position was

[15]For example, President Clinton voiced his support for minimum international labour standards (BBC 1999d).

[16]See Chapter 2: methodology.

protectionism. The newspapers' lines were very similar with almost seven out of ten articles either criticising it or making no reference. The BBC coverage was less barbed but still, over half of the sample did nothing to support protectionism. From the negative perspective, the *Guardian's* reporting of the progressive reformers and the liberalisers was very balanced with each receiving no positive coverage in around a third of articles. In contrast, the BBC was 1.8 times as likely to criticise or ignore the progressives than the free traders, a slightly larger ratio (45:25) than the clearly pro-liberalisation *Times* (54:32).

In terms of articles that gave significant exposure to the four positions, liberalisation clearly had the advantage across the board. Some 49% of BBC articles contained detailed or brief free-trade discourse, compared to 47% for the *Guardian* and 40% for the *Times*. The figures for progressive reform were 37, 37 and 22%, respectively. Hence, by margins of 12, 10 and 18 points, advocates of free trade had more coverage than those who argued for progressive reform of the WTO.

By applying a simple weighting formula to these data,[17] the dominant discourse of the samples becomes evident. Figure 3.2 illustrates the relative positions of the BBC, *Guardian* and *Times*. The latter clearly gave the most positive exposure to liberalisation which had almost twice as much sympathetic or neutral coverage than progressive reform. The *Guardian*'s support for the progressive agenda was marginally higher than for the liberalisers (39:44) and in its entirety, this newspaper achieved greater balance than the BBC which leaned towards liberalisation (46:31), but not to the same extent as the *Times*. The BBC did, however, provide considerably more coverage of protectionist arguments than either newspaper. The fundamentalists had minimal support all round, and the *Times'* predilection to overtly criticise this position pushed its coverage to *minus* five points.

The central debate was clearly between liberalisers and progressive reformers. Hence, for the final part of this analysis the coverage of their mediated contest was assessed. Articles that contained detailed explanations of both the liberalisation and the progressive positions (row C in Table 3.4) were the most likely to deliver balanced and detailed

[17]The weighted total was calculated by multiplying the frequency of articles in the 'detailed coverage' category by 3; 'brief coverage' by 2; 'acknowledged' by 1, 'critical coverage' by minus 1 and 'no mention' by zero. See Chapter 2.

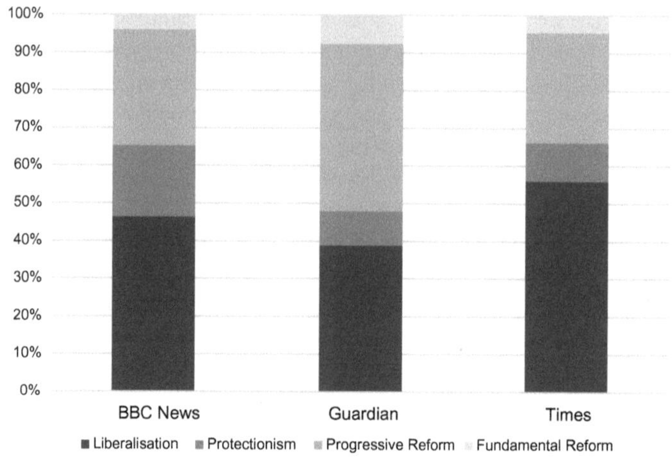

Fig. 3.2 Weighted coverage of political positions[18]

Table 3.4 Coverage of the liberalisation versus progressive reform debate

	Coverage		*BBC News*		*Guardian*		*Times*	
	Liberalisation	*Progressive*	*Frequency*	*%*	*Frequency*	*%*	*Frequency*	*%*
A	Detailed	Brief	41	32	23	19	23	29
B	Brief	Detailed	15	12	24	20	9	12
C	Detailed	Detailed	33	26	22	18	8	10
D	Other combinations		38	30	53	43	38	49
Total			127	100	122	100	78	100

information to the reader, and the BBC was the most adept in this respect, with 26% of articles compared to 18% in the *Guardian* and 10% in the *Times*. Also, the BBC had relatively few articles that gave neither side exposure (row D). In contrast, nearly half of the *Times*' and 43% of the *Guardian's* articles lacked any detail about either or both positions. The data also show that the BBC gave greater exposure to the liberalisers with almost a third of articles combining detailed coverage of this position and brief coverage of the progressive arguments (row A). In contrast, the progressives dominated in just one-eighth of BBC articles

[18]This chart understates the liberalisation figure of the *Times* by 5% because the charting software doesn't accommodate the *minus* 5% score for fundamental reform.

(row B) and overall, the BBC's tendency to favour free trade in articles that pitched the two positions against each other (row A/B) was very similar to the *Times*, with ratios of 2.7:1 and 2.4:1, respectively. The *Guardian* clearly gave more detailed coverage to the progressives than the other news organisations (row B) and this newspaper was the most balanced with almost identical numbers of articles favouring each of the two sides (rows A and B).

Critical Discourse Analysis

The quantitative analysis gives substantial clues about the political content of the BBC, *Guardian* and *Times*' reporting. Sources associated with fundamental reform were generally ignored by all three and consequently, their arguments were rarely acknowledged, and they were never explored in detail. To a lesser extent, the protectionists were also sidelined, and the primary debate pitched the liberalisers against the progressive reformers. Based on the evidence so far, the *Times* clearly favoured the former and the *Guardian* gave considerable exposure to the latter. The BBC's position, however, was more difficult to isolate: by some measures its journalistic output displayed balance and gave detailed coverage to the progressive agenda; and by others, it was comparable to the *Times*.

To gain a deeper understanding of the coverage of economic globalisation, critical analysis of journalistic discourses was undertaken. Before discussing the findings, however, it is important to emphasise that the BBC is bound by impartiality obligations and so one would not expect its journalists' descriptions of people and causes to be as explicitly judgemental as their print colleagues'. Nor did the BBC have editorials, letters pages[19] or, with a few exceptions, opinion pieces in which partisan views would be most evident. Nevertheless, close inspection of a sample of BBC articles and comparison with the newspapers' coverage confirms that liberalisation was the favoured position.

As noted above, around a third of the BBC items were published in a special report, the *Battle for Free Trade* (BBC 1999n). This title immediately positioned the issue as unambiguously combative and, with the inclusion of the word 'free', suggested a righteous outcome. It also

[19] In 1999, the BBC News website did have not have reporters' blogs nor the 'Have Your Say' reader comment facility.

implied that antagonistic forces were competing for a common, pre-established objective. Similarly, the previous BBC supra-frame, *World Trade Wars*, established confrontational expectations from the outset.[20] Published on December 13—ten days after the Conference finished—the *Battle for Free Trade* table of contents was essentially the home page of the section, and hence, it was crucial in setting the parameters of understanding for the audience, and a useful starting point for this part of the analysis. The lead paragraph set the scene:

> The failure to launch a new round of global trade talks in Seattle amid mass protests highlights deep divisions over the issue of free trade, once seen as the engine of world economic growth.

Retrospectively at least, the BBC acknowledged the role of protest in challenging the belief that free trade is universally beneficial, and thus gave some credence, albeit implied, to the arguments of the WTO critics. In the six photographs on this page, however, there was scant evidence of the human or environmental impact of economic globalisation: only one featured a person, another showed a river and forest, and the other four were rather insipid shots of container ships and cities. The running order, the subtitles and the introductions to each of five subsections also tended to conceive trade as a complex and unruly beast with few hints of a human dimension, except when explanation was given by sagacious journalists:

> **World trade talks collapse**
> The WTO's attempts to launch a new trade round in Seattle end in failure after four days of bitter disputes and street protests
>
> **Trade bullies and blocs**
> Trade has been growing faster than world output. But a free trading system has been difficult to fashion
>
> **Free trade flashpoints**
> It should be simple. But even constructing an agenda has stymied trade talks, as the BBC's Andrew Walker explains

[20]The bellicose theme was also evident in several article headlines. For example, 'Hippies declare web war on WTO' (BBC 1999f) and 'Body blow for free trade' (BBC 1999h).

> **Arguments and controversies**
> Everyone is in favour of free trade - but everyone interprets it differently. The BBC's Chris Giles supplies a guide for the perplexed
>
> **China moves to join the WTO**
> Advocates of free trade are encouraged as China reached a deal with the USA that moves it closer to joining the WTO

On the basis of these introductions, one might expect a thorough and impartial assessment of the various perspectives on world trade. However, analysis revealed support for one political position in particular. On November 23, a week before the Conference, the third article on the list gave a balanced assessment of the arguments for and against the liberalisation of agriculture and services. Despite this synopsis, the author narrowed the debate by stating that the protectionists were fighting an unstoppable force and were just delaying the inevitable: 'These countries all know that there is no escape from further liberalisation of agriculture' (Walker 1999). The journalist concluded his article by normalising 'political pain' and paraphrasing unnamed experts.

> **Taking the pain**
> Trade negotiations always require governments to accept political pain. Most economists will tell you that removing your own trade restrictions is good for you, even if others don't reciprocate

The second sentence clearly awarded intellectual superiority to 'free trade', and although Walker ended by acknowledging that some human suffering was inevitable, he suggested that, despite the inevitable hardship that some people will experience, everyone should have faith in liberalisation.

> But there are losers within countries who can see very clearly that their problems are due to the removal of trade barriers. The gains are often spread more thinly among many people who don't necessarily know that trade may be raising their standard of living. (ibid.)

The fourth item in the running order was published on the same day as Walker's piece, and it too conceived liberalisation as the inevitable, virtuous outcome. The title—'Arguments and controversies'—placed the article at the fulcrum of the trade debate and yet the introduction unequivocally stated: 'Everyone is in favour of free trade' (Giles 1999). This is a powerful assertion and, given such intellectually credible opposition to liberalisation it is highly contentious, and yet ironically, it was used to introduce competing arguments. Like Walker's piece, this article was pitched as a definitive guide to the debate, and again, it focussed on concepts and arguments rather than the impact of trade on people. The article was titled 'Finding a way through the trade morass' and began: 'Keep your wits about you—the new round of global trade talks starting in Seattle will throw up plausible sounding arguments from all sides'. The author then identified the 'sides' but gave no indication of their relative power. He also erroneously stated that all were included in the imminent Conference.

> National governments, international trading blocks, trade unions, environmentalists, farmers, multinational companies and many other pressure groups will be represented and will try to convince the world their vision of the future for world trade is best.

From the outset, the article promised to give a balanced assessment of the various positions, but the author then hinted that one viewpoint had a greater claim: 'They'll all try to paint themselves as the good guys, but they can't all be right'. The article went on to discuss the different perspectives in plain terms, but the final paragraphs accepted the position of the developed world elite:

> If totally free trade is not on the agenda, then trade we have must be managed. And even though the WTO will come under fire from many… it's the only management system for world trade we have.

The author restricted the debate further by discounting bilateral agreements—'much less transparent, much more complex and inefficient'—and in the last paragraph, Giles dismissed the fundamentalist position, gave little hope for reform, and clearly supported a WTO-led regime.

> The WTO can be changed and improved but criticising everything the WTO stands for might mean the world ends up with a much worse system of managing its trade, completely dominated by the world's big trading blocs. (ibid.)

It is important to reiterate the timing and placement of these two articles. Both were published a week before the Conference began; both featured prominently on the index page of a special BBC report; and both were offered as explanatory articles by impartial experts. To a large extent, the majority of the article texts were devoid of overt political opinion and gave measured exposure to conflicting arguments. But in both cases, the authors placed the WTO version of 'free trade' as a foregone conclusion and framed the debate as technocratic disputes among the political elite. This pattern was also evident in other BBC articles, with titles and introductions suggesting a range of perspectives would be given comparable exposure and yet close reading often revealed acceptance of the WTO's vision of world trade. For example, the 'Arguments and controversies' section also listed the following articles:

> Stop environmental destruction
> Free trade: good for all
> Does free trade benefit the poor?

The first two titles could easily be the rallying cries of the environmentalists and liberalisers, respectively, and the third—one of 12 published by the BBC the day after the protests became violent—asked a central question from the broader debate. The lead photograph—a sitting protestor, hands outstretched with peace signs, facing a sea of menacing riot police—had echoes of King Canute, and the opening paragraph heralded the arrival of a worthy and yet still distant goal: 'For the first time, the prospect of a genuinely free-trading world is in sight' (Gallagher 1999). The rest of the article provided a relatively balanced, albeit disjointed, synopsis of the pros and cons of free trade but the narrative never really addressed the title's question. However, Gallagher's choice of contextualising words before the end quote—from a senior member of the British political elite—confirmed the futility of dissent:

> But they (critics) may not have a choice. Whether they like it or not, it is here to stay. "Globalisation, the very rapid movement of capital across the world, new technology, it's a transformation of the whole world system," says…Claire Short. (ibid.)

In these terms, globalisation is conceived as a reified force that guides the trajectory of free trade. It's a *fait accompli*: there is no alternative, opposition is pointless, and the only option is to embrace the future. This narrative is consistent with Tony Blair's call to fellow left-of-centre parties, quoted in the *Times*: 'not become the immobile keepers of out-of-date dogma in the face of the new facts of globalisation' (Bremner 1999a).[21] Indeed, these three articles are symptomatic of the BBC's reporting throughout the period which generally did little to challenge the elite belief that liberalisation was the preordained endgame.

Nevertheless, as stated in the title of the BBC's special report, a 'battle' still raged, and at the beginning of the sample period the combatants were identified as the free trade advocates (particularly the UK and US governments), and the protectionists (typified by old-school Chinese Communists and recalcitrant EU socialists). When the protests began, however, opposition to came from a different quarter and the publications' allegiances became more defined. Although progressive reformers were given some exposure and credibility by all three news organisations, the *Times* often described members of this group in terms heavy with insinuating associations. On November 27, for example, a *Times* journalist bracketed *all* dissenters as outsiders:

> They encompass trade unions, environmental clubs, human rights groups, assorted religions, farmers, Third World supporters and animal welfare activists, plus countless students whose stated aim is to cause a ruckus. (Brodie 1999)

On the eve of the Conference, a *Times* leader was particularly dismissive of the critics (note the speech marks, italics added):

> At least 1,200 non-governmental organisations have formed a coalition to protest at the "evils" of globalisation. They have been joined by *anarchists, utopians, millenarians* - anyone, indeed, who believes that the ills of the world can all be laid at the door of the richer countries, America in particular. (*Times* 1999)

The newspaper continued the ridicule by association two days later (italics added):

> ... a *motley crew* of steel workers, environmentalists, poverty campaigners and *feminist witches* has succeeded in outwitting the most powerful governments in the world and hijacking the WTO agenda. (Murray 1999)

[21] 'Modernisation', 'change' and 'reform' were defining words of the first half of Blair's tenure as prime minister. See Chapter 4.

And an article in the *Sunday Times* pushed the scorn towards insult:

> Fat old union bosses and multi-pierced grunge kids who last saw shampoo in 1992 joined hands with right-wing militia groups from the Rocky Mountains and frizzy-haired professors who still keep their Vietnam posters in the sideboard ... the anti-corporate, protectionist, isolationist bandwagon. (Sullivan 1999)

Despite labelling WTO critics in such disparaging terms, the *Times* occasionally acknowledged the intellectual basis of the opposition. One journalist, for example, agreed with the protestors that the WTO's 'rapid expansion into politically contentious territory' had illuminated a 'democratic deficit' (Murray 1999). Nevertheless, the *Times*' general timbre was intolerant of dissent and even Greenpeace was branded 'largely elitist' and involved in illegal acts[22] that were the 'first step towards the type of violent disruption' seen at previous demonstrations (Riddell 1999).

In contrast, as shown in the quantitative analysis, the *Guardian* gave credence and support to the progressive reformers and its narrative often humanised the critics. On December 1, for example, the title of a leader cast the protestors as representatives of the world's citizenry and victims of oppression: 'Powerless people; Robocops face down protesters in Seattle and London: the globe's citizens are helpless before the future'. The article also gave a considered explanation of the protestors' unconventional tactics. Whereas the *Times* stated that their goal was to: 'cause a ruckus' (Brodie 1999), the *Guardian* leader writer said the protestors had: 'resorted to the demo and the TV-friendly stunt for the simplest, oldest of reasons: they have no other way of making their voice heard' (*Guardian* 1999c). This newspaper's description of the protest itself also created a very different picture to that of the *Times* (see above):

> More than 60,000 people marched in carnival spirits on the conference hall. Environmentalists, students, and an eclectic array of causes, joined steel workers and dockers to fill the city centre with colour and noise. (Elliott and Vidal 1999b)

The subheading of an *Observer* article four days later framed the 'real battle for Seattle' as 'a showdown between the world's most powerful

[22] Destroying genetically modified crops (Riddell 1999).

nations and a new alliance of the Third World with ecologists and human rights groups' (Vidal 1999d). The contrast between the peaceful demonstrators and the oppressive, futuristic law-enforcers was highlighted in the opening paragraph:

> "Shame, shame, shame on you," chanted the protesters beyond the lines of Darth Vader-style police, the armoured cars, the horsemen, the National Guard and the dogs. The tear gas was heavy on the air, the police were now firing plastic bullets into the weeping crowd and the Ministerial Round of the Seattle world trade talks was in crisis. (ibid.)

Whereas the protestors were 'colourful', 'eclectic' and in 'carnival spirits' (Elliott and Vidal 1999a), the 'Robocops' and 'Darth Vader-style police' were presented as the paramilitary wing of liberalisation. Some *Guardian* articles even playfully ridiculed the elite per se: for example, John Vidal (1999b) described a meeting at which: 'Three hundred greatly stretched suits from the powerful Alliance of Trade Expansion are jawing about the protests going on in the street far below' and in another article, he gently mocked a turgid and pompous WTO working party meeting (Vidal 1999c).

The *Guardian's* preferred discourse was clearly sympathetic to the progressives and sat in stark contrast to that of the *Times*. Although the BBC's reporting lacked the venom of the latter, it too lumped progressive reformers in with the fundamentalists and presented them as a disruptive, leaderless army. On the morning of the first day of the protests, for example, one BBC article predicted imminent conflict:

> Among the protesters were those from environmental groups, trade unions and the least developed countries...Some 50,000 critics of global capitalism arrived in the west-coast city at the weekend, in what is being dubbed the "Battle in Seattle". (BBC 1999a)

In a sidebar in the same article, BBC journalist Andrew Walker described the various events as 'mostly good-humoured ... with music, an inflatable dolphin and people dressed as turtles parading through the streets' (ibid.). Another article, also published on November 30, broke the movement into constituent parts:

> Anarchists, environmentalists, union members, human rights activists and religious groups have descended on Seattle with a common purpose - to protest against the World Trade Organisation. (BBC 1999j)

'Anarchists' also featured in the *Times*' description of the protestors (see above). Indeed, in language similar to that used by *Times* journalists, the BBC reporter cast doubts on the intellectual strength of the protestors' cause by highlighting the New Age spirituality of one particular group: 'Among the protesters are Wiccans, feminist neo-pagan lovers of nature and magic, who say the WTO values free trade over the Goddess' (ibid.).

When accompanied by photographs of violent protest or demonstrators in fancy dress, such descriptions immediately created a distance between dissenters and the conventionally dressed, well-organised and tightly focussed, pro-free trade elite. Furthermore, the reformers' more rational concerns were diluted by their association with 'anarchists', 'witches', 'turtles' and 'inflatable dolphins' and, hence, their credibility became open to question. It was also noticeable that, unlike the *Guardian*, neither the BBC or the *Times* made negative comments about the appearance of the police or the delegates.

Other BBC stories appeared to give significant support to the protestors' arguments, but the disruption narrative was still more prominent. An article on December 1, for example, contained an explanation of the broad reformist position and noted the support of President Clinton who agreed that labour and environmental issues should appear in trade discussions and 'strongly, strongly agreed' that the demonstrators should be included in the negotiations (BBC 1999d). And yet, with a headline of 'Seattle declares civil emergency', a lead photograph of a window being kicked in by a pair of anonymous demonstrators,[23] four more photos of rioting and protest, and the first third of the article devoted to details of the civil unrest, it is debatable if this news item helped readers better understand the critics' arguments. Of course, photographs of violence, arrests and general disorder were natural complements to the *Battle for Free Trade* supra-frame. But in addition to repeatedly using the aforementioned image in arguably a misleading context, the BBC also published photographs of violence at *previous* demonstrations, before the WTO Conference even began, and warned the current cohort of protestors *might* follow suit (BBC 1999i).

Photographs of violent protest were used by the BBC throughout the period, even as accompaniments to sober debates about the WTO and genetically modified crops (BBC 1999e). There were, of course,

[23]This photograph was also the lead image for three more BBC articles which further imprinted the association with violent dissent and anarchy in readers' minds.

exceptions[24] but overall, the BBC's portrayal of WTO critics had much in common with the pro-liberalisation *Times*. Indeed, the words of BBC reports tended to award greater credibility to the liberalising elite than the critics, but this was done far more subtly than the *Times*. For example, in the article entitled 'Does free trade benefit the poor?' (Gallagher 1999) anonymous critics *claimed* that the WTO is 'trampling on less powerful countries in the name of commerce', whereas the named sources *said* their beliefs. Although this was not a universal tendency, 'claim' was frequently applied to dissenters' positions but not to the elites'. For example (italics added):

> They (protestors) *claim* the clothes are manufactured in sweatshop conditions in developing countries. The company (Gap) has *denied* the allegations. (BBC 1999p)

> … the USTR (United States Trade Representative) will counter the *claims* of the protestors with *information* of its own. (BBC 1999q)

> The Electrohippies *claim* their attack will target three WTO websites. (BBC 1999f)

The BBC's proclivity to construct news around the discourse of the Western elite was particularly apparent in articles about China which, as noted above, dominated the BBC's pre-Conference coverage. *Guardian* and *Times* articles around this time noted that China's trade deal with the USA was an important step towards full WTO membership and would have a seismic impact on businesses, workers and consumers across the world (Burke 1999; Hutton 1999). Western leaders were eager to emphasise the commercial benefits of the agreement: President Clinton, for instance, presented the deal as unequivocally beneficial for American business—and therefore, Americans—and believed that Chinese exposure to the global business community would improve openness and, ultimately, enhance human rights in China (Elliott and Denny 1999). Significantly, both the left-of-centre *Guardian* and the pro-liberalisation *Times* also scrutinised the human impact of the deal.

[24]For example, some BBC articles that conceived the WTO–globalisation as a development, environmental or labour issue used images of life in Africa, plants and workers, respectively.

The *Times*, for example, noted: 'WTO entry is likely to hurt workers in China as much as those in America' (August 1999) and discussed the inevitable consequences of '…a new tide of cheap Chinese goods heading west' (Mortishead 1999a). The *Times* also highlighted objections about China's human rights record and the likely impact on manufacturing industry jobs (MacIntyre 1999). In the *Guardian*, Will Hutton (1999) stressed the historic gravitas of the moment in which: 'a communist economy of 1.3 billion people surrendered to globalisation and the market' and predicted that increasing the global workforce by 600 million would have a significant impact on the employment and spending patterns of the rest of the world.

With such coverage in the newspapers, one may have expected the BBC to also critically analyse the broader implications of China's future accession to the WTO. However, close examination of the 29 BBC articles that featured the search terms in the context of 'China and world trade' confirmed that, despite such extensive coverage,[25] arguments held by the Western elite largely went unchallenged. Indeed, 21 articles from this subset gave detailed or brief exposure to free trade compared to six for protectionism. Progressive reform arguments were given no substantial exposure and were minimally acknowledged in just six news items. Fundamental reform was not even acknowledged, and five articles made no reference whatsoever to any political position. In comparison with the newspapers, the BBC articles lacked analytical depth and most merely echoed the position of the Western elite. For example, the agreement was described as a 'market opening deal' (BBC 1999k) which involved China 'coming in from the cold' (BBC 1999o). However, unlike the newspapers, the BBC barely considered the downsides of the deal to the British economy and society. One article (BBC 1999c) did so in brief, dehumanised terms—'some workers…could be laid off'—and the only time detailed explanation was given, it was constructed in commercial legalese (BBC 1999g).

In the context of China, free trade was conceived by the BBC as self-evidently virtuous, rational and inevitable. This tendency was also present in the broader sample: with some notable exceptions, the descriptive tone of BBC articles was consistent with that of the liberalising, developed elite whereas other political positions were pushed to

[25] This subset represents almost a quarter of BBC articles.

the periphery. Indeed, throughout the period of analysis, BBC journalists wrote of 'battles', disagreements and opposing sides but rarely described them in any detail. In contrast, print journalists exercised far more linguistic latitude in their assessment of political arguments. *Times* writers were particularly scornful of anything vaguely anti-liberalisation. For instance, Charles Bremner (1999a) covered a meeting of the world's social democratic leaders that was expected to: 'endorse a manifesto that is likely to carry old-style gibes against capitalism'. The next day he quoted Tony Blair's opposition to such '"outdated doctrine and dogma" on the Left' and juxtaposed this assessment with that of the 'Socialist French Prime Minister' who called for: 'Marxist methods to rein in capitalism' (Bremner 1999c). In the *Sunday Times*, Irwin Stelzer conceived a misguided EU which is: 'unprepared to abandon agricultural protectionism or its Luddite attitude towards genetically modified agricultural products' (Stelzer 1999). The day before the Conference began, the *Times'* position was vividly expressed in a leader which conflated the protectionists with the WTO critics and argued dissent was both confused and futile in the face of unstoppable progress. The 'real fear of the protestors', wrote the author (italics added):

> … is not that the trade talks will fail but that they will succeed, for protectionism is a powerful force behind which shelter not only state monopolies, inefficient industries and cosseted farmers but *backward-looking and xenophobic ideologies*. (*Times* 1999)

There were, of course, exceptions. For example, Carl Mortishead (1999b) drew an explicit link between South Wales where: 'union leaders are negotiating with the owners of a mill over the future of hundreds of textile jobs' and '… (WTO headquarters on) the shores of Lake Geneva, (where) diplomats are wrangling over the text of an agenda for a summit meeting in Seattle'. Another journalist, David Selbourne argued that globalisation is the: 'grandest of all idols … (and) … worshippers are everywhere on their knees' (Selbourne 1999). But despite this reporter noting that nation states were being 'reduced to a market', in most cases the *Times* offered little regard to those who might suffer. Bronwen Maddox, for example, warned readers not to: 'overestimate the significance of … the diverse band of environmentalists and others who object to the organisation for some reason or other', and echoed the British government's view that free trade was the only answer:

> As Clare Short… said this week, if the demonstrators really want to help the world's poor countries, they should work to liberalise trade even further. (Maddox 1999)

Contrary to its support of progressive arguments, *Guardian* journalists occasionally equated liberalisation with the needs of the poor, too. Commenting on negotiations over the reduction of agricultural subsidies, for example, Larry Elliott ended an article: 'Very commendable. But not a lot of use to those in the world who suffer from undernourishment. All 790 million of them' (Elliott 1999b). Such endorsements, however, were in the minority and in general, the *Guardian* took a critical line: Madeleine Bunting, for example, described the 'rough side of globalisation' in a feature about the effects of liberalisation in Peru (Bunting 1999). In addition, the *Guardian* published opinion pieces by prominent progressive reformers (Coates 1999; George 1999) and at the end of the Conference, an editorial envisaged a future that promoted inclusivity:

> The process should be weighted more towards pressure groups and NGOs and less towards national governments and multinational business. The lesson of Seattle is that global trade means truly global participation. (*Guardian* 1999d)

The fundamental reform position, however, received short shrift in the *Guardian*, from both Elliott (1999c) and John Vidal who captured the irony of radicalism: 'If the WTO itself collapses, there will be no world forum for the poorest people to at least ventilate their concerns and protect their own interests' (Vidal 1999d). Indeed, there were few signs of support for the radicals in either the *Guardian* or the *Observer.* In the latter, William Keegan and Andrew Marr were unequivocal about the misguided idealism of those who challenged neoliberalism:

> Britain's version of Seattle was a little local demonstration outside Euston Station. Here the most prominent voices seemed to be wanting to abolish capitalism. Perhaps nobody had told them about the dismemberment of the USSR in 1991. Capitalism will be with us for some time. (Keegan 1999)

In his article, Marr was also dismissive the progressive reformers, intolerant of the protectionists and adamant that liberalised trade was a non-negotiable and indelible characteristic of globalisation. He also gave a damning verdict on an alternative manifesto offered by the radicals: 'sounds like the Communist Manifesto rewritten by Christopher Robin' (Marr 1999). Although the arguments for progressive reform of the WTO were awarded exposure and credence by the *Guardian,* this newspaper accepted that managing, rather than challenging, neoliberal globalisation was the only option for the left:

> Globalisation has created some ineluctable universal economic rules by which countries now abide or die - stability, low debt, low inflation. The aim of social democrats is to prove the iron will of the market does not rule alone and it is compatible with social justice. (*Guardian* 1999a)

Summary

There were clear differences in the characteristics of the three news organisations' journalism over the period covered in this case study. The *Times* and the BBC both tended to reproduce the discourse of liberalisation, whereas the *Guardian* consistently expressed sympathy for the arguments of the progressive reformers. Newspaper journalists also tended to be much more expressive in their description of actors and arguments, and *Times* reporters in particular were pointedly critical of opposition to liberalisation. Despite these differences, however, there were considerable and significant similarities.

In all three publications, if globalisation was mentioned in an article, it was invariably once, and rarely the focus of the news item. That globalisation per se was not worthy of detailed analysis during this crucial period of its development was one of the most telling findings of this case study. Also, because 'globalisation' was rarely collocated with 'WTO', it is unlikely that uninitiated readers would have been aware that the debates surrounding the Conference had any relevance to the phenomenon. Furthermore, all three publications had a propensity to conceptualise the issues in the distant, abstract realms of elite politics and world trade. Only when the protests became violent did economic globalisation gain a human dimension, but instead of focussing on the long-term impact of liberalisation on families, communities, workers and the environment, the emphasis in the *Times* and BBC was on public order.

Only the *Guardian* made a concerted effort to cover the issues thematically—usually in analytical articles—and in terms that reflected the WTO critics' agenda. This is not to say, however, that the key arguments of the fundamental reformers, such as the abolition of the WTO, were discussed in detail. Indeed, in the mediated debate about economic globalisation in late 1999, radical alternatives to neoliberalism were excluded—even by the left-of-centre *Guardian*—and in very few instances were arguments for a more humanised form of economic globalisation pitched on equal terms against the dominant discourse.

References

August, O. (1999, November 23). China Will Cheat Foreign Firms Out of Free Trade. *The Times.*

BBC. (1999a, November 30). *Protests Overshadow WTO Talks.* BBC News Website. Retrieved from http://news.bbc.co.uk/1/hi/world/americas/542622.stm. Accessed January 23, 2011.

BBC. (1999b, November 1). *Hague: Cut Taxes to Prosper.* BBC News Website. Retrieved from http://news.bbc.co.uk/1/hi/business/the_economy/501546.stm. Accessed January 23, 2011.

BBC. (1999c, November 15). *China Deal to Boost Economy.* BBC News Website. Retrieved from http://news.bbc.co.uk/1/hi/business/the_economy/520874.stm. Accessed January 24, 2011.

BBC. (1999d, December 1). *Seattle Declares Civic Emergency.* BBC News Website. Retrieved from http://news.bbc.co.uk/1/hi/world/americas/544135.stm. Accessed January 24, 2011.

BBC. (1999e, December 1). *WTO "Seizing Control of GM Trade".* BBC News Website. Retrieved from http://news.bbc.co.uk/1/hi/world/americas/545136.stm. Accessed January 24, 2011.

BBC. (1999f, November 30). *'Hippies' Declare Web War on WTO.* BBC News Website. Retrieved from http://news.bbc.co.uk/1/hi/uk/543752.stm. Accessed January 24, 2011.

BBC. (1999g, December 21). *China Stock Market Shake-Up.* BBC News Website. Retrieved from http://news.bbc.co.uk/1/hi/business/573460.stm. Accessed January 24, 2011.

BBC. (1999h, December 25). *Body Blow for Free Trade.* BBC News Website. Retrieved from http://news.bbc.co.uk/1/hi/business/570162.stm. Accessed February 4, 2011.

BBC. (1999i, November 30). *Free Trade Will Boost Third World.* BBC News Website. Retrieved from http://news.bbc.co.uk/1/hi/uk_politics/543227.stm. Accessed February 4, 2011.

BBC. (1999j, November 30). *In Pictures: The WTO Protests.* BBC News Website. Retrieved from http://news.bbc.co.uk/1/hi/world/americas/543290.stm. Accessed February 4, 2011.

BBC. (1999k, November 15). *China Drops Trade Barriers.* BBC News Website. Retrieved from http://news.bbc.co.uk/1/hi/business/the_economy/520749.stm. Accessed February 4, 2011.
BBC. (1999l, November 23). *Roddick Blasts World Trade Body.* BBC News Website. Retrieved from http://news.bbc.co.uk/1/hi/uk/533315.stm. Accessed February 4, 2011.
BBC. (1999m, November 23). *Stop Environmental Destruction.* BBC News Website. Retrieved from http://news.bbc.co.uk/1/hi/special_report/1999/11/99/battle_for_free_trade/533619.stm. Accessed February 4, 2011.
BBC. (1999n, December 13). *The Battle for Free Trade.* BBC News Website. Retrieved from http://news.bbc.co.uk/1/hi/special_report/1999/11/99/battle_for_free_trade/534014.stm. Accessed March 12, 2011.
BBC. (1999o, November 16). *WTO: China Comes in from the Cold.* BBC News Website. Retrieved from http://news.bbc.co.uk/1/hi/world/monitoring/522912.stm. Accessed March 12, 2011.
BBC. (1999p, November 28). *Security Scare Hits WTO.* BBC News Website. Retrieved from http://news.bbc.co.uk/1/hi/world/americas/541879.stm. Accessed March 12, 2011.
BBC. (1999q, November 23). *Protestors Gather in Seattle.* BBC News Website. Retrieved from http://news.bbc.co.uk/1/hi/special_report/1999/11/99/battle_for_free_trade/533220.stm. Accessed March 12, 2011.
Bremner, C. (1999a, November 8). World Socialists Set to Change Credo of Blair. *The Times.*
Bremner, C. (1999b, November 23). French Farmer's Hero Invades US. *The Times.*
Bremner, C. (1999c, November 9). Rivals Jospin and Blair in Left-Wing Duel. *The Times.*
Brodie, I. (1999, November 27). 'Battle in Seattle' Looms Over World Trade Summit. *The Times.*
Buckman, G. (2004). *Globalization: Tame It or Scrap It?* London: Zed Books.
Bunting, M. (1999, December 31). Where Inequality Engulfs Jesus and Ericsson. *The Guardian.*
Burke, T. (1999, November 23). Trade Talks Sleepwalk to Seattle. *The Times.*
Chanda, N. (2007). *Bound Together: How Traders, Preachers, Adventurers, and Warriors Shaped Globalization.* New Haven, CT: Yale University Press.
Coates, B. (1999, December 8). Friends Fall Out; Bickering Between Power Groups Helped to Scupper the Trade Talks. *The Guardian.*
Conway, E. (2009). *50 Economic Ideas You Really Need to Know.* London: Quercus.
Cooke, A. (1999a, December 6). The Last Demo Circus of the Year. *Letter from America.* BBC News Website. Retrieved from http://news.bbc.co.uk/1/hi/programmes/letter_from_america/552648.stm. Accessed February 4, 2011.
Cooke, A. (1999b, December 13). Renewed Concern Over Second-Hand Smoke. *Letter from America.* BBC News Website. Retrieved from

http://news.bbc.co.uk/1/hi/programmes/letter_from_america/562507.stm. Accessed February 4, 2011.
Elliott, L. (1999a, November 26). It's All About Putting Food in Mouths. *The Guardian*.
Elliott, L. (1999b, December 2). Who Wants What from the Talks? *The Guardian*.
Elliott, L. (1999c, December 6). Unless WTO Cleans Up Its Act There Will Be More Issues for the Protesters to Trade On. *The Guardian*.
Elliott, L., & Denny, C. (1999, November 16). China Agrees to Free Trade. *The Guardian*.
Elliott, L., & Vidal, J. (1999a, December 1). WTO Protests Erupt. *The Guardian*.
Elliott, L., & Vidal, J. (1999b, December 4). Week of Division on and off Streets. *The Guardian*.
Fukuyama, F. (1992). *The End of History and the Last Man*. New York: Free Press.
Gallagher, M. (1999, December 1). *Does Free Trade Benefit the Poor?* BBC News Website. Retrieved from http://news.bbc.co.uk/1/hi/world/americas/544997.stm. Accessed March 14, 2011.
George, S. (1999, November 24). The Problem Isn't Beef, Bananas, Cultural Diversity or the Patenting of Life: The Problem Is the WTO. *The Guardian*.
Giles, C. (1999, November 23). *Finding a Way Through the Trade Morass*. BBC News Website. Retrieved from http://news.bbc.co.uk/1/hi/special_report/1999/11/99/battle_for_free_trade/532538.stm. Accessed February 4, 2011.
Guardian. (1999a, November 23). Take a Stab at Change. *Leader*.
Guardian. (1999b, November 29). Stop. I Want to Get Off; So-Called Progress Is the New Ideology. *Leader*.
Guardian. (1999c, December 1). Powerless People; Robocops Face Down Protesters in Seattle and London. *Leader*.
Guardian. (1999d, December 4). A Fable from Babel; How to Ensure Your Meeting Is Botched Chaos. *Leader*.
Hamilton, A. (1999, November 13). Africa's Special Place in Queen's Heart. *The Times*.
Hutton, W. (1999, November 21). World Trade Organisation: At Last, the Fall of the Great Wall of China. *The Observer*.
Jawara, F., & Kwa, A. (2003). *Behind the Scenes at the WTO*. London: Zed Books.
Juniper, T. (1999, November 17). Planet Profit; Is the WTO in the Pocket of Corporate Power? *The Guardian*.
Keegan, W. (1999, December 5). In My View: Grant Us Liberty from Free Trade. *The Observer*.

MacIntyre, B. (1999, November 17). China Deal Splits Election Hopefuls. *The Times.*

Maddox, B. (1999, December 2). Seattle's Riots May Have Saved the Negotiations from Looming Failure. *The Times.*

Marr, A. (1999, December 5). Comment: The Seattle Debacle Has Raised Crucial Questions About the Role of the World Trade Organisation. *The Observer.*

Monbiot, G. (2003). *The Age of Consent.* London: Perennial.

Mortishead, C. (1999a, November 16). China's Economy Braced for a Free Trade Shake-Up. *The Times.*

Mortishead, C. (1999b, November 24). Seattle Talking Shop Will Set the Agenda for Us All. *The Times.*

Murray, A. (1999, December 1). Confusion Reigns on Seattle's Parade. *The Times.*

Owen, E. (1999, December 21). Made in Spain Gains. *The Times.*

Peet, R. (2003). *Unholy Trinity: The IMF, World Bank and WTO.* London: Zed Books.

Pilger, J. (2002). *The New Rulers of the World.* London: Verso.

Riddell, P. (1999, November 29). Rebellion on the Global Village Green. *The Times.*

Robertson, R. (2003). *The Three Waves of Globalisation: A History of a Developing Consciousness.* London: Zed Books.

Selbourne, D. (1999, December 30). All That Is Solid Melts into Blair. *The Times.*

Stelzer, I. (1999, December 5). Trade Disaster as Clinton Fights Lewinsky Legacy. *Sunday Times.*

Stiglitz, J. (2002). *Globalisation and Its Discontents.* London: Penguin.

Sullivan, A. (1999, December 5). A Grungy Day of Glory for the Flagging Left. *Sunday Times.*

Times. (1999, November 29). Chance in a Millennium. *Leader.*

Vidal, J. (1999a, November 22). Genetic Patenting Row Looms Over Trade Talks. *The Guardian.*

Vidal, J. (1999b, December 1). Unequal Terms; World Leaders Band Together to Save the WTO's Fading Image. *The Guardian.*

Vidal, J. (1999c, December 3). Secret World of WTO Deal Makers. *The Guardian.*

Vidal, J. (1999d, December 5). The Trade Talks Collapse: Real Battle for Seattle. *The Observer.*

Vidal, J., & Wintour, P. (1999, December 5). Clinton Calamity as Trade Talks Fail. *The Observer.*

Walker, A. (1999, November 23). *Free Trade Flashpoints.* BBC News Website. Retrieved from http://news.bbc.co.uk/1/hi/special_report/1999/11/99/battle_for_free_trade/532317.stm. Accessed March 12, 2011.

CHAPTER 4

Union Canutes Cannot Halt PFI

The Reporting of Private Finance in British Public Services in 2002 and 2007

Introduction

Although the Private Finance Initiative (PFI) was a flagship policy of Tony Blair's Labour government, it was conceived by the preceding administration (Craig and Brooks 2006: 133). PFI was presented in 1992 by the Conservative chancellor of the exchequer as a way of bringing private sector management, efficiency and 'fresh flows of investment' into parts of the UK economy that were 'traditionally regarded as the exclusive domain of the public sector' (Pollock et al. 1997). The rationale for PFI was clear: if private companies financed, built and managed projects, the government could procure the services on behalf of the public with relatively small payments over a protracted period.[1] Also, huge upfront capital investment could be avoided and thus, public sector debt would be minimised. Over the next five years, however, many recognised that PFI had limitations and the most vocal criticisms came from the opposition Labour Party. In 1996, for example, Shadow Chief Secretary to the Treasury, Alistair Darling, warned: 'Apparent savings now could be countered by the formidable commitment on revenue expenditure in years to come' (in Elliott and Atkinson 2007: 131).

[1] With contracts between 30 and 60 years, PFI is akin to a mortgage (Schifferes 2002a).

Jones (2002).

G. J. Merrill, *The Political Content of British Economic, Business and Financial Journalism*, https://doi.org/10.1007/978-3-030-04012-3_4

In 1997, however, the new Labour government fundamentally revised its opinion of PFI. As Chancellor, Gordon Brown was eager to fulfil his pre-election promise to reverse two decades of under-investment in public services but equally, he was hamstrung by a commitment to adhere to spending limits imposed by his Conservative predecessor (Craig and Brooks 2006: 134). Two months after the 1997 general election, health minister Alan Milburn said: 'When there is a limited amount of public-sector capital available, as there is, it's PFI or bust' (in Monbiot 2007). Indeed, PFI provided an ideal solution to Brown's conundrum and consequently, became the default model for financing public works (Smith 1999: 2). The extent of Labour's *volte-face* became evident during its first term in office: in 2000 the government announced some £20 billion worth of public projects would be privately funded by 2003 (Monbiot 2001: 63) and by 2001, 450 PFI contracts had been signed (House of Commons Library 2001). In comparison, the preceding Conservative government had approved a mere 50 PFI contracts in the four years to 1997 (Osler 2011). The Labour government's commitment to PFI meant that within four years: 'more capital projects (had) been undertaken for a given level of public expenditure and public service capital projects (had) been brought on stream earlier' (ibid.).

This was a compelling argument and yet even organisations usually sympathetic to the Labour Party, particularly trade unions, were raising concerns. The most common was the cost of finance. It is widely agreed that governments can always borrow more cheaply than the private sector and, by extension, public enterprise is the most cost-efficient way to build infrastructure (Unison 2011; Osler 2011). There were also concerns about the disparities between the capital value and the lifetime payments of PFI projects. For example, the building cost of Swindon hospital was £76 million, whereas under the 30-year PFI contract the state would pay £500 million (Osler 2002: 122). PFI projects also have high set-up costs, including tortuous tendering procedures and protracted negotiations. According to the trade union Unison, the first 15 NHS trust hospitals to adopt PFI spent £45 million on advisers (Unison 2011) and Richard Brooks[2] estimated that, by the end of 2005, advisers and consultants had earned around £15 billion from PFI (Craig and Brooks 2006: 136). Officially, PFI was only to be used if it proved to

[2]Richard Brooks is a prolific journalistic critic of PFI. He has written numerous articles for *Private Eye* on the subject.

be better value for money than the traditional method of financing, but it became 'the only game in town' accounting for 90% of all completed schools and hospitals in the first five years of the Labour administration. By 2002, the government had committed to more than £100 billion worth of future payments (*Guardian* 2002b; BBC 2002a).

Other critics believed that the problems with PFI ran far deeper and expressed concerns about the increasingly blurred delineation between government and business (Whitfield 2001; Osler 2002; Ramsay 1998). Allyson Pollock[3] argued that British businesses, particularly the construction industry, had been supportive of PFI since its inception (Pollock 2005), and with the most obvious opportunities for outright privatisation already exhausted, PFI provided an innovative route into previously sacred territory (Monbiot 2001: 9; Whitfield 2001: 5). In 1997, at the start of Labour's first term in office, Gordon Brown was eager to convince the City of London of his business credentials, and the Confederation of British Industry (CBI) requested, and was subsequently given, direct involvement in designing PFI rules (Ramsay 1998; Monbiot 2001: 97).

Private finance was clearly a deeply political issue: if public service provision was driven by commercial rather than social imperatives, argued the critics, then the nature of health, education and other services may be changed irrevocably (Pollock 2005: 57; Osler 2002: 119). While the government asserted that whether an asset is built and owned by the public or the private sector was irrelevant, others argued that the means of public service provision fundamentally changed the ends (Blair 2002a; IPPR in Hutton 2002: 232; Whitfield 2001).

Despite senior Labour politicians avoiding public debate about PFI over the previous five years, the competing arguments were forced into the open at the Labour Party Conference in September 2002. Although delegates subsequently defeated a motion to establish PFI as official government policy, and 63% of the public supported the unions' call for a review of PFI (Travis and Maguire 2002), the government remained committed to private finance. In May 2007, however, some of the sceptics' concerns were confirmed with the publication of a unfavourable parliamentary report (HCCPA 2007). It revealed that 750 PFI schemes

[3] In the early 2000s, Professor Allyson Pollock was head of the Public Health Policy Unit at University College London and is arguably the most learned and vociferous critic of PFI in the health service.

costing over £54 billion had been approved, but it also found that the government was being 'outwitted' when negotiating with consortia (Hencke 2007).

Private Finance on the News Agenda

For a period of nine weeks pivoting on each of these two key events, the BBC News website, the *Guardian/Observer* and the *Daily* and *Sunday Telegraph*[4] were searched for articles that contained 'PFI', 'PPP', 'private finance initiative' or 'public private partnership'. The initial analysis revealed two major differences between 2002 and 2007: first, the relative visibility of the search terms. In 2002, 89% of articles featured 'PFI', whereas 'PPP' appeared in 17%. In 2007, however, the proportion of articles mentioning PPP more than doubled and those featuring PFI fell by 20 points. It is important to stress that these acronyms are closely related but not synonymous[5] and the rise in hits for PPP may simply be due to an increase in contracts that were not pure PFI.[6] A second and more notable difference between the two years was the quantity of articles. For 2002, the search generated 258 items, exactly three times more than 2007 which yielded 86. Although the periods were the same length and the search terms identical, the disparity in the number of articles can be explained by the nature of the respective focal points.

The 2002 Labour Party Conference debate was a set-piece confrontation between the trade unions and a Labour government, and such fraternal squabbles have far greater news value than the publication of a report from a Westminster committee room. The massive journalistic presence at the Conference guaranteed extensive coverage of the conflict.[7] In addition, one would expect speculation in advance

[4]For the sake of brevity, references to the *Guardian/Observer* sample will henceforth be shortened to the '*Guardian*'. Similarly, the *Daily/Sunday Telegraph* will become the '*Telegraph*'.

[5]Public–private partnership (PPP) can be defined as: 'any collaboration between public bodies, such as local authorities or central government, and private companies' and, hence, PFI is one type of PPP (BBC 2003b).

[6]An alternative interpretation, given by an anonymous journalist, is that the Labour Party deliberately avoided using 'PFI' in the mid-2000s because of its association with projects that appeared to offer poor value-for-money.

[7]At the Conference, there were 26 reporters and editors from the *Guardian*; all of the *Telegraph's* political team and some leader writers; and around 200 BBC staff (Addley and Fleming 2002).

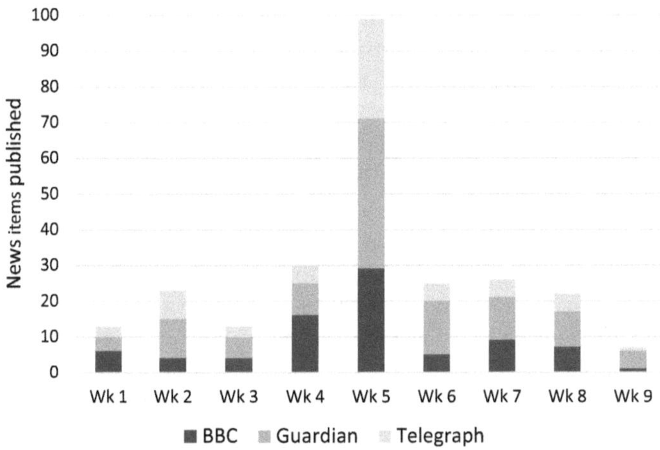

Fig. 4.1 Frequency distribution of articles (2002)

of a premeditated political scrap to generate coverage: indeed, the distribution of articles in 2002 shows a gradual increase over weeks two to four and a fall from week six onwards. Even so, the dominance of Conference week cannot be understated: it accounted for 99 of the 258 news items, including 44% of the *Telegraph's* and a third of the *Guardian's* and BBC's (see Fig. 4.1). There was no equivalent peak around the key event in 2007 and not one of the nine weeks accounted for more than a fifth of the articles published. It was also noticeable that weeks 1, 3 and 9 in 2002 had totals that were typical of 2007. Indeed, when viewed holistically, these data suggest that the spike in Conference week was an extreme aberration and 'normal' coverage of private finance in both years was in the order of ten to twenty articles per week across the three news organisations.

In 2002, the *Guardian* gave far greater exposure to private finance than either of the other two publications with 114 articles, some 40% more than the BBC and 80% more than the *Telegraph*. The *Guardian* also gave slightly more prominence to the search terms than the other two publications with 30% featuring PFI or PPP in the headline or introduction. Again, Conference week headed the rankings with the *Guardian* printing eighteen articles that mentioned a search term at the top of the news item, and the BBC and *Telegraph* each publishing nine. As with the distribution of articles, across all three media the search terms were far less prominent outside of Conference week.

Over the 2007 sample period, there was less variation with 33 articles on the BBC News website, 31 in the *Guardian* and 22 in the *Telegraph*. The search terms were also noticeably less prominent, appearing in the headline or introduction in around 20% of news items, and in 70% of articles 'PFI' or 'PPP' appeared just once, compared to about a half of the 2002 sample. The relative lack of interest in private finance in 2007 was particularly evident in the very limited coverage of the House of Commons report itself: The *Guardian* and the *Sunday Telegraph* published one article each and the BBC did not mention the report at all.

For all three news organisations, the most common categorisation was 'business' which accounted for around 30% of articles in 2002 and 2007. This was the top classification for both newspapers in both years and second for the BBC in 2002 with 16%, behind 'politics' which accounted for 44% of articles. In the same year, the *Telegraph* published twice as many articles about PFI in the business section than on the politics pages, and in 2007, some 60% of articles appeared in its financial pages. Many of the *Guardian's* articles in 2002 covered the politics of PFI but these were categorised as 'home' or 'general' news. Indeed, inconsistencies between the three publications made topic comparison challenging. For example, unlike the newspapers, the BBC employed regional classifications with 23% of articles in 2002 placed in the 'England', 'Wales', 'Scotland' and 'Northern Ireland' sections of the website. In the 2007 sample, 72% of articles appeared under 'Scotland' and 'England' and some of these were given an even tighter geographical focus ('Edinburgh', 'Cheshire', etc.). This suggests that the BBC had an increasing tendency to localise private finance rather than present it as a national issue in the general news pages. Indeed, none of the 33 BBC articles in 2007 were classified as 'politics' which contrasts sharply with the 44% in 2002.

In 2002, the *Guardian* and to a lesser extent, the *Telegraph* also covered private finance in editorials, opinion pieces, feature articles and letters to the editor, with around 20% of items falling into these categories. In 2007, over a third of the *Guardian* articles had such classifications but the absolute quantity of articles was far fewer. The relative lack of mediated debate in 2007 was also evident in the tallies for newspaper editorials: three each in 2002 compared to none five years later. The distribution of article type was also revealing. In 2002, the proportion of articles that were standard news reports or news-in-brief items accounted for around half of all three media's totals. In 2007, the vast majority of the BBC articles were standard news reports and, with the exception of seven letters to the editor in the *Guardian*, there was little indication of concerted analysis or detailed debate in any of the publications.

Taken collectively, these data suggest that although private finance was positioned on the news agenda as a matter of national political importance in 2002, it was often categorised as a business issue. In 2007, the BBC showed a tendency to localise PFI/PPP, whereas the newspapers, particularly the *Telegraph*, placed proportionately more articles on the financial pages. This shift in emphasis reflects the development of the government's private finance policy: in 2002, it was the subject of intense political debate, primarily at the Conference. But by 2007, discussion was essentially over, and PFI/PPP projects were being implemented across the country, thus promoting relatively limited coverage, primarily in the business sections.

Salience, Themes and Framing

During the pilot study, it became apparent that many of the 344 articles in the universal sample mentioned the search terms only in passing. Hence, before continuing the analysis, those articles that made merely incidental references to PFI/PPP were discarded. The 2002 sample lost 79 articles (31%) and the 2007 sample was reduced by 21 (24%). This left 179 items from 2002 and 65 from 2007 to be analysed in greater depth.

Applying this filter decimated the 2002 *Telegraph* sample which lost nearly half of its 63 articles. In fact, with the exception of Conference week, the *Telegraph* printed no more than five articles per week that gave PFI/PPP any significant exposure, and in weeks eight and nine, the *Telegraph* carried no substantial items at all. This was mirrored to a lesser extent in the BBC and *Guardian* samples, with the number of articles per week falling to five and six, respectively. The distribution of salience underlines the extent to which coverage of private finance was centred around the Conference week. Apart from this period, there was little evidence of sustained and detailed analysis in either of the sample years.

With so many articles in 2002 tied to the Labour Party Conference, it was unsurprising that the dominant primary theme was 'political' and all three news organisations demonstrated similar propensities to conceive private finance as a policy issue with between 43 and 50% of articles in this category. Overall, the second most common theme in 2002 was 'business' with the newspapers far more likely to view PFI/PPP from a commercial perspective than the BBC. Indeed, 20% of the *Guardian* and 35% of the *Telegraph* articles had business contexts, compared to just 4% of the BBC's. The remaining lower rankings were shared among a variety of other themes that, in most cases, had greater direct relevance to lay audiences. Articles that explored the effects of private finance on health, education or employment, for example, have arguably broader appeal than items focussed on politics and business which are traditionally the domains of the elite. Although politics was also the dominant primary theme in 2007, it accounted for just 26% of articles, around half of its 2002 proportion, and business fell into fifth place behind education, transport and health.

Although private finance was commonly conceptualised as a political issue, surprisingly few articles were characterised by bilateral dialogue. Indeed, in both periods the most common secondary theme for all three media was the unopposed announcement. This category included speeches, statements and predictions, and accounted for 48% of articles in 2002 and 67% in 2007. Of course, this is not to say that these articles did not include contrasting views, but active discourse between opposing parties was not their defining characteristic. The second most common secondary theme in 2002 for all three publications was 'analysis'. These articles were summations or synopses which, although they may have included conflicting opinion, were typically less indicative of vibrant debate than those in the more disputatious categories ('talk', 'fight', 'consensus', etc.) which collectively accounted for 21% of the 2002 sample.

The BBC and *Guardian* generally portrayed the debate as a series of statements—typically from politicians, trade union leaders and business people—followed by analysis. The *Telegraph* was most likely to focus on conflict with a quarter of articles defined in combative terms. The overall profile of secondary themes mirrored the lack of opposition to PFI/PPP from the Conservative Party or from within the Parliamentary Labour Party. Furthermore, ministers tended to avoid personal debate with their detractors preferring instead to funnel their arguments through the media. The only forum for interactive debate was the Conference itself, and indeed, it was in weeks four and five in which the majority of articles with disputatious secondary themes appeared. In the 2007 sample, two-thirds of articles revolved around announcements, and, with the exception of 11 BBC articles which focussed on specific projects rather than private finance per se, there was scant indication of active opposition.

As the introduction to this chapter illustrated, the arguments for and against PFI were multifaceted and, at times, rather complex. Hence, to make sense of this issue, it would be reasonable to assume that the public needed access to news items that placed PFI in wider contexts. This need was fulfilled to an extent in both years: in 2002, 36% of the universal sample and 44% in 2007 were thematic articles. However, news items that focussed on immediate events and episodes were still in the majority in both years—56 and 51%, respectively—but there were considerable differences between the three media. In 2002, three-quarters of *Telegraph* articles were episodic compared to 59% in the *Guardian* and 45% on the BBC website. The *Guardian* and the BBC were particularly keen to explain private finance in the context of broader debates: the former printed 27 articles and the BBC published 30 news items that gave the reader an understanding of *why* the issue was contentious. Indeed, in 2002 the BBC achieved an almost equal split between episodic and thematic articles. Parity was also achieved in 2007 by the *Telegraph* but this time, the BBC's reporting was predominantly episodic with 20 of the 30 articles focussed on the short term. In contrast, 70% of the *Guardian* articles in 2007 were thematic.

The union-led debates at the Labour Party Conference clearly prompted all three media, the *Guardian* in particular, to give extensive and detailed coverage to private finance and frame it as a contested political issue. Beyond the three weeks straddling the Conference, however, PFI/PPP did not appear to be significantly more newsworthy than in 2007. Indeed, perhaps the most striking findings are in the similarities, rather than the differences, between the two years and the three media. In both cases, the search terms tended to be found in articles on the politics and business pages, and the articles were invariably short-format news or analysis items, with only around 40% of items highly salient to PFI/PPP. There was very little direct debate between those holding disparate views; the unopposed announcement was the defining secondary theme, and the majority of articles were focussed on recent events rather than broader debates. Whereas private finance was framed as an active and contentious political issue in 2002, five years later, it was conceived as largely unproblematic. With short news reports about the progress of individual projects dominating the coverage, private finance in 2007 was generally portrayed as uncontested.

Source Analysis

The next step in assessing the political content of the publications' reporting involves analysing the extent to which a plurality of source types was present in articles. The average number of named sources per article for each media was close to two which suggests that differing opinions were generally present. However, this index is deceptive as significant numbers of articles did not have multiple sources.[8] In 2002, just over 40% of BBC and *Telegraph* articles and around half of the *Guardian's* contained just one or no named sources. Five years later, the figures were 53, 56 and 40%, respectively. Although this initial analysis suggests a rather patchy adherence to the journalistic convention of including multiple points of view, it reveals nothing about the exposure awarded to different groups and political positions. Hence, sources were organised into four categories: political elite; business; trade unions and workers; and other sources.

Figure 4.2 shows the proportion of named sources in each category. In both years and across all three publications, the political elite were the most cited group. The BBC clearly had the greatest propensity to quote politicians and civil servants, with this group accounting for over half of named sources in 2002 and 2007. The *Guardian* and *Telegraph* were relatively consistent with around 40% of named sources taken from the political elite, but there were noticeable differences in the frequencies of business and labour sources. The *Telegraph* gave preference to business in 2007 with 11 citations compared to three for labour, and even in 2002, when trade union leaders were vociferous critics of PFI, the ratio was still tilted in business' favour (18:13). In contrast, on the BBC website in 2002, trade union and worker sources outnumbered business voices by a factor of three, and by a quarter in the *Guardian*. In all three media, however, the ratio shifted towards business in 2007 and, with the exception of the BBC, the views of workers and their trade union representatives were rarely aired. The fourth category, 'other sources', accounted for around 10–20% of the totals and 'journalist' was the most

[8]The averages were also inflated by 60 articles that contained three or more named sources.

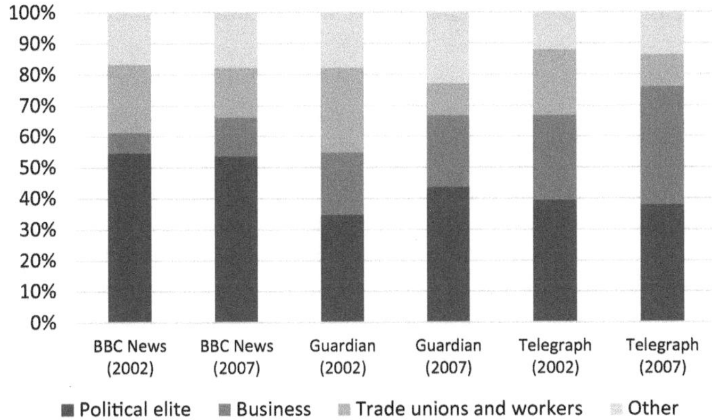

Fig. 4.2 Constitution of named sources (2002 and 2007)

common sub-category in both years, typically as the author of an opinion piece. Journalists were as prevalent as sources in the BBC sample as in the *Guardian*, and in some cases (e.g. Marr 2002; Assinder 2002a), the BBC journalist subjectively framed private finance and guided the reader's understanding in the process.

Research-oriented sources[9] were quoted 12 times in the 2002 universal sample and three in 2007, and members of the public and user group spokespeople[10] were cited on five and nine instances, respectively. There was no significant difference between the media in the propensity to quote sources from the 'grassroots' of politics but the BBC and *Guardian* each cited eight party members in 2002 while the *Telegraph* quoted none. Given the inherent, multifaceted complexity of private finance, the relative dearth of academics and economists is particularly noteworthy. One may have expected journalists to make extensive use of learned information but none of the publications did so. Similarly, given that the *raison d'être* of PFI/PPP is to provide high quality, value-for-money ***public*** services in exchange for tax revenue, the effective exclusion of workers and those who use and pay for the services is striking.

[9]This category includes academics, scientists, economists and think tanks.

[10]For example, parent–teacher, passenger and hospital user associations.

Table 4.1 Incidence of partisan named sources (2002 and 2007)

Named sources	*BBC*		*Guardian*		*Telegraph*	
	2002	*2007*	*2002*	*2007*	*2002*	*2007*
Prime minister and cabinet ministers	50	6	32	6	21	6
Business actors	10	7	30	9	18	11
Total	60	13	62	15	39	17
Trade union and professional association representatives	29	3	38	2	13	1
Advocates to sceptics	2.1 to 1	4.3 to 1	1.6 to 1	7.5 to 1	3.0 to 1	17.0 to 1

Figure 4.2 strongly suggests that the debate was dominated by elite sources that were generally in favour of private finance. As described in the introduction, British companies and industry associations welcomed PFI/PPP and, in some cases, pushed for greater private sector involvement in public services. More significantly, although it would be erroneous to assume that all of the 'political elite' were PFI advocates, the prime minister, the chancellor of the exchequer and cabinet ministers were unequivocal supporters (Table 4.1).

In 2002, the BBC featured members of this troika as named sources on 50 occasions compared to 29 for the representatives of trade unions and professional associations who were universally sceptical of PFI. *The Telegraph* also favoured the troika over worker representatives by 21 to 13, whereas the *Guardian* gave greater access to the latter (32:38). In 2007, far fewer sources were named by all three media but in each case, the trio of political PFI advocates outnumbered sceptical spokespeople by at least two to one.[11] If business sources are added to the pro-PFI political triumvirate, the dissenting voices of the trade union movement were firmly in the minority in both years and across all three publications. PFI advocates were far more visible than the sceptics across the board. In 2002, the *Guardian* featured 1.6 advocates to every sceptic compared with 2.1 for the BBC and three in the *Telegraph*. In 2007, the ratios were considerably higher, reflecting the increased relative frequency of business sources and the virtual disappearance of trade union

[11] The simplified ratios were: BBC 2:1; *Guardian* 3:1; *Telegraph* 6:1.

voices. Indeed, these data add credence to the earlier observation that the PFI/PPP debate had largely evaporated by 2007.

With such a strong dominance in frequency of appearance, it is unsurprising that PFI advocates also tended to be the most prominent sources. Despite the impetus for the debate coming from the unions, the prime minister was the most common first named source on the BBC website in 2002 and second in the *Telegraph*, behind the senior managers of PFI contractors. Blair shared the top spot in the *Guardian* with national trade union leaders which suggests a degree of parity, but if other political PFI advocates are added, it is clear that trade union spokespeople were considerably less likely to set the parameters of the debate than the Labour Party troika of prime minister, chancellor and cabinet ministers, and indeed business representatives.

Overall, the first voice belonged to a member of the troika in 28% of articles, with a similar proportion in each of the three media. In contrast, business people led in 18% of articles and trade union leaders in 11%. The BBC awarded equal billing to these latter two groups—with 9% each—but only one *Telegraph* article featured a union representative as the first source, and in the *Guardian* business outscored unions by 15 articles to 12. Also notable in 2002 was the near invisibility of opposition Conservative politicians who appeared just ten times as a named source and not once as an unnamed source.[12] Patterns were much harder to identify in 2007 as the distribution of first sources was scattered across more categories. Nevertheless, there was still evidence that preference was awarded to PFI advocates. Worker representatives were the first source in just 6% of articles, whereas spokespeople from PFI contractors accounted for 14%. As in 2002, senior cabinet ministers headed the list and led the debate in 17% of articles.

For the final phase of source analysis, Conservative politicians and Labour Party spokespeople were added to the troika, thus giving a more representative group of 'political PFI advocates'. Likewise, minority parties were combined with trade union and professional association representatives to create a more complete group of 'PFI sceptics'. Unnamed sources were also added according to their likely allegiance and the composite figures are shown in Table 4.2. Overall, the advocates had the

[12] In 2002, Conservative MPs accounted for 2.2% of all named and unnamed sources. Although this group fared better proportionately in 2007 (4.2%), it was striking that the official parliamentary opposition made such a limited contribution to this debate.

Table 4.2 Presence of groups of sources (2002)

Source group	*BBC News (n=69)*	*Guardian (n=76)*	*Telegraph (n=34)*	*Overall (n=179)*
	% of articles	*% of articles*	*% of articles*	*% of articles*
Political PFI advocates	57	34	56	45
Business	19	35	39	26
PFI sceptics	33	36	30	37
No or 'other' sources only	28	21	15	23

greatest presence in 2002, appearing in 45% of articles compared to 37% for the sceptics and 26% for business sources. However, these aggregates obscure considerable differences. The BBC and *Telegraph* gave far more exposure to the advocates than the sceptics and only in the *Guardian* was there parity between the groups. Indeed, the *Guardian* achieved remarkable balance with advocates, sceptics and business sources each appearing in about a third of articles. In contrast, business people appeared in 39% of *Telegraph* articles but just one in five on the BBC News website. It is important to stress, however, that the business community was in favour of PFI, and consequently, these data suggest that only around a third of each publications' articles in 2002 contained a sceptical viewpoint. The data for 2002 also revealed that in almost half of the articles, one of the three groups aligned with political positions had a source monopoly. The PFI advocates went unchallenged by other groups in 21% of articles, compared to 15% for business and 11% for the PFI sceptics.

Coverage of Political Positions

The source analysis strongly hints at the likely political content of news items, but it makes no allowance for journalistic input and interpretation. An article with a monopoly of business sources, for example, could conceivably be laden with criticism about private finance in public services. Nor does source analysis measure the quantity of words. Hence, to assess the political content of the sample, a holistic reading of each article was taken. This incorporated the appearance and prominence of actors; the

Table 4.3 Exclusion of political positions (2002 and 2007)

% of articles making no reference to...	*2002*			*2007*		
	BBC	*Guardian*	*Telegraph*	*BBC*	*Guardian*	*Telegraph*
Privatisation	77	82	82	97	95	79
PFI advocacy	16	0	6	3	0	7
PFI scepticism	19	24	26	70	30	33
Social alternatives	86	80	82	70	85	100

quantity of words attributed to each; and an assessment of the general tone. In this way, it was possible to assess the coverage given to each of the four political positions identified in the pilot study.[13]

Table 4.3 demonstrates that two positions—privatisation and social alternatives—were totally absent from around four-fifths of the 2002 sample. In 2007, their exclusion was even more pronounced with only 8% of articles making any reference to increased private involvement in public services, and 9% mentioning social alternatives. The majority of this latter category were published by the BBC and focussed on the SNP's pledge to introduce an alternative to PPP in Scotland.[14] It was particularly ironic that social alternatives were largely excluded from the debate, given the traditional model of public finance that has prevailed in the UK since 1945. Indeed, if an actor argued for the maintenance of the status quo, it was coded as 'social alternatives', but as the broad coverage of the PFI sceptical position confirms, the vast majority of dissent could be described as contrary opposition rather than constructive criticism.[15] With privatisation and social alternatives effectively ignored, this data set confirms that the mediated debate was dominated by advocacy and scepticism.

The table also shows that scepticism was ignored in far more news items than advocacy in both years and across all three media. This can partially be explained by the prevalence of articles that perfunctorily

[13]See Chapter 2.

[14]For example, BBC (2007c).

[15]See below—critical discourse analysis.

reported announcements or the delivery of private finance projects, or the commercial health of contractors.[16] In such cases, PFI was implicitly acknowledged as a 'fact of life'. In 2002, a tenth of articles paired a minimal acknowledgement of PFI/PPP with no mention of scepticism. In 2007, over a third of news items fell into this category, including 60% of the BBC sample. Indeed, as previously noted, sceptical sources—and the associated arguments—had virtually disappeared from reports in 2007, and to a large extent, private finance had become depoliticised and a non-contentious issue. Indeed, a weighted index of the political content of samples[17] revealed a considerable fall in all three media: the BBC sample dropped from 178 units of political content to 56 points; the *Telegraph* from 73 to 32; and the *Guardian* saw the largest relative decline from 132 to 16. This contrast can largely be explained by the low frequency of articles in 2007—and the extreme aberration of Conference week in 2002—but this was exacerbated by a dearth of items giving detailed explanations of political positions and, as highlighted above, a tendency to exclude privatisation, social alternatives and, to an extent, PFI scepticism.

Although the 2007 sample lacked quantity and diversity of perspectives, Fig. 4.3 confirms that the reporting was not devoid of politics. Of the three publications, the BBC's coverage of the private finance debate in 2002 and 2007 exhibited the greatest balance; the *Guardian* clearly favoured the sceptics; and the *Telegraph* was most sympathetic to PFI advocacy and, to a lesser extent, privatisation. These positions tally neatly with the newspapers' traditional political allegiances, and in 2002, the BBC ably fulfilled its commitment to political impartiality with near-perfect equality between advocacy and scepticism.

Political sympathies are confirmed in Table 4.4. The *Telegraph* gave preferential coverage to PFI advocacy over PFI scepticism in 32% of articles (row A) and vice versa in 9% (row B). The *Guardian* favoured scepticism in a fifth of articles and advocacy in 14%, and again, the BBC came

[16]For example, Henry (2007) and Gow (2002b).

[17]The weighted total was calculated by multiplying the frequency of articles in the 'detailed coverage' category by 3; 'limited coverage' by 2; 'acknowledged' by 1, 'critical coverage' by minus 1, and 'no mention' by zero. See Chapter 2.

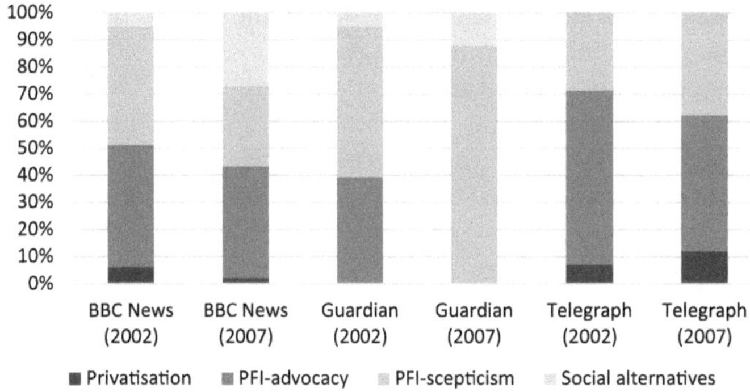

Fig. 4.3 Weighted coverage of political positions (2002 and 2007)

Table 4.4 Coverage of the advocacy versus scepticism debate (2002)

	Coverage		*BBC News*		*Guardian*		*Telegraph*	
	Advocacy	*Scepticism*	*Frequency*	*%*	*Frequency*	*%*	*Frequency*	*%*
A	Detailed	Limited	11	16	11	14	11	32
B	Limited	Detailed	7	10	16	21	3	9
C	Detailed	Detailed	19	28	9	12	5	15
D	Other permutations		32	46	40	53	15	44
Total			69	100	76	100	34	100

closest to equality with 16% of news items leaning towards advocacy and a tenth to scepticism. The Corporation also published by far the highest proportion of articles that provided detailed accounts of both positions (row C). It is also important to note that around half of all articles across the board contained no substantial debate between advocates and sceptics (row D).

Critical Discourse Analysis

The analysis thus far demonstrates that the mediated debate predominantly pitched PFI advocates against PFI sceptics. Few sources argued for privatisation or, in particular, social alternatives and, consequently, these two perspectives were effectively excluded from the debate. Hence, the next stage assesses the extent to which the media narrative reproduced those of the most favoured source groups, namely senior government ministers; trade union leaders; and business.

To better understand the combatants' respective discourses, it is important to first consider the macro-narrative that dominated Tony Blair's tenure as Labour Party leader. This was underpinned by the acceptance of contemporary capitalism, if necessary at the expense of traditional Labour principles. Such apparent pragmatism was based on the belief that the 'real world' was immutable, and hence, political parties, party members and citizens must modify their expectations. This assumption was the essence of 'New Labour', the 'rebranding' of the party which was introduced to the public at Blair's first party conference as leader in 1994 when he launched the campaign to rewrite Clause Four of the party's constitution which would formally drop Labour's defining commitment to public ownership. Although the plans were resisted by some in the Party, the rewrite was finally approved in April 1995.

The *new* Clause Four endorsed: 'the enterprise of the market and the rigour of competition ... joined with the forces of partnership and co-operation', and these words: 'for the first time made it explicit that Labour was in the business of managing capitalism rather than transcending it' (Anderson and Mann 1997: 33). In his victory speech, Blair stressed that the rewrite of Clause Four was the first of many steps. Indeed, change and modernisation were at the heart of New Labour philosophy from the outset. Crucially, it was the Labour Party and Britain that would be changed rather than capitalism or 'the world', and Blair's numerous reiterations snuffed out any chance of a resurgence from the radical left.

On the day the new Clause Four was approved, Tony Benn observed: 'the (broadcast) media tonight are dancing on the grave of socialism' and he cited an article by Blair—in the next day's *Sunday Mirror*—which argued for a reduced role in Labour Party policy making for those whom had dissented, particularly the trade unions (Benn 2002: 316; Sopel 1995: 299). Indeed, Benn had previously noted Blair's insistence that he would ignore Conference defeats (2002a: 273) and saw signs in Blair's 1994 speech of a divisive narrative thread that complemented the acceptance of the market:

> … by attacking Marx and saying he would end Clause Four, Blair opened up a huge and unnecessary debate… in the hope of isolating the left and making them look like troublemakers. (ibid.)

Labour secured a huge popular mandate in 1997, and in advance of the following general election in 2001, the manifesto introduced the next modernising step: '… a big ambition for Britain - a mission for reform of public services' (Blair in *Guardian* 2001). The manifesto reaffirmed the 1997 pledge of no increase in income tax and focussed on quantifiable improvements in public services with more nurses, doctors, teachers and police officers. It also confirmed that companies would have greater involvement:

> Where private-sector providers can support public endeavour, we should use them. A "spirit of enterprise" should apply as much to public service as to business. (Labour Party 2001: 17)

Labour won a second landslide in 2001 and public service reform was high on the agenda at the Party Spring Conference a year later where Blair, eager to fulfil the manifesto pledge, angered union leaders by using the phrases 'reformers versus wreckers' and 'small C conservatives' to describe those whom resisted reform (BBC 2002e). Indeed, the discourse of senior Labour ministers in the first period of this case study—autumn 2002—conceived PFI as an essential component of an all-encompassing modernisation of the public sector which was both desirable and unassailable (Brown in Jones 2002a). As Chancellor Gordon Brown stressed in his 2002 Party Conference speech, there was no place for the policies of yesteryear (emphases added):

> If we *retreat* from the PFI and still say that schools and hospitals have got to be built, we will end up with the *old* quick fixes and *retreat into unsustainable borrowing*. That I am not prepared to do. (in Elliott and Wintour 2002)

In these terms, alternatives to PFI that involved government borrowing did not represent the status quo so much as a retrograde step. According to the New Labour philosophy, the policies of the past were incongruous with the present by definition, and they certainly had no role in the future.

Although, in his speech in early September 2002 at the TUC Conference, Blair had been pointed in his criticism of: 'self-indulgent rhetoric from a few that belong, frankly, in the history books' (in Maguire 2002b), he was generally vague about the location of this anachronistic resistance and he usually avoided using inflammatory labels. At the Party Conference, however, Gordon Brown was more direct and branded the unions' stance as 'ideological dogma' (in BBC 2002a). Consequently, the unions—and other members of the 'old left'—were positioned as the enemy within, whose contrary views were outdated, divisive and therefore, easily dismissible.

Faced with such a finely honed, coherent and tightly coordinated onslaught, the PFI sceptics were fighting a rear-guard action. There was clearly an intolerance of dissenting views and, as Tony Benn observed, Blair's rhetoric showed no sense of participation; it was a 'managing director's speech' (Benn 2007: 63). The Labour leadership's representation of the unions' position and motives was also disputed: TUC General Secretary John Monks, for example, maintained that the unions were eager to contribute but they had been hit with a blunt ultimatum. The exclusion of the unions from policy debates said Monks showed: 'everything that is wrong with British corporate governance'.

> The government has not said to the unions 'how can you help us to solve these problems?' Instead we just get told that we must modernise or die. (Monks in Maguire and Kettle 2002)

John Edmonds, General Secretary of the GMB union, also refuted the troublemaker charge. He too highlighted the unions' desire to 'be part of the solution' and stressed that support from the workforce, not business, was the key to improved public services (Edmonds in BBC 2002c). Other union leaders focussed on the rationale of PFI. The General Secretary of Unison, Dave Prentis, for example, accused the government of ignoring the 'evidence' and being driven by 'ideology'. He also highlighted the shortcomings of a policy that: '…wastes money, wastes time and fails any objective test of value for money' (BBC 2002c). Like Edmonds, Prentis objected that 'during a period of unprecedented public investment, huge profits are going into private pockets' when the money would be better spent on 'essential public services' (Schifferes 2002b).

Other trade union leaders reiterated their reasons for opposing to PFI and presented the union movement as the wise voice of caution (Morris in Davies, B. 2002). It was not, as the government claimed, 'outdated doctrine and practice' that motivated their actions but a wholly reasonable scepticism which, ironically, mirrored that of the Labour Party's senior figures five years earlier while in opposition. This was neatly summed up in a letter from Dave Prentis to constituency Labour parties before the debate:

> There is widespread concern that PFI is inherently flawed and we believe it is now time for the government to review its position and explore other funding options. (Prentis in Travis and Maguire 2002)

These first-person statements from union leaders during the 2002 sample period demonstrate that they saw themselves as integral members of the Labour family who had a right and a duty to express their members'—and the public's—rational concerns about PFI. Indeed, the union leaders positioned themselves as the guardians of Labour Party values (Simpson in Maguire 2002a). Tactically, the unions hoped to stimulate public support by framing PFI as poor value for money and an insidious form of privatisation. The government deflected such accusations and pointed at the Tories as the true standard-bearers of privatisation (BBC 2002a). In addition, the government emphasised that the unions were stubborn contrarians, inhibitors to the 'march of progress' (Blair in Davies, M. 2002), and blind to the inevitability of change, reform and modernisation. Ministers maintained that PFI was the only financing mechanism that could realise the Party's electoral promise to rejuvenate public services, and by objecting to PFI, the unions were selfishly denying the public new schools and hospitals. These two political discourses competed for media exposure during the 2002 sample period, and the next section considers the extent to which the publications reproduced the positions.

The Reproduction of Political Narratives

The logical starting point for assessing the BBC's preferred discourse was the index page of an 'In Depth' report called 'Private Profit, Public Gain?' (BBC 2003a). BBC editors obviously considered private finance an important issue in the first period of this case study as this report carried articles dated 3 September 2001–12 February 2003. With the title phrased as a question, the contents were immediately cast in a contentious light. Indeed, the index page invited readers to vote on whether private firms should run public services,[18] and the lower page provided hyperlinks to articles grouped in six sections generally congruent with government departments (defence; health; education; etc.). The upper three sections gave more general perspectives of PFI/PPP, and the lead section listed eight hyperlinked titles (emphases added):

> Blair denies *rift* with Brown
> Blair: *No compromise* on PFI
> Blair backs foundation hospitals
> Brown takes up private cash *battle*
> Labour's *public row* over privatisation
> Blair *woos* unions over PFI
> Brown and Prescott *maul* the unions
> Taxpayers cash 'wasted' on PFI

Although this version of the web page was last edited on February 2003, seven of these eight stories were published immediately before or during the Labour Party Conference in 2002, so this was clearly deemed to be a defining period. In these articles, conflict was the dominant theme ('rift', 'no compromise', 'public row', 'battle') and Tony Blair was the protagonist in half the items. The only other named actors—senior cabinet ministers, Gordon Brown and John Prescott—were involved in particularly belligerent scenarios. The unnamed 'unions' were both wooed and mauled, and taxpayers cash was 'wasted' (with the inverted commas suggesting that this was merely an opinion).

The second section of the index page was titled 'Union malaise' and the lead article featured a colour photograph of Tony Blair in mid-speech against a background image of a teacher and pupils. The title and standfirst read (emphasis added):

> **Unions to tackle Blair on privatisation**
> The trade unions and the government are heading for a *major confrontation* over the private finance of public services

[18] Sixty-one per cent of the public were against (BBC 2003a).

The headline suggested agreement with the unions that PFI was synonymous with privatisation, a word which was commonly used in pejorative sense (Monbiot 2001: 9). Indeed, the unions' discourse often incorporated the use of 'privatisation' to galvanise public support, but this headline was a rare glint of exposure for the PFI sceptic position in these BBC articles and the majority of titles in the remainder of this section presented the unions as self-centred and aggressive. No mention was made of *why* the unions were so animated, however, and unlike the first section list, PFI was not even mentioned. The only named actor in this section was Tony Blair who was awarded a disciplinarian role (emphases added):

Unions *flex their muscles*
Unions *warned* over 'self-indulgence'
Public sector *fears*
Why unions are *militant*
Number 10 denies *'wreckers'* apology
Union *fury* at Blair *warning*
Blair *takes on* public service *'wreckers'*
Blair speech: Key quotes
Ringside view of union *fightback*
Unions *erupt* in public services row
Don't blame it all on us —Blunkett

It is clear from the references to 'wreckers', 'muscles' and 'fury' that the unions were framed by the BBC as a problem. Indeed, the section title—'Union malaise'—explicitly linked the unions to sickness, although it is not clear if the malady afflicted the country, the Labour Party, Tony Blair or indeed the unions themselves. Either way, this illness was, according to the subsequent article titles, destructive, volatile and selfish.

The layout, the running order and the titles on this index page show that the BBC largely conceived PFI/PPP as conflict. Crucially, this was not a battle of ideas but a visceral war between named senior ministers and an anonymous mass of 'unions'. Furthermore, with one possible exception,[19] the index page gave no exposure to the preferred discourse of the PFI sceptics. In contrast, the upper half of the page resonated with the government narrative. Only in the third section—'analysis'—were questions posed that might help readers make an informed decision

[19] Taxpayers cash 'wasted' on PFI.

about the merits of private finance. It was also notable that 'business' and the private sector in general were never criticised and each of the subheadings for the 'government departments' was positive or neutral about private finance. Although the comparison is far from perfect, if 'Private Profit, Public Gain?' were a book, and the index page was the table of contents, a casual reader might conclude that this was primarily an account of how a trio of determined politicians delivered new life into public services, with the help of the private sector, in the face of blind opposition from the unions.

This is not to say, however, that the arguments of the PFI sceptics were ignored by the BBC. On the contrary, many articles with links on the index page contained substantial explanation of the dissenters' position. As the quantitative analysis showed, trade union leaders were frequently quoted, often at length, and two articles in the sample period gave them *carte blanche*. The first featured around 100 words from each of four union leaders who outlined their hopes for the TUC Conference. There was no journalistic narrative and yet the choice of title—'Trade union demands'—suggested that the leaders were far less reasonable than their own words had stated (BBC 2002c). Similarly, the outgoing General Secretary of the TGWU, Bill Morris, was the subject of an interview (Davies, B. 2002) in which he used an accounting metaphor to describe the current relationship between the government and the union movement which, said Morris, had over the last five years:

> …significantly addressed the debit side: we've delivered on every single count in terms of days lost through industrial disputes, in terms of the quality of what we do, in terms of the relationship supporting government. Now we want the government to address the credit side.

The journalist immediately added detail to Morris' statement: 'By that he means issues like low pay, the current crisis over pensions, the plight of British manufacturing and working conditions' (ibid.). For many people, these are eminently virtuous causes, yet the title of the article condensed the interview into an uncompromising and selfish position: 'Morris: Payback time for the unions'. The lead photographs in these two articles were montages of suited union leaders who, in most cases, were captured with earnest expressions. The photos had a purple tint which presented the subjects in a distinctly dim light. In other articles, lead photographs of Blair, Brown and Prescott, however, were discernibly sharper, more colourful and dynamic than the union leaders'. Furthermore, two photographs featured senior ministers with public service workers in the background, whereas in their photographs, the union leaders lurked alone in the shadows.

In the prelude to the 2002 Conference debate, BBC articles informed readers that 'left-wingers' had taken: '...control of many of the UK's unions' (Davies, M. 2002) and unions were: '... more militant than for years and are being led by more left-wingers than for almost two decades' (Assinder 2002a). Readers were also reminded that unions had been: 'previously fingered by senior ministers as "wreckers" and "the forces of conservatism"' (Assinder 2002b). A PFI critic within the Parliamentary Labour Party, Llew Smith, was described as an: 'old-fashioned socialist' (BBC 2002f), and a sceptical Conference attendee, James Conway, was 'on the left of the party' (Stone-Lee 2002). By lumping opponents of PFI in the 'left', these articles echoed the divisive, 'them and us' discourse of the government. Revealingly, Blair et al. were never referred to as being on the 'right' of the Labour Party: indeed, in an informative and otherwise evenly balanced article about private finance and the NHS, there was no recognition that 'ideology' might also guide the PFI advocates:

> Unions have been up in arms over many of these policies, but ministers insist ideology must not stand in the way of better healthcare. (BBC 2002d)

Rather than highlighting that the sceptics had effectively won the argument, the BBC article covering the crucial PFI debate was framed in personal terms. Blair, rather than the policy, was defeated, and he was the victim of fratricide (emphases added).

> **Blair suffers conference defeat**
> Tony Blair has suffered an overwhelming defeat *at the hands of his own conference* over *his* programme of using private cash to run public services. (Assinder 2002f)

However, twenty-four hours after this 'embarrassing defeat' (Assinder 2002d), the same journalist clearly enjoyed a 'defiant' prime minister's speech. Again, there was no acknowledgement of the debate, and the author celebrated the growing distance between Blair and a significant portion of the Party:

> In what all would agree was a powerful and defining speech...Blair set his sights on the horizon, pressed his pedal to the metal - and waved goodbye to a large section of the Labour movement. (Assinder 2002c)

Later, in his review of the week, Assinder conceived the speech as 'Blair's turning point' (Assinder 2002e), not because his arguments had prevailed, but because he had strengthened his reputation for dogged determination. The prime minister was 'at the top of his game' and he had told 'delegates to like it or lump it'. Blair was again credited for creating distance between himself and a disgruntled rank-and-file. Indeed, ignoring the party membership was deemed a virtue and the union-led dissent was characterised as little more than anachronistic posturing. This was the Conference, wrote Assinder (emphases added):

> ...where Tony Blair finally took the step, he has been hesitating over from day one. And it was a million-mile-long stride away from the *old comrades who were trying to flex their muscles.* (ibid.)

Assinder's admiration had echoes of an earlier article by Andrew Marr who had described Blair's speech to the TUC Conference as 'masterful', and Marr's preview of the Labour Party Conference conceptualised the debates as entertainment rather than serious politics: 'Book your tickets now', he advised (Marr 2002). Indeed, as evident in the article titles on the 'Private Profit, Public Gain?' index page, the arguments for and against PFI were secondary to the conflict. Furthermore, even when the debate was dissected, there were hints of trivialisation. For instance, the key explanatory article, 'What is PFI?' (BBC 2002b), began (emphases added):

> The *creeping privatisation of public services* under New Labour is one of the *main gripes* of the trade unions and is certain to *sour the air* at the party's conference this week. But does anyone really understand what a "public-private partnership", or a "private finance initiative" is? *Never fear.* BBC News Online has the answers.

During the 2002 sample period, the BBC journalists strongly reproduced the narrative of the Labour leadership. The contest was framed as a battle of wills, rather than ideas, between New and Old Labour with the latter desperately hanging on to *passé* 'ideology'. Private finance itself rarely featured in the analysis, and discussions about its merits and pitfalls were pushed to the periphery. Some BBC journalists expressed overt admiration for Blair's tactics and rhetoric, which were seemingly more significant than Conference's rejection of Party policy. Furthermore, the light-hearted tone of some articles contrasted sharply with the serious and wide-ranging implications of private finance to the general public.

There was no levity in the *Guardian's* coverage of PFI in autumn 2002. Indeed, the newspaper published a focussed and sombre leader on the day of the PFI debate and another before Blair's speech a day later. The former wondered why, with the Conservatives in disarray, the Labour Party only had a single-digit lead in the opinion polls. The reason, suggested the author, was:

> …Labour's tin ear towards what its supporters are saying and the cracked tone in which it often addresses them. It is not enough to say that Labour is merely a victim of modern political disengagement. Labour is also the author of too many of its own worst problems. (*Guardian* 2002a)

The next day's leader unequivocally stated the *Guardian's* position: 'The PFI needs a review: Tony Blair must address party concerns'; and the final lines were equally direct:

> The unions were right to want a review and ministers wrong to deny them. The prime minister needs to seriously address delegates' concerns today. (*Guardian* 2002b)

Two of the *Guardian's* most prominent columnists were vehement sceptics. During the TUC Conference, George Monbiot wrote an impassioned article praising the union campaign (Monbiot 2002a). The unions were not just fighting for better pay and conditions for their members, argued Monbiot, they were fighting for the future of public services:

> (the unions) see part-privatisation as symptomatic of the corporate takeover of Britain, and … in turn, as symptomatic of its willingness to side with power against the powerless.

Monbiot predicted that the unions would soon become 'the United Kingdom's official opposition' and looked forward to a time when 'a revitalised union movement will encourage the rest of us to organise more effectively' (ibid.). Like Monbiot, Polly Toynbee was in favour of a review and believed government accusations of union stubbornness were groundless. She also said there was a 'gaping hole' in Tony Blair's pamphlet, *Courage of Our Convictions* (Blair 2002b), published on page six of the same newspaper. Toynbee used emotive language to describe this void which she perceived as (italics added):

> … the convictions themselves. There is no understanding of the value of the public sphere just because it is public. There is no *warmth* that recognises the *affection* people feel for public institutions, the *trust* and *pride* felt by *stake-holding citizens who are not mere customers.* (Toynbee 2002)

The day before the debate, a comment piece in the *Observer* from TGWU General Secretary, Bill Morris, was headed with a poignant and graphic title: 'This knife in our heart… private profit will destroy our core public services' (Morris 2002). This stood in stark contrast to the title of Morris' BBC's interview: 'Morris: Payback time for the unions' (Davies, B. 2002) and, indeed, like Toynbee, Morris believed that Blair was blind to the political, moral and even spiritual arguments for public services remaining in the public sector: public services are immiscible with the private sector, wrote Morris, because the former:

> … define our society and are a measure of our humanity. They are the basis of our common capital and the embodiment of the contract between citizen and state. (Morris 2002)

However, PFI sceptics did not have a monopoly on the *Guardian's* op-ed pages. On September 30, Digby Jones, head of the CBI, compared union leaders to 'latter day (King) Canutes' (Jones 2002). Jones said PFI was part of a ceaseless 'tide of change' and the unions were only delaying the inevitable. Dissent was pointless because there was simply no alternative: the world is constantly changing, and the unions risked being flattened by the: 'impatient waves of public satisfaction'. For Jones, the consumer was sovereign, and unions had a patriotic duty to concur:

> The tax-paying, voting customer must come first, not political ideology, power broking or vested interests. Business will play its part, the government clearly is - now it is up to the unions to put country first and do the same. (ibid.)

This article's distinct neoliberal discourse sat in sharp contrast to the *Guardian's* other PFI-related content. Indeed, Jones' language resonated strongly with Blair's pamphlet, his Conference speech and an *Observer* interview (Rawnsley and Ahmed 2002), all of which were founded on the inevitability of change; the need for reform; and the centrality of the consumer-citizen. Some phrases were almost identical: Jones wrote of 'politically motivated rhetoric' and 'indulgent voices of the left' and, in his speech to the TUC Conference, Blair condemned: 'the "self-indulgent rhetoric" of his most vocal left-wing union critics' (Maguire 2002b).

Naturally, senior ministers' PFI-related speeches and statements were covered in detail by the *Guardian*, but the newspaper's accompanying narrative was, unlike the BBC's, generally neutral with no praise for resoluteness and certainly no barely disguised admiration for Blair the performer, as displayed by the BBC's Marr and Assinder (see above). Like the BBC, the *Guardian* employed bellicose language for headlines and key explanations: Tony Blair, for example, gave a 'full-blooded defence' of PFI (White and Walker 2002), 'unions square(d) up to Brown for fight on PFI' (Maguire 2002c); and the TUC declared: 'outright war on the private finance initiative' (Gow 2002c).

Despite their widespread use, however, belligerent labels in the *Guardian* tended to be less prominent, and their timbre somewhat gentler than the BBC's. For example, in the *Observer* there was a 'union-led revolt' and a 'grassroots' rebellion' from 'people parked well to the left of Tony Blair' (Rawnsley and Ahmed 2002). Elsewhere, 'increasingly vocal' critics (White and Walker 2002) were urged to 'step back from confrontation' (White 2002), while union leaders 'toughened (their) criticism' (Maguire 2002a). The BBC's grammar of division and conflict, by which, for example, militant unions 'flexed their muscles' (Schifferes 2002c) and Blair 'waved goodbye to a large section of the Labour movement' (Assinder 2002c), was absent in the *Guardian's* reporting.

As essential reading for both the Labour Party and trade union leaderships, the *Guardian* was the most obvious forum for detailed, balanced and impassioned debate. The *Telegraph*, however, had a potential editorial dilemma: its preferred Conservative Party was effectively absent from the debate and traditionally, the *Telegraph* was antipathetic to both the Labour Party and the unions. Furthermore, with such a relative dearth of *Telegraph* articles in the 2002 sample, vivid examples of political discourse were fewer in number and yet no less illustrative of this newspaper's position. This was most clearly displayed in a leader on October 1: 'Blair's day of judgement' (*Daily Telegraph* 2002b). The author awarded no significance to Conference's rejection of PFI—it was nothing more than a 'symbolic ear-boxing' for Blair—but there was unambiguous support for the prime minister's single-mindedness:

> These motions and speeches have, of course, no power to change government policy - and a good job, too. The Prime Minister is right about PFI, just as he is right about Iraq.

The next day, another editorial paid tribute to Blair's speech in which he: 'showed once again why he is the leading political operator of his generation' (*Daily Telegraph* 2002c). Echoing the BBC's Assinder and Marr, the author acknowledged that Blair: 'remains a class act, the best tactician in any party and an increasingly skilful speaker' and found little to disagree with in terms of policy:

> Nearly everything he had to say about the need to replace "the monolithic provision" of health and education with services tailored to individuals could have been lifted straight from a Right-wing pamphlet.

Blair's speech clearly plucked at the *Telegraph's* political heartstrings—another article observed 'a Thatcherite tone' (Jones 2002d)—and the only frustration with the prime minister was his apparent immunity from criticism from both sides of the political spectrum:

> Neither the malcontents on his own side nor the Conservatives have yet been able to lay a glove on him. (*Daily Telegraph* 2002c)

Perhaps surprisingly, the Labour 'malcontents' were not given divisive or pejorative labels in the *Telegraph*, nor was the debate reported in particularly warlike language. Unions were 'bitterly opposed' to PFI (Sparrow 2002) and were 'angry' about private finance (Jones 2002c). But there was no talk of 'battle', merely a less harmful 'collision course' (ibid.) with the government, upon whom the unions inflicted an 'embarrassing defeat' (Brogan 2002). Instead of mauling the unions (BBC 2002a), Gordon Brown: 'rejected out of hand their demand for a freeze (of PFI)' (Jones 2002a). Apart from a reference to a 'bruising confrontation between the unions and the Government' (Jones 2002b), the *Telegraph's* language when reporting the debate bore a closer resemblance to the *Guardian's* than the BBC's.

The Normalisation of the Business Narrative

Like the *Guardian*, there was a plurality of opinion from *Telegraph* commentators. Former Chancellor Norman Lamont backed a PFI review on the grounds of the cost of finance (*Daily Telegraph* 2002a), and Boris Johnson described PFI as 'a fraud on the public purse' (Johnson 2002). These words may suggest that Lamont and Johnson—and indeed the *Telegraph*—had sympathy with the PFI sceptics. On the contrary, the *Telegraph's* dominant discourse combined personal admiration for Blair with subtle yet persistent arguments for *more* private sector involvement in public services.

For example, while agreeing that the government needed to: 'dismantle what Blair called the "monolith" of state provision', Johnson was adamant that PFI was 'not the method' to deliver reform. His prescription was: 'to inject more private finance into health', and, one might presume, other public services too (Johnson 2002). Janet Daley thought the unions' arguments 'hysterical', and although she welcomed the introduction of the private sector, she lamented the persistent 'government monopoly of health and education' (Daley 2002). *Sunday Telegraph* columnist Matthew D'Ancona advised Blair not to worry about the unions' dislike of PFI because it introduced: 'precisely the sort of labour market flexibility to the public sector that they exist to oppose'. Instead, the prime minister should be concerned: 'that the scheme has thus far been so modest in its scale' (D'Ancona 2002).

This privatisation discourse was also present in the leader on October 1 *(Daily Telegraph* 2002b) which noted the debate on PFI had (emphases added):

> ...illuminated the fault-lines between Labour's *old-fashioned* politics of tax and spend and the Blairite project of *mobilising the private sector to rescue the public services.*

The article also speculated that Blair's speech would make 'no concessions… demanding instead that Labour ***embraces*** the private sector even more ***warmly***' (emphasis added). Throughout the *Telegraph* articles, the private sector—and business in particular—was conceived as a dynamic force that could, if freed from restrictions, 'rescue the public services' (ibid.). Large companies were also benign: the private sector was simply 'paid to build and manage government infrastructure projects' (Sparrow 2002), and, like Janet Daley, Labour Party member Phil Graham could not understand why union leaders were: 'vehemently against any kind of dealing with the private sector' (Graham 2002). There was little evidence that the unions held such an absolute 'anti-private sector' position but, on the only occasion that criticism of the business of PFI was aired in the *Telegraph*, the journalist immediately categorised the unions' focus on executive pay as part of an insidious left-wing campaign. The article's first paragraph read (emphases added):

> *Trades unionists widened their attack on corporate Britain* yesterday condemning "privatisation pay pirates" - company directors who have earned huge pay rises from Government contracts. (Millward 2002)[20]

The *Telegraph's* support for increased private sector involvement was also evident in an explanatory item in which the questions—and their sequence—indicated a priority for fiscal concerns rather than any social consideration (Batt 2002b):

> What is PFI?
> Does a PFI contract involve long-term commitments?
> Is PFI different from privatisation?
> Does PFI reduce government borrowing?
> Does PFI offer value for money for the taxpayer?
> What don't the unions like about PFI?

Noteworthy here is that 'the unions' were the only apparent dissenters and another *Telegraph* article, by the same author, dismissed union fears of the creation of a 'two-tier workforce' as a 'jibe' (Batt 2002a).

[20]The *Guardian* also covered this story, but its lead paragraph began: 'Tony Blair yesterday came under union pressure to condemn publicly the excessive pay awards given to senior directors of companies involved in a host of lucrative (PFI) projects' (Gow 2002a).

In contrast, the *Guardian* was appreciably more aware of the potential dangers of deeper private sector involvement in public services. George Monbiot (2002b) noted that PFI had 'less public support than Mrs Thatcher's poll tax' and yet one reason it had not been abandoned was it kept: 'a very powerful corporate constituency quiet'. Elsewhere, Monbiot wrote that PFI was symptomatic of 'the government's capitulation to big business' (Monbiot 2002a), a view shared, albeit in less colourful language, by other columnists (Morris 2002; Toynbee 2002). In the *Observer*, Nick Cohen also focussed on how private companies—in this case defence manufacturers—were profiting excessively from public contracts. Cohen only mentioned PFI in passing but his verdict was scathing (emphases added): 'Even a Treasury which had imposed the *state-sponsored larceny* of the Private Finance Initiative had had enough' (Cohen 2002).

One may have expected the BBC's position on the 'business of PFI' to lie somewhere between the *Telegraph's* enthusiastic support and the *Guardian's* instinctive suspicion. Yet closer inspection of the 'Private Profit, Public Gain?' index page reveals a distinct lack of scrutiny. There was, for example, no focussed assessment of the potential size of the PFI 'industry', nor did any article investigate the discrepancies between the capital cost and total payments of PFI projects. This information was in the public domain and had been highlighted by several other commentators[21] and yet, out of 53 hyperlinks on this page, only three led readers to articles that examined the extent to which companies and shareholders would benefit from PFI. Only one (Gould 2002) was published in the sample period, and although the journalist did raise questions about 'excessive profits', these were trumped by a discourse that accepted the concept of private prisons from the start of the article:

> **Liverpool's profitable prison**
> Altcourse is one of the new generation of privately built and run prisons. It was designed, constructed and financed by a private consortium, Group Four, and opened at the end of 1997. The company is now responsible for running the establishment

[21]For example, Osler (2002: 122) and Toynbee (2002).

These plain, descriptive words would have been equally at home on Group Four's corporate website. The point of contention was raised in the second paragraph, but it was framed in rather muted terms:

> Early reports about the management of the prison have been very favourable. But the financing of the project has raised questions about the amount of money than can be made … in the prison business.

The casual use of these final two words suggests that the commercialisation of incarceration was non-contentious, and there was no indication within the remainder of the article that PFI had generated impassioned debate. Similarly, the most critical article of this trio (BBC 2001) opened in celebratory mood:

> **Private company bonanza**
> Rarely do companies have such good fortune as the government's private finance initiative.... which moves the provision of public services like health and education into the private sector

In these terms, PFI is rather innocuous—services are simply 'moved'—and again, there was no acknowledgement of the surrounding debate. The second paragraph positioned the business of private finance as a source of national pride:

> UK plc, or more accurately, a small number of the country's largest companies have reported healthy profits from their involvement in PFIs, which analysts estimate could be worth £30bn in revenues a year.

The third critical BBC article (Scott 2001) pointedly asked 'Is PFI a good deal?' and the journalist purposefully answered the question. Even so this was a rare exception in the BBC sample and it is ironic, given the precision and inquisitiveness of the report's title—'Private Profit, Public Gain?'—that it was the *unions'* motives and goals, rather than those of senior managers, directors and shareholders, that were examined most closely. This is not to say, of course, that the business of PFI went unreported in 2002. On the contrary, 16% of BBC news items, a third of the *Guardian's* and nearly a half of the *Telegraph* articles in this year were placed on the business pages and the majority of these articles had purely commercial themes. But as already demonstrated, the primary debate in

2002 pitched PFI sceptics against *political* advocates and, consequently, the business of PFI—and the corporate credo of maximising shareholder value through expanding market share and profit growth—went largely unchallenged.

Although some significant *Guardian* articles did question the societal impact of the profit-focussed provision of public services, many simply reported on PFI contractors' business issues (share price, debt, personnel changes, etc.) with no reference whatsoever to the broader debate.[22] Indeed, for the BBC, the *Telegraph* and even the strongly sceptical *Guardian*, the business of PFI existed primarily in a hermetically sealed domain, outside disputed territory, and within these numerous articles, the discourse was purely commercial. In 2007, both the 'New Labour' and PFI sceptical narratives were largely absent. As noted above, business voices were more prevalent, albeit marginally, than senior ministers or trade union sources. Furthermore, some 37% of articles contained only weak references to private finance with the search terms appearing as snippets of background information. In all three media, although criticisms were occasionally raised, the dominant discourse was non-contentious.

Many BBC items were short news pieces about a non-financial issue at a school, hospital or other public sector facilities. For example, the only reference to PFI in an article about a school closing was in the fifth paragraph (BBC 2007a). Other BBC articles in this category were akin to corporate press releases that succinctly stated, for example, that new fire stations would be built in Suffolk (BBC 2007b). The only sign of a political contest appeared in three articles about the Scottish Parliamentary elections, and of these, only one gave private finance a high billing (BBC 2007c). Although the SNP was 'accused by Labour of ditching its previous *hard line* on PFI and copying its policies instead' (emphasis added), readers were given no reminder that private finance had ever been disputed in the UK as a whole. The BBC also published three articles about the public–private partnership of London Underground, and again, although there were significant financial problems, there was only the merest suggestion that PFI/PPP was contentious:

> … the overspend is expected to reach £1bn. BBC business editor Robert Peston said this equated to "taxpayers cash disappearing down a black hole". (BBC 2007e)

[22] For example, Mathiason (2002) and Macalister (2002a, b).

Crucially, the BBC did not cover the publication of the parliamentary report that provides the focal point of the 2007 sample period (HCCPA 2007), and apart from a two-paragraph, balanced assessment of the impact of PFI on the NHS, written by a surgeon and buried in an item that reviewed Tony Blair's influence on the health service (BBC 2007d), the 2007 BBC sample was characterised by muted acceptance.

Overtly pro- or anti-PFI narratives were equally rare in the newspapers. Unlike 2002, no editorials or opinion pieces focussed on private finance and, consequently, neither the *Guardian* nor the *Telegraph* portrayed the same degree of allegiance to their respective political positions. Nevertheless, the *Guardian's* reporting maintained a sceptical tone, albeit deep in article texts or in letters to the editor, most of which passed pithy judgement on private finance. There was no coverage of the SNP's plans for a social alternative, and the political debate about PFI was restricted to two articles about the Labour leadership contest (Wintour 2007; Woodward and Inman 2007).

Although the *Guardian* did cover the publication of the key parliamentary report (Hencke 2007), this article did not criticise PFI/PPP per se, merely the extent to which 'Whitehall' was being 'outwitted by sharp business people when it negotiates private finance initiative deals'. The most cutting criticism, however, came from *Observer* columnist Nick Cohen who suggested that much of Labour's increased spending on the NHS was wasted:

> ...readers are well aware that far too much of it went on extortionate PFI contracts, a pig-out at the public's expense by management consultants. (Cohen 2007)

In 2007, the business pages were the natural home for PFI-related articles in the *Telegraph*, and most displayed little or no acknowledgement of the debate. Like the BBC and *Guardian*, mentions of PFI were brief and served as background information. For example, paragraph nine of a piece about problems with 'a new generation of "super-size" schools' read:

> A £250 million private finance initiative, drawn up by Lancashire County Council, has seen nine high schools in Burnley and Pendle closed down to be replaced by five "super-schools". (Henry 2007)

However, among the purely descriptive accounts of the business of PFI, several articles had a sceptical tone. One, written by a doctor, branded PFI as: 'Perfidious Financial Idiocy… (a) "smoke and mirrors" policy (that) involves mortgaging the future to build shiny new hospitals' (Le Fanu 2007); another described how unsuccessful bidders for PFI contracts 'may pocket millions of pounds in compensation from the NHS' (Donnelly 2007a); and a third reported:

> Developers will be handed huge swathes of land worth hundreds of millions of pounds, if the NHS fails to maintain a string of controversial Private Finance Initiative contracts. (Donnelly 2007b)

The use of the words 'pocket' and 'handed' suggest that the gains were ill-gotten, with private contractors benefiting from corporate welfare at the expense of NHS budgets. Even so, the *Telegraph* was only a part-time watchdog of taxpayer interests, and other news items conceived PFI as a boon for companies and investors. One article in the business section of the *Sunday Telegraph* speculated positively about the prospects of industry-friendly policies from the new prime minister—'(Gordon) Brown is said to want to surprise those who fear a return to socialist business-bashing'—and although PFI 'represents absolutely terrible value for taxpayers' money', the article reassured readers that 'the PFI bandwagon will continue to roll' (Roberts et al. 2007). Also in the business section of the same newspaper, a detailed analysis of the market in PFI equity focussed on the prospects for continued profitability and the threat of changes in legislation. The danger came not from companies profiteering at taxpayers' expense but from the state which might 'claw back a share' in which case, PFI would stand for 'punish freeloading investors' (Halligan and Russell 2007).

Summary

Although criticisms were occasionally aired in 2007, none of the three publications deemed PFI/PPP worthy of rigorous debate, and the focus was on the delivery of projects or the impact of private finance on service providers. It was only in the weeks straddling the 2002 Labour Party Conference that disparate narratives were given regular exposure, and at all other times, there was a lack of sustained mediated debate. Indeed, for the remainder of 2002—and the whole of the 2007 sample period—private finance was invariably presented in descriptive, rather than evaluative, terms and, consequently, it was framed as inevitable and non-problematic. Perhaps the most striking finding of this chapter, however, is the extent to which the established form of financing was absent from the debate. Not one article in either year analysed the merits of the public funding method that had prevailed for the previous half century and the arguments tended to be anti-PFI rather than pro-social alternatives.

In terms of political sympathies, the quantitative analysis demonstrated that the *Telegraph* supported more private sector involvement in public services, the *Guardian* took a sceptical view and the BBC awarded generally balanced coverage to both positions. However, this observation must be synthesised with the discourse analysis which revealed that the BBC generally reproduced the Labour government's narrative of irresistible reform and modernisation. In the process, the trade unions were portrayed as belligerent troublemakers standing in the path of progress.

It is ironic that the public generally shared the unions' opposition to private finance in public services, and yet the reporting of the debate was generally restricted to the interactions between the political elite and trade union leaders. Indeed, the news media gave only a partial representation of available opinion. In 2002, for example, grass-roots actors collectively accounted for 6% of all named sources, research sources made up just 3%, and none of the three publications had a propensity to quote either group. Hence, in both years large portions of British society were excluded from the debate. The views of front-line medical staff, teachers, parents, patients, passengers, taxpayers, academics and economists were generally ignored by the three media and consequently, the pro-PFI discourse, as promoted by the political elite and business, was, with the exception of the Conference period, uncontested.

References

Addley, E., & Fleming, A. (2002, October 2). One Think-Tank Sent 50 Staff and Closed Its Offices, the BBC Sent 200, and Even the Tories Turned Up. *The Guardian*.

Anderson, P., & Mann, N. (1997). *Safety First: The Making of New Labour*. London: Granta.

Assinder, N. (2002a, September 27). *Same Old Story for Blair*. BBC News Website. Retrieved from http://news.bbc.co.uk/1/hi/uk_politics/2284904.stm. Accessed April 14, 2011.

Assinder, N. (2002b, September 30). *Blair's Not for Turning*. BBC News Website. Retrieved from http://news.bbc.co.uk/1/hi/uk_politics/2288999.stm. Accessed April 14, 2011.

Assinder, N. (2002c, October 1). *Blair Leaves Doubters Behind*. BBC News Website. Retrieved from http://news.bbc.co.uk/1/hi/uk_politics/2290036.stm. Accessed April 14, 2011.

Assinder, N. (2002d, October 1). *Blair: Time to Speed Up Reform*. BBC News Website. Retrieved from http://news.bbc.co.uk/1/hi/uk_politics/2289296.stm. Accessed April 14, 2011.

Assinder, N. (2002e, October 3). *Blair's Turning Point*. BBC News Website. Retrieved from http://news.bbc.co.uk/1/hi/uk_politics/2295789.stm. Accessed April 14, 2011.

Assinder, N. (2002f, September 30). *Blair Suffers Conference Defeat*. BBC News Website. Retrieved from news.bbc.co.uk/1/hi/uk_politics/2288632.stm. Accessed May 7, 2010.

Batt, C. (2002a, October 4). Balfour Beatty Rejects PFI Workforce Jibe. *Daily Telegraph*.

Batt, C. (2002b, October 2). Public Works the Private Way. *Daily Telegraph*.

BBC. (2001, September 3). *Private Company Bonanza*. BBC News Website. Retrieved from http://news.bbc.co.uk/1/hi/in_depth/business/2001/ppp/1504247.stm. Accessed July 5, 2011.

BBC. (2002a, September 26). *Brown and Prescott Maul the Unions*. BBC News Website. Retrieved from http://news.bbc.co.uk/1/hi/business/2282328.stm. Accessed April 20, 2011.

BBC. (2002b, September 30). *What Is PFI?* BBC News Website. Retrieved from http://news.bbc.co.uk/1/hi/business/2284758.stm. Accessed April 20, 2011.

BBC. (2002c, September 6). *Union Leaders' Demands*. BBC News Website. Retrieved from http://news.bbc.co.uk/1/hi/uk_politics/2240692.stm. Accessed May 25, 2011.

BBC. (2002d, September 27). *NHS's Private Plans*. BBC News Website. Retrieved from http://news.bbc.co.uk/1/hi/in_depth/business/2001/ppp/1493328.stm. Accessed June 24, 2011.

BBC. (2002e, February 3). *Blair Takes on Public Service "Wreckers"*. BBC News Website. Retrieved from http://news.bbc.co.uk/1/hi/uk_politics/1798234.stm. Accessed July 1, 2011.

BBC. (2002f, October 21). *Llew Smith*. BBC News Website. Retrieved from http://news.bbc.co.uk/1/hi/uk_politics/2053938.stm. Accessed July 1, 2011.

BBC. (2003a, February 12). *In Depth—Private Profit, Public Gain?* BBC News Website. Retrieved from http://news.bbc.co.uk/1/hi/in_depth/business/2001/ppp/default.stm. Accessed June 15, 2011.

BBC. (2003b, February 12). *What Are Public Private Partnerships?* BBC News Website. Retrieved from http://news.bbc.co.uk/1/hi/uk/1518523.stm. Accessed June 15, 2011.

BBC. (2007a, April 18). *Legionella Bug Closes School Pool.* BBC News Website. Retrieved from http://news.bbc.co.uk/1/hi/england/sussex/6568153.stm. Accessed April 22, 2011.

BBC. (2007b, May 21). *County to Get New Fire Stations.* BBC News Website. Retrieved from http://news.bbc.co.uk/1/hi/england/suffolk/6677507.stm. Accessed April 22, 2011.

BBC. (2007c, April 17). *SNP Denies Private Funding U-Turn.* BBC News Website. Retrieved from http://news.bbc.co.uk/1/hi/scotland/6561845.stm. Accessed June 24, 2011.

BBC. (2007d, May 11). *Blair and the NHS: Viewpoints.* BBC News Website. Retrieved from http://news.bbc.co.uk/1/hi/health/6610911.stm. Accessed June 24, 2011.

BBC. (2007e, May 18). *'£1bn Rise' in Tube Overhaul Bill.* BBC News Website. Retrieved from http://news.bbc.co.uk/1/hi/business/6667865.stm. Accessed June 24, 2011.

Benn, T. (2002). *Free at Last: Diaries 1991–2001.* London: Hutchinson.

Benn, T. (2007). *More Time for Politics: Diaries 2001–2007.* London: Arrow.

Blair, T. (2002a, October 1). *Speech to Labour Party Conference.* BBC News Website. Retrieved from http://news.bbc.co.uk/1/hi/uk_politics/2290454.stm. Accessed April 20, 2011.

Blair, T. (2002b, September 27). The Courage of Our Convictions: Why Reform of the Public Services Is the Route to Social Justice. *The Guardian.*

Brogan, B. (2002, September 30). Unions Poised to Embarrass PM Over Public Finance Deals. *Daily Telegraph.*

Cohen, N. (2002, September 22). Our Sky-High Arms Fiasco. *The Observer.*

Cohen, N. (2007, June 10). So Much Money, but Where Are the Vaccines? *The Observer.*

Craig, D., & Brooks, R. (2006). *Plundering the Public Sector.* London: Constable.

D'Ancona, M. (2002, October 6). What Bill Clinton Told Me in McDonald's at Blackpool. *Sunday Telegraph.*

Daily Telegraph. (2002a, October 2). Former Chancellor Urges PFI Inquiry. *Leader.*

Daily Telegraph. (2002b, October 1). Blair's Day of Judgment. *Leader.*

Daily Telegraph. (2002c, October 2). Not so Bold. *Leader.*

Daley, J. (2002, October 2). How Will Blair Give Power to Patients and Parents? *Daily Telegraph.*

Davies, B. (2002, September 8). *Morris: Payback Time for the Unions*. BBC News Website. Retrieved from http://news.bbc.co.uk/1/hi/uk_politics/2235846.stm. Accessed June 30, 2011.

Davies, M. (2002, October 1). *Blair Promises to Be Bolder*. BBC News Website. Retrieved from http://news.bbc.co.uk/1/hi/uk_politics/2289788.stm. Accessed June 24, 2011.

Donnelly, L. (2007a, May 6). NHS May Pay Firms for Failed PFI Bids. *Sunday Telegraph*.

Donnelly, L. (2007b, May 20). Revealed: Land Clauses That Could Lose NHS Millions on Private Finance Deals. *Sunday Telegraph*.

Elliott, L., & Atkinson, D. (2007). *Fantasy Island: Waking Up to the Incredible Economic, Political and Social Illusions of the Blair Legacy*. London: Constable.

Elliott, L., & Wintour, P. (2002, September 30). Trust Me on Funding, Says Brown: No Retreat on PFI, Unions Are Warned. *The Guardian*.

Gould, P. (2002, September 26). *Liverpool's Profitable Prison*. BBC News Website. Retrieved from http://news.bbc.co.uk/1/hi/in_depth/business/2001/ppp/1529482.stm. Accessed July 6, 2011.

Gow, D. (2002a, September 10). Pier Pressure: PFI 'Fat Cat' Salaries Attacked. *The Guardian*.

Gow, D. (2002b, October 25). Amey Rejects Break-Up. *The Guardian*.

Gow, D. (2002c, September 12). Unions Give Green Light to Early Vote on Euro. *The Guardian*.

Graham, P. (2002, October 2). Heckling Our Ministers Signals That Old Labour Is Still Around. *Daily Telegraph*.

Guardian. (2001, May 16). Labour Launches 'Ambitious' Manifesto. *Leader*.

Guardian. (2002a, September 30). Crunch Conference: Labour Finds the Going Tougher. *Leader*.

Guardian. (2002b, October 1). The PFI Needs a Review: Tony Blair Must Address Party Concerns. *Leader*.

Halligan, L., & Russell, J. (2007, May 20). Private Finance Initiative or Punish Freeloading Investors? *Sunday Telegraph*.

Hencke, D. (2007, May 15). Sharp Business People Outwitting Whitehall Over PFI Refinancing Deals, Say MPs. *The Guardian*.

Henry, J. (2007, April 29). Super-School Pupils 'Will Be Disaffected'. *Sunday Telegraph*.

House of Commons Committee of Public Accounts [HCCPA]. (2007, May 15). *Update on PFI Debt Refinancing and the PFI Equity Market*. Retrieved from www.publications.parliament.uk/pa/cm200607/cmselect/cmpubacc/158/158.pdf. Accessed May 10, 2010.

House of Commons Library. (2001, December 18). *The Private Finance Initiative: Research Paper 01/117*. Retrieved from http://www.parliament.uk/documents/commons/lib/research/rp2001/rp01-117.pdf. Accessed April 17, 2011.

Hutton, W. (2002). *The World We're In*. London: Little, Brown.
Johnson, B. (2002, October 3). I Refuse to Discuss the Currie and Major Affair: The Thursday Column. *Daily Telegraph*.
Jones, D. (2002, September 30). Union Canutes Cannot Halt PFI Tide. *The Guardian*.
Jones, G. (2002a, September 30). 2 in 3 Voters Lose Faith in Blair Reform. *Daily Telegraph*.
Jones, G. (2002b, September 28). Blair Faces Union Anger on Private Finance Deals. *Daily Telegraph*.
Jones, G. (2002c, September 20). Brown Dismisses Unions' Anger at Private Financing. *Daily Telegraph*.
Jones, G. (2002d, October 2). Blair Calls for Bold Action to Boost Services. *Daily Telegraph*.
Labour Party. (2001). *Ambitions for Britain*. General Election Manifesto. London: Labour Party.
Le Fanu, J. (2007, May 21). Doctor's Diary: James Le Fanu on the Dangers of Financing the NHS with 'Smoke and Mirrors' Policies. *Daily Telegraph*.
Macalister, T. (2002a, September 12). Carillion Looks at Amey's Discards. *The Guardian*.
Macalister, T. (2002b, September 12). NHS to Hand over 4,800 Acres for Housing. *The Guardian*.
Maguire, K. (2002a, September 6). Unions to Take on Labour over PFI. *The Guardian*.
Maguire, K. (2002b, September 11). Blair Lashes Left as He Calls for Partnership. *The Guardian*.
Maguire, K. (2002c, September 8). Unions Square Up to Brown for Fight on PFI. *The Guardian*.
Maguire, K., & Kettle, M. (2002, September 5). Monks Warns Blair Over 'Bottling Out'. *The Guardian*.
Marr, A. (2002, September 27). *Labour's Unity Challenge*. BBC News Website. Retrieved from http://news.bbc.co.uk/1/hi/uk_politics/2284516.stm. Accessed June 24, 2011.
Mathiason, N. (2002, September 15). Universities 'Must Sell Off Assets'. *The Guardian*.
Millward, D. (2002, September 10). 'Privatisation Pay Pirates' Cost Public Millions. *Daily Telegraph*.
Monbiot, G. (2001). *Captive State: The Corporate Takeover of Britain*. London: Pan Books.
Monbiot, G. (2002a, September 10). Our Real Opposition: We All Depend on the Unions to Confront Privatisation and the Advance of Corporate Power. *The Guardian*.

Monbiot, G. (2002b, October 29). Do as We Say, Not as We Do: While Lula's Brazil Kowtows to the Free Market, Blairs Britain Only Pretends to Do So. *The Guardian*.
Monbiot, G. (2007, September 4). This Great Free-Market Experiment Is More Like a Corporate Welfare Scheme. *The Guardian*.
Morris, B. (2002, September 29). This Knife in Our Heart. *The Observer*.
Osler, D. (2002). *Labour Party PLC: New Labour as a Party of Business*. Edinburgh: Mainstream.
Osler, D. (2011, January 25). *Private Finance Initiative: An Idiot's Guide*. Retrieved from http://www.davidosler.com/2011/01/private-finance-initiativean-idiots-guide/. Accessed April 17, 2011.
Pollock, A. (2005). *NHS Plc: The Privatisation of Our Health Care*. London: Verso Books.
Pollock, A., Dunnigan, M., Gaffney, D., Macfarlane, A., & Majeed, F. (1997). What Happens When the Private Sector Plans Hospital Services for the NHS: Three Case Studies Under the Private Finance Initiative. *British Medical Journal, 314,* 1620: 1266.
Ramsay, R. (1998). *Prawn Cocktail Party: The Hidden Power Behind New Labour*. London: Vision.
Rawnsley, A., & Ahmed, K. (2002, September 29). The Blair Interview. *The Observer*.
Roberts, D., Halligan, L., Hennessy, P., Watts, R., Pfeifer, S., & Garside, J. (2007, May 6). Does Brown Have a Trick Up His Sleeve? *Sunday Telegraph*.
Schifferes, S. (2002a, September 30). *Labour's Public Row Over Privatisation*. BBC News Website. Retrieved from http://news.bbc.co.uk/1/hi/business/2287783.stm. Accessed April 20, 2011.
Schifferes, S. (2002b, September 19). *Unions to Tackle Blair on Privatisation*. BBC News Website. Retrieved from http://news.bbc.co.uk/1/hi/business/2268042.stm. Accessed June 23, 2011.
Schifferes, S. (2002c, September 12). *Unions Flex Their Muscles*. BBC News Website. Retrieved from http://news.bbc.co.uk/1/hi/business/2251651.stm. Accessed July 3, 2011.
Scott, J. (2001). *Is PFI a Good Deal?* BBC News Website. Retrieved from http://news.bbc.co.uk/1/hi/in_depth/business/2001/ppp/1496562.stm. Accessed June 16, 2011.
Smith, C. (1999). *Making Sense of the Private Finance Initiative*. Abingdon: Radcliffe.
Sopel, J. (1995). *Tony Blair: The Moderniser*. London: Bantam Books.
Sparrow, A. (2002, September 27). Brown Defies Unions on Private Cash for Hospitals and Schools. *Daily Telegraph*.

Stone-Lee, O. (2002, October 1). *Delegates Cheer Public Service Drive.* BBC News Website. Retrieved from http://news.bbc.co.uk/1/hi/uk_politics/2290515.stm. Accessed June 28, 2011.

Toynbee, P. (2002, September 27). If You're so Sure, Prove It. *The Guardian.*

Travis, A., & Maguire, K. (2002, September 26). Majority Backs Fire Strikes and Wants PFI Halted. *The Guardian.*

Unison. (2011). *Private Finance Initiative.* Retrieved from http://www.unison.org.uk/pfi/index.asp. Accessed April 17, 2011.

White, M. (2002, September 28). Unions Rebuff Blair on Services: Last Ditch Talks to Avoid Public Sector Defeat at Conference. *Guardian.*

White, M., & Walker, D. (2002, September 27). Blair Warns on Public Services. *The Guardian.*

Whitfield, D. (2001, June). *Private Finance Initiative and Public Private Partnerships: What Future for Public Services?* Centre for Public Services. Retrieved from www.european-services-strategy.org.uk/.../pfi/pfi...ppp/what-future-pfi-ppp.doc. Accessed June 24, 2011.

Wintour, P. (2007, May 14). Brown Brands Rivals' Policies Unaffordable. *The Guardian.*

Woodward, W., & Inman, P. (2007, June 6). Brown Cheers Union with Vow on Private Equity Tax Loopholes. *The Guardian.*

CHAPTER 5

How Sinful Is Your Shopping Basket?

The Reporting of Tesco in 2006, 2007 and 2008

Introduction

When measured against a commercial yardstick, British supermarkets flourished in the first decade of the twenty-first century. Over this period, supermarkets greatly increased their range of products; the number and size of stores; their presence in the convenience store market; and their geographical reach (Humby et al. 2008; Seth and Randall 2005). By 2008, the so-called Big Four—Tesco, Asda, Sainsbury and Morrison—accounted for almost two-thirds of a grocery market that was worth £120 billion a year (Competition Commission 2008: 29; Wood 2008). Supermarkets were also credited with helping to reduce inflation, creating hundreds of thousands of jobs—transforming shopping habits and redefining the economics of agriculture (Hall 2011; Bevan 2005; NEF 2003). Supporters claimed these were the inevitable consequences of adapting to changes in society, competing ferociously, and satisfying public demand for choice, value and convenience (Bevan 2005).

The primary focus of this case study is Tesco which consolidated its position as the UK's pre-eminent supermarket chain throughout the 2000s. During the decade, it became a Britain's most valuable retail brand, a corporate role model, and even a 'bellwether' for the UK economy (Foxwell 2008; Seth and Randall 2011: 43; *Sunday Telegraph* 2008). In 2000, Tesco had one-fifth of the UK grocery market; by

Jardine (2007).

G. J. Merrill, *The Political Content of British Economic, Business and Financial Journalism*, https://doi.org/10.1007/978-3-030-04012-3_5

2008, its share had risen to 28%, twice as much as its nearest competitor (Competition Commission 2008: 29); and by some estimates, Tesco took one-eighth of *all* British consumer expenditure (Simms 2007: 24). The company generated annual net profits above £1 billion every year between 2001 and 2010, and it had the highest operating profit margins of the top seven grocery retailers (Competition Commission 2008: 35). Ever-growing market share and high profit margins made Tesco increasingly attractive to investors, and from 2002 to 2008, share price growth outstripped the UK food retailing sector (Hemscott 2011). At the end of the decade, Tesco was the third largest retailer in the world, and arguably the most innovative and ambitious (Wood 2011).

It is evident that supermarkets, and Tesco in particular, have been a boon for investors, and opinion polls have confirmed widespread public support: a survey by *Which?* magazine, for example, revealed that 73% of Britons approved of supermarkets (Consumer Association 2010). However, other polls have found a 'love-hate relationship': an ICM survey discovered that 80% of people thought competition rules should be tightened, and almost half agreed that Tesco was 'too big and powerful' (Tooher and Laurance 2005). A War on Want survey found a similar proportion would welcome 'new laws to redress the balance of power between stores… and their employees… and suppliers' and just 40% of people said that low prices were intrinsically beneficial for society (Hall and Watts 2006).

Some authors, both in the USA and UK, went further and suggested that large supermarket chains are inherently insidious entities that pay minimal and begrudging attention to the needs of other stakeholders (Quinn 2000; Fishman 2007; Spotts and Greenwald 2006; Monbiot 2001; Blythman 2007; Simms 2007). Such works were part of a broader, contemporaneous narrative that disputed the belief in the inherent, self-evident virtue of markets driven by sovereign consumers and supplied, predominantly, by large corporations. Others highlighted corporations' lack of respect for local cultures; antipathy to organised labour; ambivalence to workers' and animal rights; and poor environmental records (Klein 2000; Hertz 2001; Pilger 2002). Joel Bakan (2004) was particularly pointed and personified the joint-stock corporation as a 'psychopath' with no genuine concern for the negative social consequences of its actions.

Hence, in the period covered by this book, admiration for British supermarkets was hardly universal, and as their power grew, so did criticisms from think tanks, such as the New Economics Foundation (NEF 2003); MPs from all parties (Mathiason 2005; Derbyshire 2007a); and numerous stakeholder groups including: farmers; small retailers; environmentalists (FoE 2003, 2005); development NGOs; trade unions; and heritage groups.[1] Although there was no tightly coordinated campaign and these bodies represented disparate reformist arguments, they broadly agreed that the social costs of unfettered expansion of supermarkets must be addressed. Some advocates of the status quo were eager to dismiss such objections as part of an 'ideological battle' (Bevan 2005: 5–6) and others noted 'little sign in shopper behaviour' of anxieties (Seth and Randall 2011: 43). Nevertheless, in the first decade of the century, there was a vibrant debate between advocates and reformists about the power of British supermarkets.[2]

Tesco on the News Agenda

The content analysis pivots on three dates around which one might expect the news media to be particularly interested in supermarkets. As illustrated, the early 2000s had witnessed vigorous debates about supermarket power, and on 9 May 2006, a Competition Commission investigation was launched. This promised to address several of the reformists' criticisms: it had a far wider scope than previous inquiries and included the convenience store sector, land banks, the abuse of buying power and anti-competitive pricing (*Guardian* 2006). The second key date is 23 January 2007 when the interim report was released, and the third is 30 April 2008, the publication date of the final report (Competition Commission 2008). Hence, LexisNexis was searched for articles in the *Guardian/Observer*, and the *Daily* and *Sunday Telegraph* that mentioned Tesco anywhere in the text for the five weeks straddling each of the key dates.[3] The BBC News website archive was also searched over the same 35-day periods.

The three years generated 228, 282 and 279 articles, respectively, and hence, a total of 789 items form the universal sample. At this stage, it is

[1] Andrew Simms estimated over 100 groups were involved in campaigns against supermarket power (2007: 336).

[2] See Chapter 2 for detailed descriptions of the advocate and reformist narratives.

[3] For the sake of brevity, references to the *Guardian/Observer* sample will henceforth be shortened to the '*Guardian*'. Similarly, the *Daily/Sunday Telegraph* will become the '*Telegraph*'.

impossible to determine if the 24% increase between 2006 and 2007/8 is significant. The most striking feature, however, is the disparity between the media. In each of the three years, the BBC published far fewer articles than either of the newspapers: in 2006, Tesco appeared in just 30 BBC articles, compared with 113 for the *Guardian* and 85 for the *Telegraph*, and in 2007 and 2008, the newspapers each published over twice as many articles as the BBC.

These data show that Tesco had a constant presence in the news, but it was apparent that many mentions were incidental to the story. Such articles invariably contained a single reference to Tesco, for example, as the scene of a crime, or as a source of product, wine or recipe ingredient. Some 40% of articles in the universal sample fell into this 'incidental' category and were removed by the first salience filter.[4] Incidental references were far more prevalent in the newspapers than on the BBC website: in each of the three years, between a half and a third of *Guardian* and *Telegraph* articles fell into this category, compared with a quarter of BBC articles. This reflects the intrinsic differences between commercial newspapers, with opinion pieces and consumer-oriented supplements, and a public service news website that has very few of the former and none of the latter. Hence, the post-first filter samples for the three years were 132, 167 and 172 articles, respectively: a total of 471 items. The removal of the incidental references revealed a modest peak in reporting in the middle weeks of 2007 and 2008 with 42 and 46 news items, respectively, compared with a median of 33 in each year. This pattern was reproduced by each of the media in both years and approximates to the normal distribution one would expect around an important event or announcement. In 2006, however, the first week provided the peak.

The financial pages were the most common location of articles in the newspapers. Around half of all *Guardian* and 60% of *Telegraph* articles that mentioned Tesco appeared in the business sections. Again, there was a high degree of evenness with no significant change between the years. The second most populous category for the newspapers was general/UK news, which consistently accounted for around a fifth of articles. Generally, the *Guardian* and *Telegraph* were equally likely to mention Tesco in

[4]These articles are not directly pertinent this research, but it is worth noting that these 318 seemingly trivial appearances demonstrate the extent to which Tesco has permeated British society.

features, weekend magazines and in the personal finance pages, but the former published over four times as many articles in the leaders, letters and opinion section than the latter. In contrast to the newspapers, nine-tenths of BBC articles fell into two categories: UK news[5] and business. In the absence of comparable supplements, features or personal finance sections on the BBC website, this concentration of articles was to be expected. Likewise, the BBC does not have the same variety of business articles as the newspapers (e.g. share tips, opinion pieces and stock market reviews). In addition, many BBC articles focussed on issues that might normally appear in the local press but probably not the nationals.[6] Business articles, on the other hand, tend to be national or international, and fewer of the BBC news items fell into this category than the newspapers, with the exception of 2007 when around a half appeared in the business pages.

The BBC also had a propensity to report with relative brevity. On average, four-fifths of BBC articles were standard news items compared to 40% for the *Guardian* and 48% for the *Telegraph*. This difference is again attributable to the broader range of article type in the newspapers. Whereas the BBC ran just seven long-format feature articles over the three years the *Guardian* published 41 and the *Telegraph* 28. The newspapers also mentioned Tesco in more opinionated[7] items than the BBC: there were 21 such occurrences in the *Guardian* and 45 in the *Telegraph* compared with two for the BBC.

In terms of prominence of the search term, there were again significant similarities between the *Guardian* and *Telegraph*. In all three years, Tesco appeared in either the headline or introduction of between 33 and 41% of newspaper articles and had just a single mention in around a third of items. In the BBC samples, however, Tesco was far more prominent and appeared in the headline or introduction in two-thirds of articles. The BBC was also far less like to give Tesco a single mention: on average, one in three newspaper articles made a lone reference to Tesco compared to one in seven BBC items. The composite annual figures demonstrate that Tesco appeared in the headline or introduction of 42% of articles and was mentioned just once in 30%. By this measurement,

[5] Unlike the newspapers, the BBC News website regionalises UK news into England, Scotland, Wales and Northern Ireland.

[6] For example, local council planning decisions on new store proposals (BBC 2006b).

[7] This category combines columns, opinion pieces, debates, sketches, editorials, *vox populi* and letters to the editor.

none of the years were exceptional and, apart from the BBC's tendency to feature Tesco prominently, these data give scant indication of the degree of mediated debate. Indeed, closer examination of the articles revealed that Tesco played a cameo role in some extremely pertinent and detailed articles.

For instance, Tesco made two rather lowly appearances in the *Guardian's* analysis of the announcement of the Competition Commission inquiry (Walsh 2006) and had just one mention in the equivalent article in the *Telegraph* (Reece 2006). It was noticeable that when supermarket power per se was the focus of the article, Tesco was rarely singled out. Conversely, Tesco sometimes appeared in the headline or introduction in articles that made no reference whatsoever to the broader debate. These tended to be routine news items in the business sections of the newspapers or BBC articles about local issues (see above). Consequently, it was apparent that prominence of search term was no guarantee that a news item was relevant to the objectives of this research. Hence, to further distil the sample, a second filter was applied which removed the articles with weak salience. This provided a highly refined and far more manageable sample of 294 articles, 37% of the universal sample of 789 items, to be analysed in greater detail.

For this sample, the quantity of reporting increased steadily between 2006 and 2008, and as shown in Table 5.1, most of the growth was attributable to the BBC which by 2008 was almost on a par with the newspapers. Even with the removal of peripheral articles, the *Guardian* and the *Telegraph's* distribution profiles remained highly congruent with similar quantities of coverage across the years. However, assuming particularly detailed and contextualised information is found in features, and that opinionated articles are most likely to contain strong views, the data suggest that 2007 was the peak year for concerted debate with 43% of articles in these categories compared to 38% 2006 and 22% in 2008. Again, these aggregates obscure differences: the BBC published just nine

Table 5.1 Annual distribution of articles (post-second salience filter)

	2006	*2007*	*2008*	*Total*	*%*
BBC	16	22	30	68	23
Guardian	34	35	39	108	37
Telegraph	36	40	42	118	40
Total	86	97	111	294	100
%	29	33	38		

features or opinionated articles overall, whereas the *Guardian* printed 49 and the *Telegraph* 42.

Themes and Framing

It was evident from the pilot study that the majority of articles framed Tesco in a limited number of contexts. Furthermore, many of the themes of the articles were consistent with the corporate and reformist arguments described in Chapter 2, and closer analysis of the data gave some indication of the extent to which the competing positions were given exposure. Although corporate themes were dominant overall, some 40% of articles followed broadly reformist themes, with two categories—local communities and the environment, and competition and consumers—gaining far more coverage than the other three.

The *Telegraph* was clearly the most consistent: in each year, between 44 and 52% of articles focussed on corporate themes[8] and around a third had reformist themes.[9] The *Guardian* favoured corporate contexts in 2006, as did the BBC in 2007, but the emphasis for both in the other two years was on reformist themes. Overall, the data suggest the most active year for debate was 2007 with the *Guardian* and *Telegraph* printing their highest proportion of articles with contentious reformist themes, and the former publishing an inordinately high number of articles about the Competition Commission investigation. In contrast to the newspapers, almost half of the BBC's coverage in 2007 focussed on investor and CSR issues and its peak year for reformist themes was 2008. Averaging the proportions of articles with corporate or reformist contexts revealed that the newspapers generally confirmed their traditional allegiances: across the three years, 48% of *Telegraph* articles followed corporate themes compared with 33% for reformist, whereas the *Guardian* preferred the latter to a similar degree (28:44). Similarly, the BBC appeared to favour the reformists (32:41) but it is important to note that its most common reformist theme was 'local communities and environment' (LCE) and many of the articles in this category were concerned with parochial planning issues.

[8] Investor and corporate social responsibility (CSR).

[9] Competition and consumers; local communities and the environment; supply chain; employment; and political influence.

At a macro-level, although corporate themes dominated, the media gave considerable coverage to reformist issues. LCE was the top reformist theme for all three media in all three years, except for the *Guardian* and *Telegraph* in 2008 when competition and consumers headed the list. But these were the only two of the five reformist categories to receive any significant exposure: supply chain, employment and political influence collectively accounted for less than 7% of the universal sample. It is evident that when debate about supermarket power was aired, it was primarily framed in terms of the impact on local communities and the environment and, to a lesser extent, competition on consumer prices. In contrast, workers, suppliers and those concerned with the political influence of supermarkets had very few opportunities to express their views.

The secondary theme data suggest that news about supermarkets was rarely characterised by bilateral dialog with just 17 articles—6%—defined by talk, discussion or negotiation. This is not surprising, however, given the nature of the issues. Unlike a mainstream political contest, in which the two sides are routinely pitched face-to-face, the supermarket debate was an extended and rather amorphous phenomenon that was linked to a formal investigation over three years. Hence, there was no physical forum—for example, parliament or a political conference—in which the participants could compete for media attention in set-piece encounters. This is not to say, of course, that the interaction of ideas was absent and around one-fifth of articles were classed as 'contested announcements' and a further 23% were largely analytical, so there were clearly opportunities for different viewpoints to be expressed.

The leading secondary theme across all media, however, was the uncontested announcement which accounted for 31% of items. In such articles, an organisation or person typically made a statement which the journalist relayed and contextualised but excluded conflicting views. Just over half of these 92 articles contained corporate sources only, with the BBC the least likely to include a voice from outside of the business world. In contrast, a reformist group had a monopoly on comment in less than 3% of articles. Further analysis revealed that in 11% of the universal sample, Tesco was the first-named source in an article classed as an uncontested announcement. These data suggest all three media gave considerable unchallenged coverage to the corporate sector in general and Tesco in particular.

Given that reformist arguments were often complex and interrelated, it would be reasonable to assume that the most informative articles would be those that placed the issues in a wider context and explained the various viewpoints in detail. The public need for such analysis was fulfilled to an extent with around a third of items coded as mainly or entirely thematic. Conversely, 59% of articles covered immediate events and episodes, and by definition, these gave scant indication that the issues were connected to the macro-debate. The data also revealed that the proportion of thematic articles fell over the three years from around 40% in 2006 and 2007 to 18% in 2008. Indeed, only one-eighth of the *Telegraph's* articles in 2008, and none of the BBC's, gave detailed and contextualised analysis in the period surrounding publication of the final Competition Commission report.

With around 40% of articles following reformist themes, a similar proportion revolving around contested announcements or journalistic analysis, and a third of articles giving considerable context and background, it appears there was plenty of fertile ground for mediated debate. Indeed, supermarkets were often framed as a contentious issue by all three media with the *Guardian* and the BBC showing the greatest propensity to follow the reformists' agendas and the *Telegraph* favouring corporate themes. It is important to emphasise, however, that only two of the five reformist narratives were given significant exposure and very few of the 294 articles focussed on the relationships between supermarkets and their suppliers and workers, or their involvement in British politics. It is also important to stress that even in 2007, when the debate appeared to be most active, all three publications carried numerous articles that followed investor or CSR themes. Hence, a significant proportion of all news items—44% in 2006, 34% in 2007 and 28% in 2008—were framed according to corporate agendas and were seemingly untouched by the ongoing debate.

Source Analysis

In order to gauge the extent to which a plurality of viewpoints was present in the articles, the next stage of investigation assessed sourcing patterns. This revealed a clear preference in all media for corporate sources and, although reformist spokespeople were widely quoted, many stakeholder groups appeared so rarely that they were effectively excluded from the debate. Indeed, the initial stage of source analysis demonstrated a widespread propensity to *not* feature a multiplicity of named sources.

With the exception of the *Telegraph* in 2006 and the *Guardian* in 2008, around 60% of articles contained fewer than two named sources. Given the journalistic principle of presenting multiple perspectives, this is surprising, particularly with so many articles following potentially contentious, reformist themes. It would be misguided, however, to assume that such articles were necessarily bereft of a dissenting voice. Indeed, the data also show that all three publications frequently quoted unnamed sources—337 in total over the three years—but as one might expect with 'Tesco' as the search term, the majority of these spokespeople—62%—represented the company or other corporate interests.

Although business sources often disagree, it is reasonable to assume that they shared a commitment to the primacy of profit, and hence, they would generally follow either the investor or the CSR narrative. Similarly, it is reasonable to assume that the main opposition to corporate narratives would be delivered by stakeholder organisations. These reformist groups were certainly present among the unnamed sources, but they accounted for just 13% of the total which gave corporate spokespeople an overall advantage of almost five-to-one. The *Guardian* confirmed its traditional sympathies for social movements to an extent with the highest proportion of unnamed sources from stakeholder groups, but these were still outnumbered by corporate voices by a factor of more than three. The *Telegraph* favoured business sources over stakeholders by around five-to-one, and in the BBC articles, there were eleven unnamed corporate spokespeople for every one stakeholder counterpart. The overall rankings were remarkably consistent in 2006 and 2007 but corporate sources strengthened their position in 2008 with 65% of that year's anonymous appearances, whereas stakeholder groups were relegated to joint fourth position with just 7%.

Business actors also dominated as named sources with 'other corporate' and Tesco heading the category rankings in each of the three years, and overall accounting for 44% of all appearances.[10] Corporate voices outnumbered named spokespeople of stakeholder groups by a factor of more than five in the *Telegraph*, three on the BBC News website and two-and-a-half in the *Guardian*. The peak year for stakeholders was 2006 but this was only marginally higher than 2007, and in these two years, these groups never exceeded 18% of appearances in any data set. It is important to note, however, that stakeholder groups did not have a monopoly on dissent and many 'individuals' quoted were often associated with critical views. However, although it is tempting to lump

[10]Forty-three per cent of the BBC's named sources were corporate, compared to 38% for the *Guardian* and 51% for the *Telegraph*.

farmers, independent shop owners and other local businesses in with stakeholder groups, thereby creating an arguably more representative reformist category to counter the corporate lobby, it would be misguided to assume that they share the same perspective. Nevertheless, it is noteworthy that this category's contribution was only a few points lower than the stakeholder groups' and, in all three media, 'individuals' accounted for between 11 and 18% of named citations.

Similarly, journalists might express a view on supermarket power, and reporters accounted for 10% of all named sources, with the BBC least likely to quote a journalist and the *Guardian* the most. One might also reasonably expect politicians to have contributed to this debate, and yet this group had a meagre tally: just 7% of the 492 named sources across the three years were 'political', and in just ten instances, these were either Labour or Conservative MPs. Furthermore, the total absence of the prime minister and just two appearances by government ministers confirm that the supermarket debate was contested outside of Westminster. This is not to say, however, that the debate was bereft of input from political bodies: on the contrary, Competition Commission spokespeople were quoted 16 times as a named source—and 17 anonymously—over the three years, and the Office of Fair Trading was cited 15 and 11 times, respectively.

Aggregating the named and unnamed sources confirmed the dominance of corporate sources. Figure 5.1 shows that for the BBC and *Telegraph*, business actors—Tesco and other corporate—accounted for the majority of sources in all three years, and only in the *Guardian*, did they constitute less than half of the citations.[11] Even so, stakeholder groups were still outnumbered in this newspaper by a factor of three. This was considerably lower than the BBC and *Telegraph's* ratio of five-to-one, but this figure alone illustrates that, even in a newspaper traditionally associated with social causes and left-of-centre politics, large corporations still had far more exposure than groups representing reformist concerns.[12] Stakeholder organisations accounted for almost a

[11] Corporate actors accounted for 53% of all BBC sources, 45% of the *Guardian's* and 56% of the *Telegraph's*.

[12] The ratios of corporate-to-stakeholder sources were: BBC—90:18, *Guardian*—152:51; and *Telegraph*—182:36.

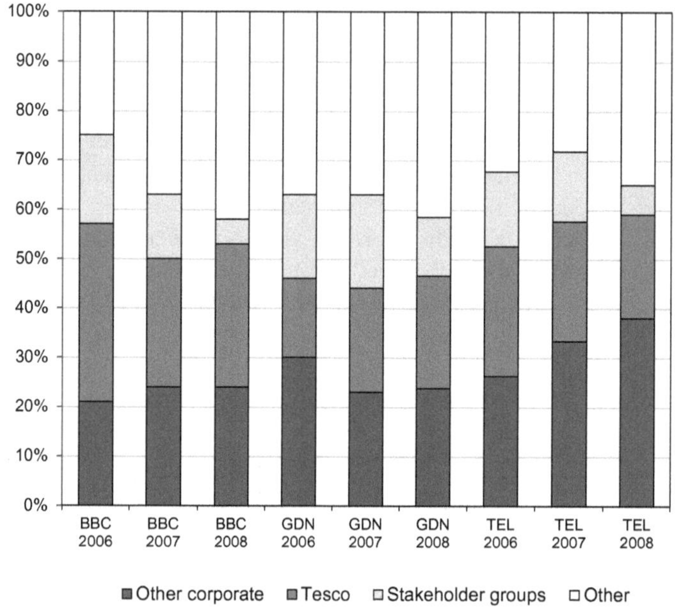

Fig. 5.1 Constitution of named and unnamed sources

fifth of *Guardian* sources in 2007 but in 2008, these groups made up just 12% and were displaced primarily by 'other categories'. This shift was mirrored in the BBC and *Telegraph* articles to a lesser extent.

These data are illuminating but as aggregates they say little about the extent and nature of debate within articles. A more representative metric is the first-named source as this person typically establishes the trajectory of the narrative. Again, the top two categories across all years and media were 'Tesco' and 'other corporate' which collectively accounted for 44% of the first-named sources, with BBC articles the most likely to open with a business voice. In contrast, stakeholder groups featured as the first-named source in 7% of articles. The *Guardian* had the greatest propensity to quote stakeholders first, but at 9% of the total, the tally was dwarfed by the 40% of items that were led by a business actor.

The supremacy of corporate sources is underlined in Table 5.2 which shows that 48% of articles totally excluded people and organisations that might hold reformist views. In contrast, stakeholder groups had a

Table 5.2 Source monopolies and debates

Articles (N=294)			*2006*	*2007*	*2008*	*Total*	*%*
Corporate source monopoly			31	40	70	141	48
Stakeholder source monopoly			4	8	3	15	5
Debates							
Corporate	followed by	Reformist	16	12	7	35	12
Reformist	followed by	Corporate	8	18	15	41	14
Other categories			27	19	16	62	21
Total			86	97	111	294	100

source monopoly in just 5% of items. Some 60% of BBC articles restricted comment to corporate voices compared to around 45% for each of the newspapers. The BBC was also the most likely to award Tesco a source monopoly with 28% of articles excluding other corporate and stakeholder spokespeople.[13]

The peak year for debate was clearly 2007, with 31% of articles in this year featuring both corporate and reformist sources.[14] In 2008, however, just one-fifth of articles included both categories, and with corporate sources enjoying monopolies in a further 63% of articles, the opportunities for mediated argument would appear slim in this year. Assuming the first-quoted party has the advantage in an article that contains conflicting views, reformist voices enjoyed a modest edge over their corporate opponents overall. This was most pronounced in 2008 (15:7) and reformists also opened the debate most often in 2007 (18:12) but corporate spokespeople clearly dominated in 2006 (16:8).

In terms of the composition of stakeholder sources, independent traders and environmental NGOs were the most quoted in all three media which reflected the emphasis on the LCE themes highlighted earlier. The *Telegraph* had the greatest propensity to quote suppliers and their pressure groups, typically the National Farmers' Union, and only the *Guardian* sought the views of trade unions or, most significantly, the

[13]The *Guardian* and *Telegraph* granted Tesco a source monopoly in 16 and 10% of articles, respectively.

[14]For the purposes of this section of the analysis, 'reformists' combine 'stakeholder groups' and 'individuals'. Although not all this latter category held reformist views, many, such as farmers and independent traders, were critical of supermarket power. Hence, the figures represent the best-case scenario for the reformists.

New Economics Foundation (NEF). As noted above, the NEF had published comprehensive critical studies about the power of supermarkets[15] and its policy director wrote a seminal book about Tesco's impact on society.[16] Naturally, this information was also readily available to the news media, as was research produced by other stakeholder groups[17] and yet journalists, particularly at the BBC, showed little interest in referring to these organisations in their reports.

Coverage of Narratives and Arguments

In comparison with corporate sources, none of the stakeholder groups were particularly well represented. Indeed, the source analysis demonstrates that the corporate sector had a clear advantage across the board. This was particularly pronounced in BBC articles which, collectively, favoured business over stakeholder groups even more than the traditionally pro-corporate *Telegraph*. The *Guardian* showed signs of sympathy to those who held reformist viewpoints but even this newspaper favoured business spokespeople overall. This is not to say, of course, that reformist views were equally rare. It is important to remember that almost 40% of articles followed reformist themes, and the relative dearth of stakeholder spokespeople does not necessarily mean that the arguments were absent. Hence, the next stage of analysis considers the extent to which the two corporate narratives and the five reformist argument strands were given exposure. The data show that the *Guardian* plainly gave the greatest coverage to the reformists, in both relative and absolute terms. In contrast, the *Telegraph* favoured corporate narratives, and although one might expect the BBC to give similar amounts of exposure to both camps, it too clearly favoured the business agenda.

By taking a holistic reading of each item, it was possible to synthesise the viewpoints of all sources—including 'political', 'individuals' and 'other sources'—with the nuances of the journalistic narrative and assess the quantity of coverage of the corporate and reformist positions. Figure 5.2 illustrates the political content of each media's annual sample

[15] For example, NEF (2003).

[16] This book (Simms 2007) was accompanied by a website that acted as a central resource for campaigning groups (Tescopoly 2012).

[17] For example, FoE (2003).

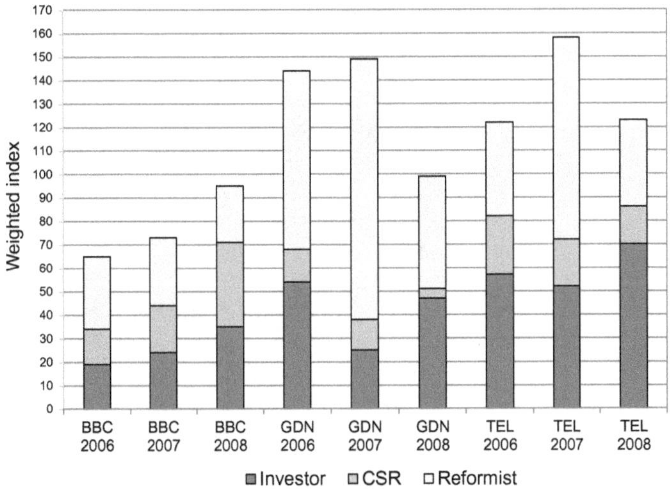

Fig. 5.2 Weighted coverage of political positions

and shows that the most concerted debate occurred in the *Guardian* and the *Telegraph* in 2007.[18] In this year, the former favoured the reformist over the corporate position—investor and CSR—by a factor of almost three whereas the *Telegraph's* coverage was marginally tilted towards the reformists. The *Guardian* also favoured the reformists in 2006, albeit by a rather modest margin. The BBC's coverage in 2006—and the *Guardian's* in 2008—was almost perfectly balanced between the two camps, but the corporate position dominated the BBC's news output in 2007 and, in particular, 2008. The *Telegraph's* weighted coverage indices for the first and last years were strikingly similar, and in both cases, corporate content outscored reformist by a factor of two.

The investor narrative was clearly more prevalent than CSR in the newspapers, with the *Guardian* giving little exposure to corporations' positive impact on society. Indeed, this newspaper exhibited net criticism of CSR in 15 articles across the three years compared to just two in the *Telegraph* and none among the BBC samples. The BBC was more likely

[18]The weighted total was calculated by multiplying the frequency of articles in the 'detailed coverage' category by 3; 'limited coverage' by 2; 'acknowledged' by 1; 'critical coverage' by minus 1; and 'no mention' by zero. See Chapter 2.

Table 5.3 Weighted coverage of reformist arguments

	BBC News			*Guardian*			*Telegraph*			*Total*	*%*
	2006	*2007*	*2008*	*2006*	*2007*	*2008*	*2006*	*2007*	*2008*		
Competition	13	13	8	29	41	13	15	35	16	183	38
Supply chain	1	5	2	8	14	6	5	16	14	71	15
LCE	17	8	13	33	51	26	14	33	7	202	42
Employment	0	3	1	3	4	2	1	2	0	16	3
Political	0	0	0	3	1	1	6	0	0	11	2
Total points	31	29	24	76	111	48	41	86	37	483	100
Three-year total		84			235			164			

to positively report CSR than the newspapers with some 26% of its coverage over the three years following the lead of companies, particularly Tesco, eager to promote themselves as good corporate citizens. In comparison, just 8% of *Guardian* and 15% of *Telegraph* articles followed the CSR narrative. It was also evident that the investor narrative per se was rarely criticised over the three sample periods, with just three instances in the *Telegraph*, two in the *Guardian* and one on the BBC News website.

Table 5.3 shows that the BBC also gave the least coverage to the five reformist arguments. As noted above, the newspapers' sample sizes were considerably larger than the BBC's, so one would expect greater exposure.[19] But the differences in the number of articles were far smaller than the disparities in weighted coverage: over three years, reformists recorded 84 points on the BBC News website, about half of the *Telegraph's* tally and a third of the *Guardian's*. The data also confirm that the reformist arguments had the greatest exposure in 2007 and the least in 2008. Indeed, in 2007 the reformists notched up a total of 226 points, some 47% more than the corporate tally. In the other years, however, the corporate position dominated with a 13% margin in 2006 and an 82% advantage in 2008.[20]

It is also evident that two reformist arguments were consistently awarded far greater exposure and credence than the others. Collectively, the 'local communities and environment' (LCE) and the 'competition' strands accounted for between 86 and 73% of the publications' coverage of reformist narratives. Arguments relating to the supply chain were in a distant third place and only the *Telegraph* showed a propensity to voice the concerns of farmers and food producers. The other two reformist arguments, however, received very little coverage in any of the media. Employment issues were barely acknowledged across the three years. Furthermore, not one article in the distilled sample of 294 made a direct reference to the political influence of supermarkets.

Critical Discourse Analysis

Although the quantitative analysis has revealed distinct patterns, it would be misguided at this point to assert that the *Guardian* was simply 'pro-reformist' or the BBC and *Telegraph* were 'pro-corporate'. Even though

[19] See Fig. 5.1.

[20] The total weighted points for the corporate and reformist positions for 2006, 2007 and 2008 were: 167–148; 154–226; and 198–109, respectively.

the analysis thus far suggests these leanings, support for the positions was far from universal or unwavering, and in all three media, both narratives enjoyed considerable exposure. Hence, to gain a deeper and more complete understanding of the political content of the samples, the next stage assesses the language used to present the various arguments and the extent to which journalists reproduced the corporate discourses.

Before embarking on the analysis, however, it is important to emphasise an inherent difference between the BBC News website and the newspapers. Unlike their counterparts at the *Guardian* and the *Telegraph*, BBC journalists are constrained by the Corporation's statutory obligations to impartiality[21] and so one would not expect reporters to describe actors, institutions or ideas in overtly judgemental terms. Similarly, within the BBC sample, there were no editorials, no opinion pieces and, with one exception,[22] no set-piece debates. In contrast, almost a fifth of newspaper articles over the three years provided fertile ground for the expression of liberated journalistic opinion.[23] For these reasons alone, the BBC's coverage was generally couched in far plainer language and was bereft of the explicit opinion that peppered newspaper reports. Nevertheless, closer examination confirmed that the BBC gave more credence to the corporate than the reformist discourse, and although its journalists did not express the investor narrative as vehemently as the *Telegraphs'*, they tended to follow the corporate line more closely than their print colleagues.

Reporting the Competition Commission Announcements

Detailed analysis of texts revealed that the *Guardian*, and to a lesser extent, the *Telegraph*, gave credence to the alternative framework of competition offered by the reformists. The BBC, however, adhered to the state-defined parameters of the Competition Commission inquiry. This was evident in articles that covered the initial announcement. The *Guardian* highlighted the gravity of the inquiry, and in reminding the reader that this is the third investigation in seven years, supermarkets

[21] See Chapter 2.

[22] BBC (2008a).

[23] This is most visible in columns, opinion pieces and editorials.

were bracketed as habitual offenders who were being carefully monitored on behalf of the public (emphases added):

> Supermarkets face third inquiry in seven years: *Watchdog* promises most *thorough scrutiny* yet: Focus on land banks and below-cost pricing. (Walsh 2006)

The *Telegraph*, however, concentrated on the companies' prospects and speculated that they might be ordered to restrain their growth: 'Supermarket inquiry could *force* the big companies to sell stores' (Murray-West 2006). The BBC's headline—'Supermarkets in competition probe'—was plain by comparison, and the use of the word 'probe' implied an exploratory examination rather than a meticulous investigation: (BBC 2006c). Indeed, the BBC also used 'probe' in headlines covering the announcement of the interim report (BBC 2007b), a more detailed account of this report (BBC 2007c), and for an article about alleged price fixing of tobacco (BBC 2008b). Only one BBC item about the regulatory authorities opened with a title that hinted at punishment for repeated wrongdoing: 'OFT in new supermarket crackdown' (BBC 2008c). It would be misguided, however, to infer any substantial meaning from such short phrases and beyond the headlines, key BBC articles did incorporate elements of the reformist discourse. For example, the 2006 opening paragraph of the article that covered the announcement of the investigation read:

> The market dominance of UK supermarket giants Tesco, Asda, Sainsbury's and Morrisons is to be investigated for the third time in seven years. (BBC 2006c)

Although there was no indication if 'market dominance' was good or bad, this paragraph echoed the title of the equivalent *Guardian* article (see above) but the second paragraph used a colloquial phrase which, like 'probe', suggested casual reconnaissance rather than thorough investigation (emphasis added):

> The stores control almost 75% of the £120bn UK grocery market and the Office of Fair Trading wants the Competition Commission *to take a look.* (ibid.)

Again, in the BBC report there was no sense of the importance of the investigation that was stressed in the second sentence of the *Guardian* article: 'In what will be a significant inquiry, the commission will look far more widely into the food retailing market than it has done in the past' (Walsh 2006). The equivalent *Telegraph* article conceptualised the investigation as an inquiry into the 'abuse of power' by the supermarkets and although its focus was on the impact of possible constraining directives on the Big Four, it at least included a quotation from the Association of Convenience Stores [ACS] (Murray-West 2006). The equivalent *Guardian* article also directly relayed the concerns of small traders and featured an additional statement from Friends of the Earth (Walsh 2006). The BBC article, however, only quoted the chief executive of the OFT (BBC 2006c), and overall, it was a perfunctory account of a routine investigation and the only objections came from unnamed 'critics' whose sole concern was that large supermarkets were: 'driving local convenience stores from the High Street'.

Although this pattern was not universal in BBC articles that covered the Competition Commission inquiry, there was a tendency to report criticism in dehumanised terms. The key article in 2007, for instance, again merely paraphrased 'campaign groups' who criticised supermarkets for 'stifling competition' (BBC 2007b), and although a second, more detailed article did briefly quote representatives from Action Aid, the ACS and an academic, their words followed a guiding narrative from the BBC's business editor, Robert Peston, who said the Commission: '…seem to imply that there is not sufficient competition at the local level' (BBC 2007c).

In 2008, the only BBC article to directly address the final report posed a polarised question in its title—'Grocery inquiry: success or failure?'—and featured first-person assessments from the chief executives of Asda and Tesco, and the British Retail Consortium (BBC 2008a). These advocate voices were apparently trumped by four reformists—a dairy farmer, an independent shop owner and representatives from FoE and the ACS—but, although readers were seemingly encouraged to formulate their own answer, the journalist's opening words suggested a satisfactory outcome had been achieved:

> The powers of the major supermarkets are set to be curbed by a series of measures recommended by the Competition Commission.
>
> Changes to the planning system should improve the number of large supermarkets consumers can choose from in a local area. And an independent ombudsman will investigate how retailers treat their suppliers. (ibid.)

It is noteworthy that competition was defined as the number of *large* supermarkets available to consumers: independent retailers were ignored and although the concerns of suppliers were mentioned, other reformist sub-narratives—environmental, employment and political influence—were excluded.

These examples illustrate that although the BBC achieved a degree of balance by quoting concerns of stakeholder groups, its reports tended to tightly adhere to the remit of the official investigation rather than those of the reformist camp, and hence, the journalistic narrative was detached from the concerns of individuals and communities. This pattern contrasted markedly with the newspapers, particularly in 2007 which, as identified in the quantitative analysis, was the peak year for debate.

Over a period of six days surrounding the release of the interim report in 2007, the *Guardian/Observer* published ten substantial articles—compared to the BBC's two—which underlined the newspapers' critical position. These included two editorials, three opinion pieces and a case study about the travails of an independent chain of shops in rural Wales (Bowers 2007). Over the same period, the *Telegraph* published nine significant articles including three opinion pieces but no editorials. Although the general tenor of this newspaper's reporting was congruent with the advocacy displayed in the titles of the key 2006 articles (see above), the reformist narrative was still evident, albeit in qualified or jocular terms. For example, in an opinion piece, editor of *Country Life* magazine, Clive Aslet wrote: 'We cling to the Competition Commission's inquiry into the grocery trade as the last hope of halting this Beelzebub' (Aslet 2007). Nevertheless, the author was more persuaded by the positives of supermarket power, such as bringing: 'fresh, cheap food to places that it could never be bought before' and although 'some of the moans (of the critics) are on target', the author was satisfied that, on balance, supermarkets acted in the public interest (ibid.).

Another *Telegraph* article visited the Oxfordshire town of Bicester, a place that had been: 'Tesco'd six times over' (Derbyshire 2007b). But like the BBC's reporting, the parameters of investigation were limited to competition among the big supermarkets, and the thoughts of local retailers and, indeed, shoppers were absent. Apart from these articles, and a letter to the editor that sang the praises of buying from independents (Holden 2007), the *Telegraph's* reporting during this crucial period was firmly underpinned by opposition to regulation. For example,

Richard Fletcher positioned the inquiry as an interrogation that had to be endured by the large supermarkets (emphases added):

> Supermarket retailers are *braced for further questioning* as the Competition Commission focuses its inquiry on a number of specific *allegations*, including predatory pricing. (Fletcher 2007c)

Another article began by raising the spectre of legislation (emphases added): 'Supermarkets could be *forced* to sell land and alter their relationships with suppliers' (Murray-West 2007), and although this article noted that 'thousands of local specialist stores (are) being killed off by big supermarkets', and aired the concerns of a dairy farmer, the reformist narrative was overshadowed by the commercial. This was also evident in two comment pieces in the business pages which, *in lieu* of an editorial in the main sections of the *Telegraphs*, most clearly demonstrated the newspapers' commitment to *laissez-faire*. In the first, *Sunday Telegraph* business editor Dan Roberts castigated supermarkets for becoming sidetracked by corporate social responsibility. 'Barely a day passes', he wrote:

> ...without another public relations stunt from one supermarket or another to show how green, healthy, and cuddly to suppliers (delete as appropriate) they all are. (Roberts 2007)

Echoing Clive Aslet (see above), the author urged the supermarkets to focus on 'the big stuff' and be proud of their central role in reducing inflation and unemployment. Tesco's greatest achievement, wrote Roberts, was putting: '...food on the nations' dinner tables with ever-increasing variety and quality and at ever-decreasing cost and inconvenience' (ibid.). In the second comment piece (Fletcher 2007b), the author's satirical eye was attracted to both the chief executive of Tesco, who delivered a 'well-rehearsed sermon' following the publication of the interim report, and unnamed 'critics', whose objections to the company amounted to little more than 'noise'. Despite acknowledgements to the plight of suppliers and independent traders, the article was founded on the assumption that market forces must remain unimpeded. Tesco is, wrote Fletcher, 'one of our most successful exports' and the company 'has driven down prices - not only benefiting customers but also helping the Government to keep a lid on inflation'. While the author noted that 'concerns about the balance of power between suppliers and retailers' identified in the 2000 inquiry were still relevant, he concluded with a redefined conundrum for the chairman of the Competition Commission, Peter Freeman, that confirmed the primacy of competition: 'The real question is, can (Freeman) work out how to stamp out these worst excesses of competitive behaviour without stifling healthy competition?' (ibid.).

It is important to reiterate that the BBC's reporting at this crucial stage of the investigation was relatively brief, dispassionate and closely followed the regulator's agenda. Compared with the *Telegraph*, the BBC used less combative language, and although there was little sense of the fear of regulation—nor overt support for *laissez-faire* economics—the BBC gave far greater credence to the status quo than to the arguments of the reformists. Even though the *Telegraph* was primarily worried about the impact of regulation on an axiomatically virtuous market, it still managed to give significant, yet piecemeal, exposure to the critical discourse.

In contrast to both the BBC and *Telegraph*, the *Guardian* strongly doubted the potential of the inquiry to address the concerns of the broader reformist movement. Although the newspaper welcomed the inquiry, an editorial printed the day after the release of the interim report underlined the *Guardian's* reformist assumptions:

> There is no doubt that … dominance can hollow out town centres, diminish local shops and impose a dreary sameness across once very different towns. (*Guardian* 2007)

The author then highlighted the inherent weakness of the current inquiry and pressed for a different strategy:

> These are important matters that deserve to be weighed carefully against the lower prices. But the Competition Commission cannot do that balancing. A wider review is needed to resolve the doublethink. (ibid.)

This line was pursued in an opinion piece in the financial pages on the same day (Pratley 2007b). One might have expected a business journalist to focus on the financial prospects of the supermarket chains—sales growth, profits, share price, etc.—but after passing a quick judgement on the findings so far ('There was nothing here to frighten Tesco or any other supermarket') the author reminded readers that:

> … the main grumbles … concern damage to local communities, town centres and the environment; treatment of workers, … and animal welfare. (ibid.)

The most frustrating aspect of the inquiry, concluded Pratley, was that these issues lay outside the official remit, and although they *could* be addressed by a government-commissioned inquiry, he didn't believe this would occur:

> … any broader investigation of supermarket behaviour and power would have to be commissioned by government itself. Don't hold your breath. It would have happened by now. (ibid.)

Finally, in a third *Guardian* opinion piece, one of the most prolific critics of supermarkets, Felicity Lawrence, said the interim report was:

> …a case of Nelson's Eye… with the commission holding its telescope to the one that has partial vision. But if its vision is poor, it is because its statutory powers require it to wear blinkers. (Lawrence 2007)

Like the rest of the *Guardian's* 'opinionated' coverage in this crucial period, Lawrence took the view that the Competition Commission report was blind to the reformist concerns and inevitably this: 'will mean victory for excessive supermarket power' (ibid.). Indeed, there was considerable consistency across the *Guardian's* reporting which took a highly critical position, namely that the scope of the inquiry was too restricted, and hence, the negative consequences of the status quo would perpetuate. In contrast, the dominant discourse of the *Telegraph* was vociferously corporate. Despite frequent acknowledgement of the victims of supermarket power, the newspaper's columnists and senior journalists vigorously objected to threat of constraint on a successful grocery industry. The dominant discourse within the BBC sample, however, was harder to determine. In general, journalists adopted the detached language of the inquiry, and apart from occasionally reflecting the views of stakeholders, its reproduction of the corporate discourse was far less impassioned than the *Telegraph's*.

The Reproduction of the CSR Narrative

Outside the weeks in which the inquiry dominated the news agenda, however, the BBC's reporting followed the corporate line more closely than even the overtly pro-business *Telegraph*. This tendency was subtly expressed but a vivid illustration can be found in the coverage of CSR themes, particularly Tesco's announcement of several environmental initiatives on 18 January 2007 (Leahy 2007). The next day, three articles in the *Guardian* analysed the announcement, followed by a leader in the *Observer* on 21 January and an opinion piece in the *Guardian* two days later. The *Telegraph* covered Tesco's announcement in two standard news items, and it also featured in a *Sunday Telegraph* opinion piece. Although the announcement generated just one article on the BBC News website, the relative lack of quantity was far less significant than the language of the article.

The primary article in the *Guardian* covered the announcement in plain, factual terms (Finch and Vidal 2007). Tesco's initiative was 'significant', wrote the authors, but it was left to commentators to consider the implications. These included one corporate voice—Tesco chief executive, Terry Leahy—and three named representatives from stakeholder groups: the green think-tank Forum for the Future, FoE and Greenpeace. These spokespeople greeted the announcement with guarded enthusiasm, a position also adopted by an opinion piece in the *Guardian's* financial pages (Pratley 2007a). Here, the author hinted at mystery surrounding the company's precise motives: 'This does not appear to be a superficial exercise. Nor is it charity or even altruism', and he also observed that 'cynics' might link the timing with the impending release of the Competition Commission's report. Although Pratley was also sceptical about the arithmetic of the proposals, he concluded the public had to trust the architects: 'One assumes it will pay for itself, but the economics seem to have slotted into place with miraculous ease' (ibid.).

Similarly, as a committed environmentalist and long-standing supermarket critic, George Monbiot was both confused and amazed at the revolution that was apparently sweeping through the sector[24]:

> The superstores' green conversion is astonishing, wonderful, disorientating. If Tesco and Wal-Mart have become friends of the earth, are there any enemies left? (Monbiot 2007)

Previously, Monbiot had 'scorned the idea of corporate social responsibility' but he was now delighted that companies he still branded as

[24]In 2005, Wal-Mart made a commitment 'to use 100% renewable energy, create zero waste and cut greenhouse emissions by 2009' (Finch and Vidal 2007). Also, Marks and Spencer had pledged to become carbon neutral by 2012 (Monbiot 2007).

'the most arrogant of the behemoths' had finally succumbed to the arguments of the environmental lobby. But, like Pratley, he believed Tesco's 'bold' commitments were: 'weevilled with contradictions and evasions'. Most importantly, argued Monbiot, the only way to achieve true sustainability is to 'consume less', and this is fundamentally incompatible with a grocery market dominated by large suppliers. This assertion challenged one of the core assumptions of neoliberalism—the primacy of growth—and although the *Observer's* stance was noticeably less critical than that of its sister paper,[25] the dominant discourse in these traditionally 'left-wing' newspapers resonated with sceptical optimism.

Doubt over Tesco's environmentalism was also apparent in the *Telegraph*, but the reasoning was based on different principles. Like the *Guardian*, the item that reported the news was a functional summary of the main points of Leahy's speech but in this article, scepticism was limited to a single paraphrased and unattributed statement:

> Environmental campaigners who have criticised Tesco's green record, welcomed the announcement as a step in the right direction. (Derbyshire 2007c)

Using the Tesco announcement as a news hook, a second article focussed on the consumer and asked: 'How sinful is your shopping basket?' (Jardine 2007). An independent expert, Joanna Yarrow, reviewed the contents of the journalist's Tesco basket with 'disdain' and gave the supermarket a 'green rating' of just three out of ten. This tallied with a similar *Guardian* article on the same day which reported that Tesco had scored a 'D' in a National Consumer Council environmental report (Hickman 2007). The *Sunday Telegraph* business editor, Dan Roberts, categorised the environmental initiatives as peripheral to the supermarkets' primary goals (Roberts 2007). By focussing on their green credentials, wrote Roberts, Tesco et al. were distracted by 'window dressing' and, particularly with the Competition Commission report imminent, 'there is a real danger that the most powerful pro-market arguments are lost'.

[25] The *Observer* leader framed corporate environmentalism as good for business: 'It is a simple, clever idea, born of commercial logic… Tesco recognises the growing power of climate-conscious consumers and wants, quite reasonably, to profit from them' (*Observer* 2007).

These sentiments tallied with the *Telegraph's* dominant discourse around the key Competition Commission announcements (see above) and confirmed the newspapers' strong commitment to the corporate agenda.

In contrast to the newspapers' reporting, however, the single BBC article was an unquestioning reproduction of Tesco's announcement (BBC 2007d). Headed with a photograph of the company's chief executive, the article's title personalised the commitments—'Tesco boss unveils green pledges'—and a prominent pull-quote from Leahy could equally have been said by the head of Greenpeace: 'If we fail to mitigate climate change, the environmental, social and economic consequences will be stark and severe'. The only other source quoted in the BBC article was the head of the government-funded Carbon Trust, who unconditionally supported the initiative. Unlike the newspaper articles, the journalist expressed no scepticism, either in the narrative or by proxy through spokespeople from stakeholder groups. Nor was the announcement connected to the broader debates surrounding supermarket power nor, indeed, the imminent publication of the interim report.

This article was indicative of the BBC's reporting of Tesco's CSR initiatives in general. As noted in the quantitative analysis, the BBC gave far more exposure to the 'good works' of supermarkets than the newspapers and rarely did the narrative challenge the company's claims. For example, both the *Daily Telegraph* and the BBC covered Tesco's intention to build flats for staff in London (Fletcher 2007a; BBC 2007a). Whereas the *Telegraph* journalist limited his report to the bald facts and passed no judgement, the BBC article quoted the words of a Tesco spokeswoman who hoped the scheme would be:

> ..."beneficial for staff retention" in London, where (Tesco) suffer from a high turnover of workers..."It is being led in London because there is more need for affordable housing... the sites in London are more constrained so you need to be a lot more imaginative". (BBC 2007a)

Again, the BBC report contained no balancing perspective from, for example, a housing charity that might explain *why* there is such a dearth of affordable housing in London. Nor did the article consider the other side of the affordability equation and consult a trade union representative who might describe the extent and implications of poor pay in the capital, nor indeed did the journalist interview a Tesco staff member. Even though the actual number of homes available in the pilot project was negligible,[26] the article portrayed Tesco as an altruistic company that prioritises the welfare of its employees. Also in 2007, the BBC was the only publication to cover a new partnership with the Open University that would allow students to put Tesco loyalty card points towards the cost of their degrees (BBC 2007e). Like the housing article, the quantity and positivity of the words far outweighed the actual significance of the news[27] but this time, there was a dissenting voice, albeit quoted at the end of the article. Although the president of the National Union of Students was worried about: 'the extent to which consumerism is becoming integral to the student experience', she too agreed that the plan was 'well-intentioned' and she offered no direct criticism of Tesco.

The Reproduction of the Investor Narrative

Over the three years, the BBC also published other Tesco CSR announcements that were ignored by the newspapers.[28] The Corporation's reporting of such news was not totally devoid of criticism but typically, journalists reproduced Tesco's CSR narrative, and in sharp contrast to the *Guardian* and *Telegraph*, all BBC articles covering CSR initiatives were sympathetic. The sample periods conveniently coincided with the announcement of Tesco's annual results in 2006 and 2008, and this presented an ideal opportunity to compare the language used to interpret the same events across the three media. Although the differences between the BBC and the newspapers were less pronounced than around the Competition Commission announcements or when covering CSR, the BBC was again the least likely to deviate from Tesco's preferred discourse.

On 25 April 2006, the BBC published a standard news item that reported the details of Tesco's annual results (BBC 2006a) and a feature-length analysis of the company's overseas expansion (Stamp 2006). The former's headline described Tesco's record profit as 'bumper' and

[26] Tesco: 'allocated 13 of the 250 flats it is building …to staff.' This equates to 6% of the total (BBC 2007a).

[27] The article stated: 'To receive this £40 fees discount, students would need to have spent £1,000 in the store' (BBC 2007e).

[28] Such as 'All Tesco bags 'to be biodegradable'' (BBC 2006d) and 'Shares windfall for Tesco staff' (BBC 2007f).

although the opening paragraphs prioritised growth achievements[29] the fourth described a rather incongruent, detached and arguably insignificant CSR initiative: 'The retailer also said it would dedicate £100m to a new fund to invest in environmental technology' (BBC 2006a). Criticism was limited to an accusation, halfway into the piece, about Tesco's considerable 'land bank', which chief executive Terry Leahy dismissed ('There is no such thing…') and, at the foot of the article, a brief synopsis of the case for a competition inquiry.

Although Leahy's view was contrasted with that of an unnamed FoE representative, this final section of the article was sub-headed 'Not dominant' which, although speech marks were used, presented the null hypothesis as the strongest proposition. The BBC feature article (Stamp 2006) also included criticism of Tesco but again, the reader was not made aware of any arguments against constant growth until the middle of the article. Furthermore, there was no indication in the opening paragraphs that international expansion had a downside. Indeed, the journalist was evidently impressed as soon as he entered Tesco's headquarters' building:

> In the lobby of Tesco's head office, you can't help noticing a row of clocks telling the time in 12 different countries. Unlike for some businesses, this display of internationalism is no empty gesture. (ibid.)

Although the tone was upbeat—Tesco was 'stacking up sales' and 'expanding at full throttle'—the views of dissenters were present, and to an extent, both BBC articles in 2006 contained contrasting perspectives. But the lowly placement of reformist arguments; the use of the word 'critic' as a label for anonymous dissent; and, most importantly, the priority given to Tesco's financial achievements demonstrated the articles' adherence to the corporate narrative.

In contrast, the reformist discourse was much more evident in the *Guardian* articles in 2006. In a standard news item covering Tesco's results, for example, the Competition Commission inquiry featured in the standfirst: 'Rise and rise of Tesco: Chain rings up £2.2bn profit as inquiry looms: … Competition body to look at pricing and property' (Finch 2006). This latter fact was far more prominent than in the equivalent BBC article, and although the *Guardian* piece carried much of the same investor-focussed information, it devoted more space and gave

[29] 'Profits 17% higher', 'UK sales rising 10.7%' and 'foreign sales up 23%' (BBC 2006a).

greater credence to reformist concerns. Towards the end of the article, for instance, the journalist illustrated the trade-off between high profits and the plight of workers and suppliers:

> The group (Tesco) cut costs and held its margins - suggesting that suppliers were asked to cut their prices. The Transport and General Workers Union, which has more than 100,000 members working in farming, food processing and distribution, said Tesco's profits were in stark contrast with its suppliers'.[30]

Another *Guardian* journalist demonstrated the ability to construct business journalism with a social dimension in a feature article about Tesco's first store in China (Watts 2006). Unlike the author of the BBC feature about the company's overseas expansion, the reporter balanced the views of a Tesco executive and a stock market analyst with two stakeholders—a shop worker and a shopper—who might be affected by the arrival of a foreign company. The author also quoted supermarket wages in China—'usually less than £70 for a 160-hour month'—and in doing so, this article was a far more humanised representation of Tesco's activities than the equivalent piece in the BBC. In a third article on the same day, Neil Pratley suggested that the company's growth was impervious to public criticism:

> Tesco's shareholders need not worry yet. Acres of hostile coverage in the press and the arrival of the word Tescopoly into dinner party conversation seem to have had precisely zero effect on the group's financial performance. (Pratley 2006)

In quoting the title of the definitive book about Tesco's power and influence (Simms 2007), the author perhaps assumed that the issue was high in the *Guardian* reader's consciousness. Pratley also suggested that Tesco cannot be trusted: '(Tesco's) selective disclosure ... hints at the reason why it generates so much suspicion'. As noted above, it is somewhat unusual for a business journalist to take such a critical position.

[30]The article continued: 'Farming is on its knees and food processors are issuing repeated profit warnings as they struggle to meet the demands of the Tesco monopoly,' said Brian Revell, the T&G national organiser for food and agriculture (Finch 2006).

But again, this is indicative of the *Guardian's* consistent and, at times, strident, criticism of Tesco and large supermarkets.

Perhaps surprisingly, the *Telegraph's* primary news item about Tesco's 2006 annual results was an assault on the environmental initiatives that were announced alongside the financial data. The latter only appeared in the middle of the article and the first half elaborated on the provocative title: 'Tesco accused of going green to boost reputation' (Murray-West and Wallop 2006). The grounds for the attack was a statement from a spokesperson from FoE who said the relative insignificance of the initiatives amounted to 'greenwashing'. The article also included criticism from the Association of Convenience Stores and an environmental consultancy that had ranked Tesco bottom of five retailers in its ethical index, and overall, the chief executive's words were greatly overshadowed by the reformists'.

In the context of other *Telegraph* reporting around the announcement, however, this article was an aberration. In a comment piece, Henry Wallop framed Tesco's annual results as the latest checkpoint in an endless race: even though the company had posted record profits, the rate of increase was down, the 'shine was taken off', and other supermarkets were 'nipping at Tesco's heels' (Wallop 2006a). Although the author mentioned Leahy's insistence that the environmental initiative was not 'a PR stunt', reformist organisations and their arguments were totally excluded. Likewise, an anonymous comment piece in the City section (*Daily Telegraph* 2006) was wholly focused on the strategic genius of Tesco. It began:

> Tesco and its chief executive, Sir Terry Leahy, have had the monopoly on forward thinking in the supermarkets sector, at least over the past decade, which is why it has come to dominate.

Such was the praise for Leahy that the title suggested that he had the powers of a soothsayer ('Watch Terry Tesco, he knows how the wind's blowing'). The author also revealed a belief in the inherent virtue of the market: Tesco 'had the foresight to buy up land to give it a pipeline of sites that it can roll out' and although some small businesses and communities had suffered from the company's growth, this was simply an inevitable consequence of Darwinian capitalism: 'The chain has admittedly been the death knell for many local shops but a large number of these offered poor choices at high prices' (ibid.). As for Leahy's 'greening' of Tesco, the author dismissed the charge, made in the leading article[31] that this was 'a vacuous political statement to buy off the "green lobby"' and explained that it was just another part of the corporate strategy (emphases added:) '...simply the latest *investment*, and there will be more to come, in what in Terry Tesco's judgment will be *the next big thing* for supermarkets' (*Daily Telegraph* 2006).

In these terms, environmentalism is good for business because it will become fashionable and Tesco, under Leahy's guidance, is the trend-setter. Whatever a financially successful company does, according to the *Telegraph's* dominant discourse, is self-evidently honourable. Indeed, three days later, the newspaper's *Questor* column placed a 'buy' notice on Tesco shares (Wallop 2006b). The author described 'suspicion' of Tesco as: 'one of the great mysteries of modern life' and wondered how '15 million shoppers every week' could represent anything other than unequivocal endorsement. Before justifying the share tip, the author reminded readers of the controversy surrounding the company and trumped it with a pithy synopsis of Tesco's positive impact on society:

> If you read some reports you might believe that Tesco is responsible for all of society's ills, rather than the largest private-sector employer, creating significant amounts of wealth. (ibid.)

These sentiments echoed an opinion piece in the *Sunday Telegraph* (Stevenson 2006) which first acknowledged the opposition to Tesco's activities and then promptly suggested that the criticisms were overblown (emphasis added):

> No one would claim Tesco is an unqualified force for good. Allegations that it is destroying town centres and squeezing suppliers out of existence have gained widespread credence because there is a *grain of truth* in them.

Like *Questor*, the author posited that such accusations were nothing more than 'paranoia (that) says as much about us, and our distrust of success, as it does about the company itself', and therefore, any restriction on Tesco's natural trajectory was unjustified and abhorrent (emphasis added): '(The) Competition Commission should think carefully before pursuing a *vendetta*'. The *Telegraph's* discourse around

[31] Murray-West and Wallop (2006).

the 2006 annual results revolved around the belief that corporate success must not be punished, and this tallied strongly with the editorial line during the key dates for the inquiry (see above). There was also consistency in the *Guardian's* focus on the reformist agenda and its purposeful representation of the views of individuals and other stakeholders. The BBC, however, gave only minimal credence to the reformist discourse and tended to follow Tesco's corporate narrative most enthusiastically.

This reporting pattern was also evident in a BBC article that covered the announcement of Tesco's results in 2008. The text incorporated a hyperlink to a four-minute audio interview with Terry Leahy (BBC 2008e) that focussed entirely on Tesco's ability to maintain growth in difficult financial times. Neither the grocery market inquiry nor any of the concerns of the reformists were put to Leahy by the journalist. Similarly, although the audio piece and the article (BBC 2008d) were published two weeks before the final Competition Commission report, the latter made the barest reference to the inquiry: Tesco 'said it was continuing to work with the Competition Commission on the final stages of their investigation'. Instead, the article dissected the company's 'sparkling results' that had 'confounded analysts… whom had predicted that the wheels had started to wobble on the Tesco juggernaut' (ibid.).

The newspapers also showed demonstrably less interest in Tesco's financial performance in 2008 than two years earlier. The single *Guardian* article that covered the news (Finch 2008) led with details of an environmental announcement that accompanied the key data ('Tesco labels will show products' carbon footprints') and the first half of the article was a faithful reproduction of Tesco's CSR message. No sceptical source countered Leahy's promises to create: 'a revolution in green consumption' and 'bring the environmental movement into the mass market' and overall, the article reproduced both elements of the corporate discourse, CSR and investor, and excluded the reformist.

The *Telegraph's* coverage of the 2008 annual results focussed on the debate between unnamed 'critics' of the performance of Tesco's US operations, and Terry Leahy who: 'rubbished reports that Fresh & Easy … is struggling' (Hall 2008). The chief executive was presented as a strong leader who 'hit back' at the sceptics and put up a 'staunch defence of the chain'. No other source was cited in the article, and no reference was made to the Competition Commission inquiry nor the reformist arguments. It is fitting that the second *Telegraph* article in 2008 was another 'buy' notice from *Questor* (Essen 2008). Two years previously, the column had tipped Tesco (see above) and this time, the author was unequivocal in her assessment of the company's prospects: 'We think that the shares are worth buying'. This statement implied that the Competition Commission and the reformist arguments had been dealt with and no longer represented serious menace. Indeed, these parties were so insignificant that neither were mentioned, and the most pertinent issues, according to the author, were a 'perceived slowdown' in Tesco's domestic sales growth and unspecified 'problems' with its US operations (Essen 2008).

Overall, the *Telegraph's* coverage of Tesco's 2008 results resonated with a sense of business as usual. The Competition Commission and the arguments of the reformists were now irrelevant, and these perceived threats to Tesco's growth, which had generated such strong opinion from the newspapers two years earlier, had dissipated. Similarly, by reproducing the dual corporate narratives, the *Guardian* article seemed to accept Tesco's position, as both a successful commercial enterprise and a responsible corporate citizen. Indeed, unlike in 2006 when the views of reformists and the Competition Commission featured in all three articles, the *Guardian* in 2008 followed the corporate lead. Likewise, in 2008 the BBC's reporting of Tesco's record results focussed entirely on the company's future. The impending Competition Commission final report was a mere side-note, and the arguments of the reformists were totally excluded from the debate which now centred squarely on Tesco's ability to further enhance its profits.

Summary

With some 40% of the 294 articles in the refined sample placing Tesco in the context of reformist arguments, one might presume that concerns about supermarket power received significant and detailed coverage. This is true to an extent, but it is important to note five points about the extent and nature of the mediated debate. Firstly, the most vibrant and detailed discussions were clustered around the three key dates, and at other times, the coverage of Tesco was largely bereft of opposing viewpoints. Indeed, outside of the weeks immediately surrounding the Competition Commission announcements, reporting clearly favoured the status quo with the investor and CSR narratives far outweighing the reformist arguments. This was evident in all three media and suggests that the normal pattern of reporting tends towards the corporate position.

Secondly, three of the five reformist narratives—supply chain, employment and political influence—were virtually excluded from the debate and only two—local communities and the environment, and competition and consumers—were given regular exposure. Thirdly, corporate voices were dominant and accounted for between 40 and 60% of all sources in each of the nine data sets. In contrast, spokespeople from stakeholder organisations never accounted for more than 18% of sources in a data set and were outnumbered by business representatives by a factor of at least three-to-one. Fourthly, although one might expect the BBC to have the most balanced sourcing profile, it clearly gave preference to corporate spokespeople, and in this respect, it was very similar to the *Telegraph*, and only in the *Guardian* were non-corporate sources in the majority. This pattern was mirrored in the coverage given to the competing narratives: The *Guardian* largely gave the greatest exposure and credence to reformist arguments while the BBC and the *Telegraph* generally favoured the corporate position.

Finally, it is also important to stress that the refined sample represents just 37% of the articles that were picked up by the original search. As noted, Tesco was mentioned in each of the remaining 495 articles and, although these citations were devoid of overt support for the corporate or reformist positions, their apparent neutrality confirmed that Britain's most powerful supermarket has an indelible, far-reaching and immeasurable cultural presence.

References

Aslet, C. (2007, January 24). Sainsbury's Is Too Clever for My Own Good. *Daily Telegraph*.

Bakan, J. (2004). *The Corporation: The Pathological Pursuit of Profit and Power*. Toronto: Viking Canada.

BBC. (2006a, April 25). *Tesco Has Bumper £2.25bn Profit*. BBC News Website. Retrieved from http://news.bbc.co.uk/1/hi/business/4941236.stm. Accessed March 1, 2012.

BBC. (2006b, April 24). *Vote in Favour of New Tesco Store*. BBC News Website. Retrieved from http://news.bbc.co.uk/1/hi/scotland/south_of_scotland/4939772.stm. Accessed March 4, 2012.

BBC. (2006c, May 9). *Supermarkets in Competition Probe*. BBC News Website. Retrieved from http://news.bbc.co.uk/1/hi/business/4753707.stm. Accessed July 12, 2012.

BBC. (2006d, May 10). *All Tesco Bags to be 'Biodegradable'*. BBC News Website. Retrieved from http://news.bbc.co.uk/1/hi/uk/4758419.stm. Accessed July 21, 2012.

BBC. (2007a, January 15). *Tesco to Build Homes for Workers*. BBC News Website. Retrieved from http://news.bbc.co.uk/1/hi/england/london/6264059.stm. Accessed March 4, 2012.

BBC. (2007b, January 22). *UK Grocers Face Competition Probe*. BBC News Website. Retrieved from http://news.bbc.co.uk/1/hi/business/6287923.stm. Accessed July 16, 2012.

BBC. (2007c, January 23). *Grocery Probe Eyes Local Market*. BBC News Website. Retrieved from http://news.bbc.co.uk/1/hi/business/6289479.stm. Accessed July 16, 2012.

BBC. (2007d, January 18). *Tesco Boss Unveils Green Pledges*. BBC News Website. Retrieved from http://news.bbc.co.uk/1/hi/business/6276351.stm. Accessed July 12, 2012.

BBC. (2007e, February 6). *Tesco to Offer 'Clubcard Degrees'*. BBC News Website. Retrieved from http://news.bbc.co.uk/1/hi/education/6335399.stm. Accessed July 21, 2012.

BBC. (2007f, February 9). *Shares Windfall for Tesco Staff*. BBC News Website. Retrieved from http://news.bbc.co.uk/1/hi/business/6345137.stm. Accessed July 21, 2012.

BBC. (2008a, April 30). *Grocery Inquiry: Success or Failure?* BBC News Website. Retrieved from http://news.bbc.co.uk/1/hi/business/7374952.stm. Accessed July 2, 2012.

BBC. (2008b, April 25). *Retailers in Tobacco Price Probe*. BBC News Website. Retrieved from http://news.bbc.co.uk/1/hi/business/7366348.stm. Accessed July 16, 2012.

BBC. (2008c, April 28). *OFT in New Supermarket Crackdown*. BBC News Website. Retrieved from http://news.bbc.co.uk/1/hi/business/7369838.stm. Accessed July 16, 2012.

BBC. (2008d, April 15). *Tesco Sees Profit Rise to £2.8bn*. BBC News Website. Retrieved from http://news.bbc.co.uk/1/hi/business/7347769.stm. Accessed July 21, 2012.

BBC. (2008e, April 15). *Tesco Announce £2.8bn Profits*. BBC News Website. Retrieved from http://news.bbc.co.uk/1/hi/business/7349285.stm. Accessed July 21, 2012.

Bevan, J. (2005). *Trolley Wars: The Battle of the Supermarkets*. London: Profile Books.

Blythman, J. (2007). *Shopped: The Shocking Power of British Supermarkets*. London: Fourth Estate.

Bowers, S. (2007, January 24). Smaller Players Struggle to Beat Aggressive Pricing. *The Guardian*.

Competition Commission. (2008, April 30). *Groceries Market Investigation: Final Report.* Retrieved from www.competition-commission.org.uk/rep_pub/reports/2008/538grocery.htm. Accessed May 10, 2010.

Consumer Association. (2010, February). Supermarkets—Are You Left Satisfied? *Which? Magazine.* Retrieved from http://www.which.co.uk/your-account/which-magazine-archive/february-2010/. Accessed November 18, 2011.

Daily Telegraph. (2006, April 26). Watch Terry Tesco, He Knows How the Wind's Blowing. *Daily Telegraph.*

Derbyshire, D. (2007a, January 20). Rainbow Coalition Out to Save the High Street. *Daily Telegraph.*

Derbyshire, D. (2007b, January 24). Bicester, the Town That Has Been Tesco'd Six Times Over. *Daily Telegraph.*

Derbyshire, D. (2007c, January 19). Carbon 'Footprints' and More Wind Turbines at Tesco Stores. *Daily Telegraph.*

Essen, Y. (2008, April 16). It's Worth Adding Upbeat Retail Giant to Your Shopping Basket. *Daily Telegraph.*

Finch, J. (2006, April 26). Rise and Rise of Tesco: Chain Rings up 2.2bn Profit. *The Guardian.*

Finch, J. (2008, April 16). Tesco Labels Will Show Products' Carbon Footprints. *The Guardian.*

Finch, J., & Vidal, J. (2007, January 19). You've Checked the Price and Calorie Count, Now Here's the Carbon Cost. *The Guardian.*

Fishman, C. (2007). *The Wal-Mart Effect: How an Out-of-Town Superstore Became a Superpower.* New York: Penguin.

Fletcher, R. (2007a, January 24). Commission's Supermarkets Probe Goes Local. *Daily Telegraph.*

Fletcher, R. (2007b, January 24). It Is Tricky Ensuring Healthy Competition Is Not Stifled. *Daily Telegraph.*

Fletcher, R. (2007c, January 29). The Fate of Supermarket Giants Lies in His Hands. *Daily Telegraph.*

Friends of the Earth (FoE). (2003, February). *Briefing: Super Markets or Corporate Bullies?* Retrieved from http://www.foe.co.uk/resource/briefings/super_markets_corporate_bullies.pdf. Accessed November 18, 2011.

Friends of the Earth (FoE). (2005, June). *Briefing: The Tesco Takeover.* Retrieved from http://www.foe.co.uk/resource/briefings/the_tesco_takeover.pdf. Accessed March 17, 2012.

Foxwell, A. (2008, May 12). Tesco Brand Is UK's 'Most Valuable'. *Daily Telegraph.*

Guardian. (2006, May 10). Supermarkets Face Competition Inquiry. *The Guardian.*

Guardian. (2007, January 24). Supermarkets: Wanting it Both Ways. *The Guardian.*

Hall, J. (2008, April 16). Sir Terry Defends Tesco's US Stores. *Daily Telegraph.*

Hall, J. (2011, June 9). Tesco "Not Too Big" Says Clarke. *Daily Telegraph.*

Hall, J., & Watts, R. (2006, May 14). To Check out the Big Four. Supermarkets Face a Backlash. *Sunday Telegraph.*

Hemscott. (2011). *Share Price of Tesco Compared to FTSE-100 and Food Retailers, 2002 to 2008.* Retrieved from http://www.hemscott.com/companies/company-chart.do?companyId=622&from=2/1/2002&to=1/5/2008&returnPeriod=5&comparisons=100@IT,63@GRP. Accessed November 18, 2011.

Hertz, N. (2001). *The Silent Takeover: Global Capitalism and the Death of Democracy.* London: William Heineman.

Hickman, L. (2007, January 19). Green Grocers? How Supermarkets Measure Up. *The Guardian.*

Holden, C. (2007, January 25). Shopping Around. Letter to the Editor. *Daily Telegraph.*

Humby, C., Hunt, T., & Phillips, T. (2008). *Scoring Points: How Tesco Continues to Win Customer Loyalty.* London: Kogan Page.

Jardine, C. (2007, January 19). How Sinful Is Your Shopping Basket? *Daily Telegraph.*

Klein, N. (2000). *No Logo.* London: Flamingo.

Lawrence, F. (2007, January 25). The Supermarket Inquiry Is Blind to the Real Issues. *The Guardian.*

Leahy, T. (2007, January 18). *Tesco, Carbon and the Consumer.* Speech. Retrieved from http://www.tescoplc.com/index.asp?pageid=17&newsid=356. Accessed July 20, 2012.

Mathiason, N. (2005, November 6). Foes Home in on Tesco. *The Observer.*

Monbiot, G. (2001). *Captive State: The Corporate Takeover of Britain.* London: Pan Books.

Monbiot, G. (2007, January 23). If Tesco and Wal-Mart Are Friends of the Earth, Are There Any Enemies Left. *The Guardian.*

Murray-West, R. (2006, May 10). Supermarket Inquiry Could Force the Big Companies to Sell Stores. *Daily Telegraph.*

Murray-West, R. (2007, January 23). Competition Inquiry Could Force a Giant Supermarket Land Sale. *Daily Telegraph.*

Murray-West, R., & Wallop, H. (2006, April 26). Tesco Accused of Going Green to Boost Reputation. *Daily Telegraph.*

New Economics Foundation (NEF). (2003, December 15). *Ghost Town Britain II: Death on the High Street.* Retrieved from http://www.neweconomics.org/sites/neweconomics.org/files/Ghost_Town_Britain_II.pdf. Accessed November 18, 2011.

Observer. (2007, January 21). The Future Is the Low Carbon-Emission Politician. Leader.

Pilger, J. (2002). *The New Rulers of the World.* London: Verso.

Pratley, N. (2006, April 26). Property Could Trip up Tesco. *The Guardian.*

Pratley, N. (2007a, January 19). Viewpoint: Going Green Is Not Without Cost. *The Guardian.*

Pratley, N. (2007b, January 24). Viewpoint: We Are Rolling in the Aisles of Our Choice. *The Guardian*.
Quinn, B. (2000). *How Wal-Mart Is Destroying America (and the World)*. Berkeley, CA: Ten Speed Press.
Reece, D. (2006, May 10). Big Stores' Opponents Should Be Careful What They Wish For. *Daily Telegraph*.
Roberts, N. (2007, January 21). Supermarket Sweep. *Sunday Telegraph*.
Seth, A., & Randall, G. (2005). *Supermarket Wars: Global Strategies for Food Retailers*. London: Palgrave Macmillan.
Seth, A., & Randall, G. (2011). *The Grocers: The Rise and Rise of Supermarket Chains*. London: Kogan Page.
Simms, A. (2007). *Tescopoly: How One Shop Came Out on Top and Why It Matters*. London: Constable.
Spotts, G., & Greenwald, R. (2006). *Wal-Mart: The High Cost of Low Price*. New York: Disinformation Company.
Stamp, G. (2006, April 25). *Foreign Growth Key to Tesco Goals*. BBC News Website. Retrieved from http://news.bbc.co.uk/1/hi/business/4781458.stm. Accessed July 21, 2012.
Stevenson, T. (2006, May 2). Galbraith's Concerns Over Power of Big Firms Still Valid. *Sunday Telegraph*.
Sunday Telegraph. (2008, May 4). Tesco, BP and Lloyds TSB Head Telegraph 20.
Tescopoly. (2012). Retrieved from www.tescopoly.org. Accessed July 21, 2012.
Tooher, P., & Laurance, B. (2005, February 13). Giants That Must Be Curbed. *Mail on Sunday*.
Wallop, H. (2006a, April 26). Rivals Nipping at Tesco's Heels. *Daily Telegraph*.
Wallop, H. (2006b, April 29). Why You Should Stop Worrying and Learn to Love Tesco Shares. *Daily Telegraph*.
Walsh, F. (2006, May 10). Supermarkets Face Third Inquiry in Seven Years. *The Guardian*.
Watts, J. (2006, April 26). Tesco … Every Little Frog Helps. *The Guardian*.
Wood, Z. (2008, April 20). Waitrose Pans Tesco Town Rule. *The Observer*.
Wood, Z. (2011, February 25). How Tesco Chief Sir Terry Leahy Changed the Way Britain Shops. *The Guardian*. Retrieved from http://www.guardian.co.uk/business/2011/feb/25/tesco-sir-terry-leahy-retires. Accessed November 18, 2011.

CHAPTER 6

Summary and Discussion

Introduction

Although this book focusses on events that occurred in the 1990s and 2000s, it is extremely relevant to understanding the contemporary British news media. Indeed, the main findings tally with much of the pre- and post-2008 Financial Crisis research in this sphere. In terms of sourcing patterns, for example, journalists habitually gravitate to members of the political and business elite. This implies a deep-seated modus operandi among practitioners which spans the mainstream news media. Irrespective of the political position of the publication, journalists tend to give only limited exposure and credence to interpretations from beyond the 'consensus'. This deficit of perspectives has been noted in previous studies, but as a highly detailed comparative analysis across multiple news providers, this book makes a significant contribution to debates about the news media's propensity to ignore, criticise or demonise some political interpretations. The failure by journalists, therefore, to adequately interrogate the root cause of the Crisis—the Credit Boom of the 2000s—should not have been a surprise: the episode may have been exceptional, but the reporting patterns were predictable.

G. J. Merrill, *The Political Content of British Economic, Business and Financial Journalism*, https://doi.org/10.1007/978-3-030-04012-3_6

A Deficit of Perspectives

Despite the manifest differences in political content in the four organisations' news product, it is important to first stress the similarities that were revealed. Collectively, the case studies suggest that the British news media has generally converged around a set of common assumptions that determine which EBF issues reach the agenda, how the news is reported, and which interpretations are awarded exposure.

In each of the three case studies, there were pronounced spikes in coverage around the key event, after which the issue slipped off the news agenda. This was particularly apparent with economic globalisation and private finance which presented editors with the compelling news value of vigorous exchanges between well-defined combatants in a specific place. In comparison, the supermarket debate was rather amorphous and muted, and did not have a physical location to compare with the streets of Seattle or the Labour Party Conference, nor were the opposing parties so clearly defined. Even so, the three news providers gave the greatest and most detailed attention to supermarket power around the time of the Competition Commission announcements.

Similarly, the media tended to frame economic globalisation, private finance and Tesco as either political or business issues, and only on relatively few occasions were they given a human angle. Global trade, for example, was frequently framed in abstract terms and its impact on workers, the environment and consumers were rarely considered. Similarly, private finance was primarily conceived as a battle of wills between two wings of the Labour movement rather than a debate that had considerable implications for all British citizens. Again, the supermarket case study was an exception to a point, in that many articles adopted themes sympathetic to stakeholders, but the tendency to place the activities of Tesco in a commercial context remained.

The propensity to favour elite interests was reflected in sourcing patterns. In each case study, greatest access was awarded to spokespeople from mainstream political organisations, including regulators and lobbying groups, and large companies. Indeed, the implied definition of 'business' generally equated to multinational corporations and the financial services sector, and small enterprises, family firms and the self-employed were excluded. Workers were rarely quoted either, and trade union leaders only made frequent appearances in the private finance case study around the time of the Labour Party Conference. A particularly striking finding, however, was the near-invisibility of independent experts: academics, research organisations and economists were absent from the vast majority of articles. Voices from stakeholder organisations, such as NGOs, social movements and community groups, had greater presence but they were outnumbered by the political-corporate duet. Citizens were also largely excluded from the mediated debates. This was particularly apparent in the private finance case study in which front-line staff (doctors, nurses, teachers, etc.), the users of public services (patients, parents, etc.), taxpayers and citizens were rarely consulted.

With such a disparity in access, it was inevitable that the news media gave only sporadic exposure to ideas that challenged neoliberalism. Arguments for reform of the World Trade Organisation (WTO) *were* present in the globalisation case study, as were those of the sceptics in private finance, and the various strands of dissonance in the supermarket debate. However, the more radical viewpoints were given no sustained coverage or credence. Indeed, the news organisations were united in their definition of the limits of debate: economic globalisation was a contest between the rich world elite who supported 'free trade' and those calling for progressive reform of the WTO, but the views of the developing world and groups campaigning for a fundamental rethink were omitted. Similarly, instead of airing arguments for the maintenance of the traditional public sector funding model, journalists focussed on the often-heated exchanges between Tony Blair's 'modernising' government and trade union leaders who formed the vanguard of opposition to the Private Finance Initiative (PFI).

The supermarket debate was somewhat more complex but again it was simplified, as a contest between the advocates of the status quo, and consumers and, to a lesser extent, local communities, but not workers, suppliers or those concerned about supermarkets' political influence. Crucially, the quantitative analyses demonstrated that although issues *were* contested around the key events, reporting over the rest of the sample periods tended to be constructed in non-problematic terms. Hence, despite sometimes-spirited debate, all news organisations normalised three tenets of neoliberalism: the WTO's vision of globalisation; private finance in public services; and oligopolies led by dominant companies.

Political Divergence

The critical discourse analyses added detail and colour to patterns uncovered by the quantitative data. In particular, they emphasised differences in the political constitution of the news. Across all three case studies, the *Guardian-Observer* most consistently gave exposure to ideas from the left, and this tendency was confirmed in its journalistic narratives. Editorials, opinion columns and, in some cases, standard news items were often consistent with the arguments of the moderate WTO critics; these newspapers described the effects of globalisation in human terms and expressed sympathy for the treatment of protestors by riot police. Similarly, the *Guardian-Observer* took a sceptical line on private finance, it was critical of the underpinning political philosophy and sometimes argued its case in emotive language. In the context of supermarket power, these newspapers often framed the debate in broad, social terms, they were dubious about corporate social responsibility (CSR) and, unlike the other publications, there were hints of compassion even in its business reporting. It must be noted, however, that dissident narratives coexisted with considerable amounts of news constructed in plain, descriptive language which did little to challenge the status quo.

The *Guardian-Observer* exhibited few signs of radicalism and yet it tended to challenge elements of neoliberalism in a way that was rarely evident in the *Times-Sunday Times* and the *Telegraphs*. Indeed, the political positions of these organisations were unequivocally on the right and this was most apparent in editorials and opinion pieces that adopted an axiomatic, free market discourse. In the context of economic globalisation, *Times-Sunday Times* journalists were intolerant of dissent and were scathing in their descriptions of protestors. Conversely, 'free trade' was conceived as self-evidently virtuous and inevitable. The *Telegraphs* took similar positions in the other two case studies, although their preferred discourse was somewhat less damning of the opposition. These newspapers subtly pressed for greater private sector involvement in public services, and in the supermarket debate, journalists were overtly antagonistic to regulation. Restrictions on commercial activities were anathema for the *Telegraphs*, and by promoting *laissez-faire* as the only viable principle, the newspapers reproduced a Darwinian form of the corporate narrative.

Contrary to a widely held belief that the BBC favours left-wing interpretations, this study places the Corporation on the right of the spectrum. Reporting across the three case studies tended to follow the discourse of the political and business elite and overall, BBC journalistic narratives had more in common with the newspapers of the right than the *Guardian-Observer*. These tendencies were evident in the descriptions of protestors in Seattle and the belittling of their arguments by senior BBC journalists. In the case of private finance, BBC journalists reproduced the New Labour discourse: Tony Blair's dogged determination and his rhetorical skills were admired; trade union leaders were portrayed as defenders of outdated beliefs; and, despite Party policy being rejected in a Conference vote, the marketisation of the public sector was presented as a virtuous *fait accompli*. In the supermarket debate, the BBC, like the *Telegraph*, generally gave preference to the investor narrative. But, whereas the *Telegraph* saw CSR as a distraction, the BBC framed Tesco as a responsible corporate citizen. The tenor of the BBC's coverage may have lacked the conviction of the *Telegraph's*, but its journalists followed both elements of the corporate line more faithfully.

The Debates Continue

By virtue of its timing and broad subject matter, this book will inevitably be slotted alongside works focussed on the 2008 Financial Crisis. In one respect, this would be misguided because the intention was not to explore the same specific episode. Furthermore, by concentrating on a unique and relatively recent event, such tightly focussed studies are rather parochial and ignore the history and indelible characteristics of EBF news. Nevertheless, this study *does* contribute to this sub-corpus because it confirms that mainstream British journalism tends to follow elite agenda.

As illustrated in Chapter 1, the inadequacies of journalism in the prelude to the Crisis were the logical result of a production process that, despite leaps in technology, has remained largely unchanged for decades. The failure by journalists, therefore, to adequately interrogate the root cause of the Crisis—the Credit Boom of the 2000s—should not have been a surprise: the episode may have been exceptional, but the reporting patterns were predictable. Hence, this study can be placed with critical post-Crisis works that have revealed a tendency to produce news that favours elite interests, particularly investors (Butterick 2015; Shaw 2016; Berry 2016; Knowles et al. 2017).

This propensity was underlined in Dean Starkman's 2014 study of the American news media's role in the Financial Crisis. Like Damian Tambini in the UK (2010), Starkman also asked a question that is absent from much post-2008 work, namely whether EBF journalists have a watchdog role that would benefit citizens rather than investors. The three case studies uncovered little evidence of this type of journalism. Assuming there are multiple interpretations of economic and business issues, for the news media to perform its Fourth Estate duties and sufficiently equip the citizenry with the information needed to make political decisions, journalists need to give exposure to a wide range of perspectives. In much the same way that Mike Berry (2012) found alternatives to the 'banking bailout' were rarely discussed on BBC Radio 4s *Today* programme, this study reveals that none of the four news media organisations awarded *sustained* coverage to dissenting interpretations. Thus, it can also be situated alongside other British and international research that has highlighted the marginalisation of arguments that challenge the 'consensus' as defined by the political and corporate elite.

The definition of the 'consensus' is vital for understanding reporting patterns. According to Berry, the news media reflects 'shades of opinion at Westminster' rather than across the broader civil society (ibid.: 267–268). Political views close to this point are awarded exposure and significance, but those on the periphery are considered in a zone of deviance and are thus are unworthy of impartial coverage. Hence, the protestors at Seattle, the trade union leaders at the Labour Party Conference, and supermarket workers and suppliers were promoting ideas so detached from the political-corporate 'consensus' that they did not merit fair treatment. Consequently, an air of inevitably was evident across the case studies: globalisation, for example, was presented in numerous contexts, from war to motorsport, and on the few occasions it had an economic context, it was invariably conflated with neoliberalism and, moreover, presented as a mystical force which was 'stalking the land' (Travers 1999).

Similarly, despite widespread public opposition and the Conference defeat, PFI was positioned as the rational next step in Tony Blair's 'modernisation' of Britain. A grocery market dominated by a handful of large companies was also conceived as natural and benign. Tesco was mentioned in passing in 40% of the universal sample of 789 articles which reflected its unproblematic omnipresence in British society. Furthermore, the company's political influence was never questioned, and outside the periods around the Competition Commission announcements,

Tesco was rarely criticised. Hence, neoliberalism was normalised by the news media. For this reason, the empirical elements of this book complement a largely theoretical body of work that has noted the reification of the market and the portrayal of neoliberalism's inevitable supremacy.

Perhaps the most logical categorisation for this book, however, is alongside the landmark content studies of the Glasgow University Media Group (GUMG) from the 1970s to the 1980s. Indeed, this study was partly inspired by these works and employs similar methods, and by focussing on relatively recent issues, it goes some way towards reinvigorating the British critical tradition. The findings relating to the representation of dissenting perspectives are consistent with these earlier studies, and it is important to note that four decades after the GUMG's first work was published, the mainstream news media appears to have no greater inclination to reflect the views of those who challenge elite interpretations. For the GUMG, the dissenting voices belonged to trade unions and workers, whereas this study identified a wider range of stakeholder organisations that offered competing visions.

In addition, the globalisation case study, and to a lesser extent private finance, revealed evidence of the delegitimisation of dissent through negative representations of groups and individuals. The *Times-Sunday Times'* disparaging descriptions of protestors in Seattle, for example, and the BBC's portrayal of trade union leaders as trouble-makers diverted attention from their arguments. Elite actors and groups, however, were not criticised in the same manner. Such representations also echo notable studies of the British news media's portrayal of left-wing politicians. Although the mediated globalisation and private finance debates were rarely personalised, the collective radical voice was frequently placed in a similar frame as the 'loony left' of the Labour Party in the 1980s, and more recently, the 'hard left' leadership of Jeremy Corbyn (Curran et al. 2018; Schlosberg 2016; Couldry and Cammaerts 2016).

This book also contributes to debates about the BBC. Because the Corporation has a statutory obligation to impartiality, it arguably presents the greatest hope for improving public knowledge of economics, business and finance and alternative thinking in these areas. The empirical chapters, however, suggest that the BBC is falling short of such normative expectations. It is important here to highlight the BBC's own understanding of impartiality. This is central to its public service remit and it is useful to quote two subsections of the most recent Editorial Guidelines in detail (emphases added):

> **Breadth and Diversity of Opinion**
> Across our output as a whole, we must be *inclusive*, reflecting a breadth and diversity of opinion. We must be fair and open-minded when examining the evidence and weighing material facts. We must give *due weight to the many and diverse areas of an argument.*
> ...
>
> **Due Weight**
> Impartiality does not necessarily require the range of perspectives or opinions to be covered in equal proportions either across our output as a whole, or within a single programme, web page or item. Instead, we should seek to achieve 'due weight'. *For example, minority views should not necessarily be given equal weight to the prevailing consensus.*
> Nevertheless, *the omission of an important perspective, in a particular context, may jeopardise perceptions of the BBC's impartiality....* (BBC 2018)

When the findings of the three case studies are synthesised, the extent to which the BBC effectively reflected a 'breadth and diversity of opinion' is debatable. Furthermore, what constitutes 'due weight' is clearly a subjective assessment. As noted above, the political content of the BBC's EBF reporting has more in common with the newspapers of the right than the centre-left *Guardian-Observer*. This is significant when one considers that public opinion evidently spans the political spectrum.

Despite the widespread acceptance of neoliberalism by the elite, a range of belief still exists among the citizenry. For example, a survey conducted at the height of the private finance debate found that 63% of respondents supported the trade unions' call for a review of PFI (Travis and Maguire 2002). Furthermore, one year after the Financial Crisis, scepticism about neoliberalism was a global phenomenon: a survey of 29,000 people in 27 countries revealed widespread disenchantment. In just two countries did more than one-fifth of people think capitalism was working well and a higher proportion considered it 'fatally flawed' (BBC World Service 2009). These are clearly not 'minority views' and hence, one might expect the BBC to award them the appropriate level of exposure and credence.

As noted in Chapter 2, this book was partly inspired by Alan Budd's report on the impartiality of the BBC's business journalism (2007). Budd's comprehensive mixed-method study was illuminating, but the lines of inquiry did not extend beyond the Corporation.

In some respects, this study is the logical extension of Budd's work because it compares the BBC's journalistic output with that of news organisations that are overtly political, thus giving benchmarks of what constitutes left- and right-wing interpretations. This brings the focus back to the definition of the 'consensus', and the findings of this book resonate with Phillip Schlesinger's classic work in which he noted discordance between the BBC's output which is generally 'supportive of the existing order' and the Corporation's operating principles which claim that it has 'no place in the political spectrum' (1978: 167). The BBC is a vital component in British power structures and its journalists are adept at consistently producing news that adheres to the agenda of the elite which inevitably: 'uphold the established society' (Hetherington 1985: 41). Four decades after Schlesinger's study, Tom Mills (2016) arrived at a similar conclusion, and this book adds further supporting evidence to arguments that the BBC's journalism reproduces and reinforces the views of political and business elite.

Towards a More Critical EBF Journalism

Although this study contributes to knowledge about EBF journalism, its empirical foundations are restricted to three case studies and four news organisations. Furthermore, despite the multiple sampling points over a ten-year period, it is temporally limited. To address questions about representativeness, therefore, a similar methodological approach could be applied to other issues and publications, and hence, a more complete picture of the nature of EBF journalism would emerge.

Future studies could look at the coverage of post-Crisis economic issues such as austerity; the impact of immigration; the representation of a new generation of protest groups, like Occupy Wall Street, and income and wealth inequality. Similarly, analysis could be extended to mid-market and 'red top' newspapers which have far larger readerships than the broadsheets analysed in this study and online news organisations. The BBC also offers opportunities for more research. Its news website was chosen for this study partly because it provides easy access and, as a text-based medium, its content is comparable with newspapers. But the Corporation's broadcast output has arguably greater impact, and so the analysis of prime-time TV news coverage of economics and business would be illuminating, particularly when compared with other broadcasters.

Research about the contribution of the alternative news media to public debate would also be useful. Some British magazines and websites take a critical perspective of economics and business and do not follow the mainstream news agenda. Consequently, they have the ability to be prophetic. *Private Eye*, for example, revealed the inadequacies of private finance in British public services way before the mainstream media took an interest, and the *New Internationalist* has been covering the global inequities of neoliberalism for decades. Alternative publications have limited audiences, but they are arguably the most intriguing element of the news media because they can perform Fourth Estate functions in ways that the mainstream cannot.

There are also opportunities to extend the knowledge of the sociology of EBF journalism. This study has focussed on the news product only which itself is the result of a multifaceted process that has not yet been investigated in depth. Although there has been some interview-based research that has explored journalists' sourcing strategies, and their role perceptions, there is a need for a comprehensive study that analyses how EBF news is made. By considering the various human, economic, bureaucratic and technological factors involved in the production process, such a study would help explain the patterns and tendencies revealed in the case studies. A comparative study of different news organisations would be particularly illuminating.

From the perspective of the general public, there is clearly a need for EBF journalism that is more representative of a fuller diversity of perspectives. These exist in the alternative news media but this, by definition, sits on the edge of public consciousness. Even so, there is a strong case for a new approach to mainstream journalism that promotes greater public understanding and engagement, while also giving more coverage to ideas that reside on the periphery. There are compelling arguments why this form of journalism should colonise the mainstream. In the UK, for example, MediaLens promotes the view that journalists should focus on the needs of humanity. Indeed, the founders of this organisation believe that the failings of mainstream journalism can be traced to a well-intended but ultimately unachievable principle:

> Not only is journalistic "objectivity" impossible, the attempt to achieve it is morally abhorrent. How can we remain neutral in a world afflicted by poverty and war? (Edwards and Cromwell 2009: 239)

This compassionate ethos is shared by the investigative journalist John Pilger who tells: '…stories of humanity from the ground up, not from the point of view of the powerful and those who, in one way or another, want to control or exploit us' (in Hayward 2001: 1). While such opinions carry noble intentions, however, they are utopian because the mainstream media is seemingly hardwired to prioritise the agenda of the political and corporate elite. Some argue that improved training will help journalists understand the complexities of economics, business and finance and then be better equipped to challenge their sources. It is important to note, however, that journalist knowledge is just one factor in a complex production process. Hence, without a seismic shift in editorial priorities, working practices and organisational structures, significant change in the news product is unlikely.

This synopsis paints a depressing picture for those hoping for EBF news that routinely offers wider interpretations of the economic environment. Trade unions, NGOs, left-wing research organisations, social movements and other stakeholder groups are perennially frustrated by the lack of media interest in their causes. However, if an issue *does* gain the news media's attention, then the immutability of journalistic practice can work in their favour. Over the last two decades, the rise in prominence and public support of some issues traditionally associated with the left—for example, Fair Trade, climate change and Make Poverty History—demonstrates that once-radical ideas *can* capture the news media's interest and be covered sympathetically if they can be pushed onto the agenda. Although mainstream news organisations favour elite voices, the highly mechanised production process is still geared to include multiple perspectives.

Perhaps critical organisations might collaborate and form a social news agency, along the lines of the Press Association, that is dedicated to channelling press releases, research and packaged items direct to newsrooms. If these organisations can consistently generate material that is congruent with editors' conceptions of news values, provoke debate with strong arguments, high-profile spokespeople and supporting data, and follow up with timely, helpful and personalised PR support, then mainstream publications may begin to include left-of-centre thinking as a matter of course. Naturally, this would require much planning, coordination and compromise by groups that are only loosely connected in their political beliefs. In the meantime, if the British public want to explore radical perspectives, their only effective choice is the alternative news media.

References

BBC. (2018). *Editorial Guidelines: Section 4—Impartiality*. Retrieved from https://www.bbc.co.uk/editorialguidelines/guidelines/impartiality/breadth-diversity-opinion. Accessed August 29, 2018.

BBC World Service. (2009). *Wide Dissatisfaction with Capitalism—Twenty Years After Fall of Berlin Wall*. Opinion Poll Produced in Conjunction with PIPA and Globescan. Retrieved from www.globescan.com/news_archives/bbc2009_berlin_wall. Accessed January 1, 2010.

Berry, M. (2012). The Today Programme and the Banking Crisis. *Journalism, 14*(2), 253–270.

Berry, M. (2016). No Alternative to Austerity: How BBC Broadcast News Reported the Deficit Debate. *Media, Culture and Society, 38*(6), 844–863.

Budd, A. (2007). *Report of the Independent Panel for the BBC Trust on Impartiality of BBC Business Coverage*. Retrieved from http://www.bbc.co.uk/bbctrust/our_work/other/business_news.shtml. Accessed January 1, 2010.

Butterick, K. (2015). *Complacency and Collusion: A Critical Introduction to Business and Financial Journalism*. London: Pluto Press.

Couldry, N., & Cammaerts, B. (2016). *Journalistic Representations of Jeremy Corbyn in the British Press: From Watchdog to Attack Dog*. London School of Economics. Retrieved from http://www.lse.ac.uk/media@lse/research/pdf/JeremyCorbyn/Cobyn-Report-FINAL.pdf. Accessed February 13, 2017.

Curran, J., Gaber, I., & Petley, J. (2018). *Culture Wars: The Media and the British Left* (2nd ed.). Abingdon: Routledge.

Edwards, D., & Cromwell, D. (2009). *Newspeak in the 21st Century*. London: Pluto Press.

Hayward, A. (2001). *In the Name of Justice: The Television Reporting of John Pilger*. London: Bloomsbury.

Hetherington, A. (1985). *News, Newspapers and Television*. Basingstoke: MacMillan Press.

Knowles, S., Phillips, G., & Lidberg, J. (2017). Reporting the Global Financial Crisis. *Journalism Studies, 18*(3), 322–340.

Mills, T. (2016). *The BBC: The Myth of a Public Service*. London: Verso.

Schlesinger, P. (1978). *Putting Reality Together (BBC News)*. London: Constable.

Schlosberg, J. (2016). *Should He Stay, or Should He Go? Television and Online News Coverage of the Labour Party in Crisis*. Media Reform Coalition. Retrieved from http://www.mediareform.org.uk/wp-content/uploads/2016/07/Corbynresearch.pdf. Accessed February 13, 2017.

Shaw, I. (2016). *Business Journalism: A Critical Political Economy Approach*. Abingdon: Routledge.

Starkman, D. (2014). *The Watchdog that Didn't Bark: The Financial Crisis and the Disappearance of Investigative Reporting*. New York: Columbia University Press.

Tambini, D. (2010). What Are Financial Journalists For? *Journalism Studies, 11*(2), 158–174.

Travers, H. (1999, December 8). For Richer or Poorer. *The Guardian*.

Travis, A., & Maguire, K. (2002, September 26). Majority Backs Fire Strikes and Wants PFI Halted. *The Guardian*.

Index

G. J. Merrill, *The Political Content of British Economic, Business and Financial Journalism*, https://doi.org/10.1007/978-3-030-04012-3

FSC
www.fsc.org
MIX
Papier | Fördert
gute Waldnutzung
FSC® C083411

Kolibri 360 GmbH
Ferdinand-Jühlke-Straße 7
99095 Erfurt, Deutschland
produktsicherheit@kolibri360.de